KANT'S *GROUNDWORK*
OF THE METAPHYSICS
OF MORALS

Immanuel Kant's *Groundwork of the Metaphysics of Morals* of 1785 is one of the most profound and important works in the history of practical philosophy. In this introduction to the *Goundwork*, Sally Sedgwick provides a guide to Kant's text that follows the course of his discussion virtually paragraph by paragraph. Her aim is to convey Kant's ideas and arguments as clearly and simply as possible, without getting lost in scholarly controversies. Her introductory chapter offers a useful overview of Kant's general approach to practical philosophy, and she also explores and clarifies some of the main assumptions which Kant relies on in his *Groundwork* but defends in his *Critique of Pure Reason*. The book will be a valuable guide for all who are interested in Kant's practical philosophy.

SALLY SEDGWICK is Professor of Philosophy and Affiliated Professor of Germanic Studies, University of Illinois at Chicago. She is editor of *The Reception of Kant's Critical Philosophy: Fichte, Schelling, and Hegel* (2000).

CAMBRIDGE INTRODUCTIONS TO KEY
PHILOSOPHICAL TEXTS

This new series offers introductory textbooks on what are considered to be the most important texts of Western philosophy. Each book guides the reader through the main themes and arguments of the work in question, while also paying attention to its historical context and its philosophical legacy. No philosophical background knowledge is assumed, and the books will be well suited to introductory university-level courses.

Titles published in the series:

DESCARTES'S *MEDITATIONS* by Catherine Wilson

WITTGENSTEIN'S *PHILOSOPHICAL INVESTIGATIONS* by David G. Stern

WITTGENSTEIN'S *TRACTATUS* by Alfred Nordmann

ARISTOTLE'S *NICOMACHEAN ETHICS* by Michael Pakaluk

SPINOZA'S *ETHICS* by Steven Nadler

KANT'S *CRITIQUE OF PURE REASON* by Jill Vance Buroker

HEIDEGGER'S *BEING AND TIME* by Paul Gorner

HEGEL'S *PHENOMENOLOGY OF SPIRIT* by Larry Krasnoff

KANT'S *GROUNDWORK OF THE METAPHYSICS OF MORALS* by Sally Sedgwick

KANT'S *GROUNDWORK OF THE METAPHYSICS OF MORALS*

An Introduction

SALLY SEDGWICK

University of Illinois at Chicago

CAMBRIDGE UNIVERSITY PRESS
Cambridge, New York, Melbourne, Madrid, Cape Town, Singapore, São Paulo, Delhi

Cambridge University Press
The Edinburgh Building, Cambridge CB2 8RU, UK

Published in the United States of America by Cambridge University Press, New York

www.cambridge.org
Information on this title: www.cambridge.org/9780521604161

First published 2008

Printed in the United Kingdom at the University Press, Cambridge

A catalogue record for this publication is available from the British Library

Library of Congress Cataloguing in Publication data
Sedgwick, Sally S., 1956–
Kant's Groundwork of the metaphysics of morals: an introduction / Sally Sedgwick.
p.   cm. – (Cambridge introductions to key philosophical texts)
Includes bibliographical references (p.   ) and index.
ISBN 978-0-521-84345-4
1. Kant, Immanuel, 1724–1804. Grundlegung zur Metaphysik
der Sitten.   2. Ethics.   I. Title.   II. Series.
B2766.Z7S43   2008
170–dc22
2008007735

ISBN 978-0-521-84345-4 hardback
ISBN 978-0-521-60416-1 paperback

For Peter

Contents

Preface

Immanuel Kant's *Groundwork of the Metaphysics of Morals* of 1785 is one of the most profound and important works in the history of practical philosophy. In this Introduction to the *Groundwork*, I provide a guide to Kant's text that follows the course of his discussion virtually paragraph by paragraph. I have aimed to convey Kant's ideas and arguments as clearly and simply as possible, without getting lost in scholarly controversies. I have tried to produce a guide that is easy to use. The organization of all but my first chapter mirrors that of Kant's discussion in the Preface and three sections of the *Groundwork*. I subdivide my chapters into topic headings that track the progression of his arguments. I frequently provide page references to the Academy edition of the *Groundwork*, so that the reader can match up my discussion with the relevant passages in Kant's text.

Although I have strived for accessibility throughout this work, the reader will discover that I have not always succeeded. In part, this reflects the fact that Kant's own narrative in the *Groundwork* is not uniformly accessible. He is particularly obscure when he turns his attention to methodological matters. Moreover, he sometimes relies on arguments he has provided in other texts. This is most obviously the case in the third and most challenging section of the *Groundwork*, where he sets out to demonstrate the reality of human freedom.

In my introductory chapter, I offer an overview of Kant's general project in practical philosophy. I try to give my reader some sense of the big picture. In addition, I review key assumptions that underlie Kant's argument in the *Groundwork*, assumptions he defends in the context of his theoretical philosophy. This is background material that I hope will aid my reader in understanding some of the more elusive arguments of the *Groundwork*, including the argument of Section III.

Unavoidably, every chapter of this guide touches upon matters of great complexity. The student should not be discouraged by this. It is possible to appreciate much of the basic project of the *Groundwork* without mastering each of Kant's argumentative moves. Likewise, it should be possible to benefit from much of this guide without comprehending every part of it. Although I have written this book primarily for the student who is reading the *Groundwork* for the first or second time, some of my discussions are likely to be of interest only to the more experienced reader.

I have accumulated a number of debts in connection with this work. First, I am indebted to Hilary Gaskin of Cambridge University Press for the invitation to take on the project, and for editorial assistance along the way. I owe thanks as well to the anonymous readers engaged by the Press who commented on my initial proposal, and years later, on the submitted manuscript. I am grateful to the College of Liberal Arts and Sciences at the University of Illinois at Chicago (UIC) for reducing my teaching responsibilities over these past three years, and to my department at UIC for providing an exceptionally collegial environment in which to work. In addition, I thank Rolf-Peter Horstmann and the Alexander von Humboldt-Stiftung for the support that made possible a research trip to Germany in the spring of 2004, when the book was in its early stages. During that visit, Manfred Baum gave generously of his time to explore with me the potential shape of the project and some of the challenges I would encounter. I have also benefited from the philosophical expertise of Stephen Engstrom, David Hilbert, Tony Strimple, and Rachel Zuckert, who either commented on drafts or discussed interpretative difficulties with me. I am grateful to Cameron Brewer for providing indispensable technical assistance in preparing the manuscript for submission. Finally, I owe special thanks to my most cherished consultant, Peter Hylton, who lived with and supported this project on a daily basis. Needless to say, the imperfections of this work are my responsibility alone.

Abbreviations of Kant's works

CPR	*Critique of Pure Reason*
CPrR	*Critique of Practical Reason*
MM	*Metaphysics of Morals*
MM I	*Metaphysics of Morals, Doctrine of Right*
MM II	*Metaphysics of Morals, Doctrine of Virtue*
Prolegomena	*Prolegomena to Any Future Metaphysics that Will be Able to Come Forward as a Science*
Religion	*Religion Within the Boundaries of Mere Reason*

CHAPTER I

Introduction

I. KANT'S LIFE: A BRIEF BIOGRAPHICAL SKETCH

Immanuel Kant was born on April 22, 1724 in Königsberg (now Kaliningrad), a major trading port on the Baltic Sea in what was then East Prussia. He was the fourth of nine children of a master harness-maker.[1] His parents were devout observers of the Protestant sect known as Pietism.[2] Although his mother died when he was only thirteen, she had a profound impact on his life. She recognized his special gifts early on and encouraged their development. As Kant wrote in a letter, she "awakened and broadened" his ideas, and "implanted and nurtured" in him the "first seed of the good."[3]

From the age of eight to sixteen years Kant attended the Collegium Fridericianum, a Pietist school dedicated to the instruction of mathematics, history, geometry, and, above all, Latin. Although he enjoyed studying Latin as well as Greek at the Collegium, he described his

---

[1] Manfred Kuehn. *Kant: A Biography* (Cambridge University Press, 2001), p. 28. Uwe Schultz claims that Kant was the fourth of eleven children, in *Immanuel Kant* (Reinbek bei Hamburg: Rowohlt Taschenbuch Verlag, 2003), p. 7.

[2] Pietism was a Protestant movement founded in the mid-seventeenth century to protest the highly scholastic and creed-bound form of Lutheranism at that time in Germany. Pietists emphasized good works over worldly success, and the importance of one's personal devotional life over public displays of faith. For more on the Pietism of Kant's day and its influence on Kant, see Ernst Cassirer, *Kant's Life and Thought*, trans. James Haden (New Haven, CT: Yale University Press, 1981), p. 18; Theodore M. Greene, "The Historical Context and Religious Significance of Kant's Religion," in his translation of Kant's *Religion Within the Limits of Reason Alone*, pp. xxviii–xxx; Manfred Kuehn, *Kant: A Biography*, pp. 34–45.

[3] The passage in full: "I shall never forget my mother, for she implanted and nurtured the first seed of the good in me; she opened my heart to the influence of Nature; she awakened and broadened my ideas, and her teachings have had an enduring, beneficent effect on my life." Quoted in Cassirer, *Kant's Life and Thought*, p. 13.

experience there as that of "youthful slavery."[4] The school imposed upon its students a particularly zealous form of Pietism, and Kant resisted its insistence upon public displays of devotion. Already as a boy, he was drawn to the ideals of tolerance and freedom of conscience.

In 1740, the year Frederick the Great ascended the throne of Prussia, Kant matriculated at the University of Königsberg. Although his family was of modest means, he avoided pre-professional subjects such as law, medicine, and theology. Under the inspiration of his favorite teacher, Martin Knutzen, Kant immersed himself in the study of natural science and philosophy. It was Knutzen who introduced him to the writings of the two thinkers who had the greatest impact on his early intellectual development: Isaac Newton and Christian Wolff.

Kant's father died in 1746, leaving him without the financial means to continue his university studies. Kant earned an income for a number of years as a private tutor, then returned to the University of Königsberg in 1755 to write the essay required for completing his degree. In that essay he defended his own theory of atoms and their forces. For approximately the next fifteen years, he worked both at the Royal Palace Library and as a lecturer at the university, where he taught a wide range of subjects such as maths, natural science, logic, anthropology, geography, metaphysics, moral philosophy, and theology. It was not until 1770, when Kant was forty-six, that he was finally appointed Professor at the University of Königsberg.[5] His most important philosophical work, the *Critique of Pure Reason*, appeared in 1781. He taught at the University of Königsberg until 1797, seven years prior to his death.

Kant's predilection for regularity in his daily routine has been the subject of much commentary. He was up every morning at 5 a.m. to prepare his lectures, and in bed every night at 10 p.m.[6] Apparently, he was so punctual in taking his evening constitutional that the housewives of Königsberg could set their clocks by it. (He is

---

[4] J. M. Greene, "The Historical Context and Religious Significance of Kant's Religion" p. xxviii.
[5] Kant was appointed "Ordinary Professorship in Logic and Metaphysics." This was an appointment at the highest rank.
[6] U. Schultz, *Immanuel Kant*, p. 25.

said to have missed his daily walk only once, when he received a copy of Rousseau's *Émile* in the post.) Although he permitted himself few frivolities and governed his life by the principles of hard work and self-discipline, he is reported to have had a convivial and even playful nature.[7] As a young man, he was an avid billiards player. Even before he was a famous author, he was one of the most sought-after guests of Königsberg. He frequently entertained friends for the midday meal, and looked forward to these occasions as breaks from the hard labors of philosophy. He seems to have most enjoyed the company not of family or university colleagues, but of town merchants and businessmen.[8]

Kant died of natural causes at the age of seventy-nine years and ten months on February 12, 1804.

2. THE SUBJECT MATTER OF THE *GROUNDWORK*

2.1 *The* Groundwork *is a treatise in practical philosophy*

In the most general terms, practical philosophy is concerned with the norms or rules of human conduct. It considers how we *ought* to treat one another and ourselves. For Kant, the task of the practical philosopher is that of determining, on the one hand, what it is to be a good or virtuous person. As he sometimes puts it, practical philosophy seeks to discover the conditions under which we are worthy of happiness.[9] But practical philosophy, on Kant's conception, also investigates the nature and limits of political power. What laws ought a state to enforce? What institutions should it promote, and what rights should it guarantee?

Written in 1785, the *Groundwork of the Metaphysics of Morals* is the first of Kant's three major works in practical philosophy. He published the *Critique of Practical Reason* in 1788, and the two parts of the *Metaphysics of Morals* in 1797 and 1798. Kant did not, however, confine his attention to the area of practical philosophy. He made important contributions to metaphysics, the philosophy of science,

---

[7] E. Cassirer, *Kant's Life and Thought*, p. 24.   [8] U. Schultz, *Immanuel Kant*, p. 49.
[9] See, for example, Kant's discussion beginning at A 805/B 833 of the *Critique of Pure Reason*. The question "What should I do?" belongs to the domain of "practical" or "moral" philosophy. The answer to this practical question, in his words, is: "Do that through which you will become worthy to be happy."

aesthetics, and the philosophy of religion as well. As a systematic philosopher, he sought to demonstrate the interconnection of these various domains of inquiry as parts of an overarching whole. One consequence of this insistence upon systematic unity is that his works in practical philosophy cannot be adequately appreciated in isolation from his other philosophical writings. This feature of Kant's approach will become apparent in our study of the *Groundwork*, since he often relies in that text on claims he has argued for elsewhere. The idea of human freedom he defends in Section III, for example, depends for its justification on his account of the conditions of human experience articulated in the *Critique of Pure Reason*.

2.2 *The* Groundwork *is a not a text in applied ethics*

We might expect from a treatise on practical philosophy a compendium of dos and don'ts, a guide to how we should conduct ourselves in particular situations. Although Kant intended his theory to have relevance for everyday life, the *Groundwork* is nothing like a guidebook. For one thing, it contains very little discussion of concrete cases. On the rare occasion in which Kant considers an example of a particular moral problem, his treatment is highly abstract. He seems to have had no interest in analyzing cases in detail.

It would be a mistake to conclude from the abstract character of Kant's discussion in the *Groundwork*, however, that he had no concern whatsoever to articulate or defend practical rules in that text. On the contrary, he devotes a great deal of attention to one rule in particular, the rule he calls the "categorical imperative." He identifies this rule as the most basic principle by means of which we measure moral value. On his account, it is this rule that ultimately determines what we ought to do in specific cases. The *Groundwork* is nonetheless not a work in applied ethics. Rather than provide a case-by-case analysis of concrete moral problems, it is concerned with a different task. That task is suggested in the work's title. The German word for "groundwork" is "*Grundlegung*," which literally translates as "laying the ground." The *Groundwork* lays the ground for practical philosophy in this sense: it provides philosophical support or justification for the supreme rule upon which all practical philosophy is based. As Kant writes in his Preface:

The present groundwork is ... nothing more than the search for and establishment of the *supreme principle of morality*. (392)

For Kant, the project of laying the ground is not just different from but also *prior to* that of identifying and applying specific practical rules. We can illustrate this priority by means of an example. Suppose you are considering whether to be dishonest in a particular situation. You ask a friend for advice, and she supplies a rule: "One ought to never be dishonest in cases like that." You might respond simply by accepting your friend's rule and conforming your behavior to it. Alternatively, you could demand that she justify her judgment. If you chose the latter course, you would be inquiring into the rule's ground; you would be searching for the principle upon which the rule was based. You would be requiring an argument establishing its legitimacy.

Kant's view is that, as rational creatures, we should not follow moral rules uncritically. We should satisfy ourselves that the principles governing our conduct are well grounded or justified. His *Groundwork* is intended to meet this need for justification. As he indicates in the above-quoted passage, the task of the *Groundwork* is to search for the supreme principle of morality and demonstrate that this principle is warranted as the only possible supreme moral law. Kant concedes that specific applications of the law would be useful in illustrating its adequacy, but he provides very little by way of applications in the text (392).[10]

2.3 *Relation of the* Groundwork *to the* Metaphysics of Morals

In his Preface, Kant asserts that the *Groundwork* is a preparatory work. It is preliminary, he says, to a "metaphysics of morals," a text he says he intends to publish someday (391). The text he says he will someday

---

[10] Strictly speaking, none of Kant's other major works in practical philosophy are texts in applied practical philosophy either. He provides a far more extensive discussion of particular duties in his *Metaphysics of Morals* than in the *Groundwork* or the *Critique of Practical Reason*. But his level of discussion in the *Metaphysics of Morals* is still quite abstract. He considers duties that apply generally to human nature, but he does not specify on a case-by-case basis the duties that obligate us in particular situations. Kant tells us in Section 45 of the *MM II* that a complete account of duties would require an appendix to that text in which applications of the moral law are modified to fit varying circumstances (469). He never provides such an appendix, however. Mary Gregor provides an informative account of Kant's various levels of discussion in the Introduction to her 1964 translation of Kant's *Doctrine of Virtue*, PA, pp. xvii–xix.

publish is the two-volume work that appeared in 1797 and 1798, the *Metaphysics of Morals*. As we will see in a moment, the *Groundwork* supplies and justifies the principle that provides the foundation for that later work. We can better appreciate Kant's task in the *Groundwork* if we first consider what he has in mind by a "metaphysics of morals."

i. On the two divisions of Kant's Metaphysics of Morals

Kant writes in the Preface to the *Metaphysics of Morals* of his aim to provide the "metaphysical first principles" of a "doctrine of right" and a "doctrine of virtue" (*MM* 205). The *Metaphysics of Morals* is thus comprised of two parts or divisions: *The Metaphysical First Principles of the Doctrine of Right* (1797) and *The Metaphysical First Principles of the Doctrine of Virtue* (1798).[11] Both the *Doctrine of Right* and the *Doctrine of Virtue* specify duties; both, that is, supply rules of conduct we are obligated to obey. Each *Doctrine*, however, specifies a different class of duties.

Kant writes in the Introduction to his *Metaphysics of Morals* that all practical lawgiving can be distinguished "with respect to the incentives" (*MM* 218). By this he means that we can distinguish the two classes of duties with regard to the way in which each requires us to act. In the case of the class of duties Kant sometimes identifies as "ethical" – the class he discusses in his *Doctrine of Virtue* – the motivation derives from the idea of duty alone. These duties command that we cultivate in ourselves certain dispositions. Duty obligates us, for example, to cultivate in ourselves the dispositions to be kind to our neighbor and to perfect our talents. These duties bind us even though we cannot be externally coerced into performing them. We cannot be externally coerced for two reasons. First, ethical duties or duties of virtue imply no correlative right. Because we violate no one's rights if we fail to answer the command of these duties, the state has no right to punish us. Second, even if the state did have the right to compel us, it could not in fact do so. This is because duties of virtue require of us something that is not susceptible to external

---

[11] The German word for what is usually translated as "morals" in Kant's title is "*Sitten*." Kant remarks in his Introduction to the *MM* that "*Sitten*" refers to "manners and customs" (216). The translation of "*Sittlichkeit*" as "morals" in the title *MM* is not a mistake because Kant himself uses the terms "*Sitten*" or "*Sittlichkeit*" and "*Moralität*" interchangeably, for example, at (219).

coercion – namely, dispositions. In Kant's view, dispositions can no more be externally compelled than beliefs or opinions.

Consider, now, a second class of duties, the class Kant discusses in the *Doctrine of Right*. The incentive to obey these "juridical" duties is not just internal but also external. These duties, unlike duties of virtue, admit of external coercion. They admit of external coercion because they command actions rather than dispositions or intentions. If I trespass on your property, the state may rightfully punish me. The state has a right to punish me, because in trespassing, my action is incompatible with your right to express your outer freedom (*MM I* 250, *MM II* 381).

ii. Ambiguities in Kant's use of the terms "morality" and "ethics"

We use the terms "morality" and "ethics" in broad as well as narrow senses. The more typical use is perhaps the narrow one. In the narrow sense, the terms "morality" and "ethics" refer to duties that cannot be coerced by the state, duties whose incentive is internal (duties of virtue, as Kant calls them). Sometimes, however, we use the terms more broadly to refer to *all* practical obligations, including externally coercible obligations. We use the term "ethics" broadly, for instance, when we characterize the question of the state's right to impose the death penalty as an ethical one.

The reader should be prepared for the fact that Kant, too, uses the terms "morality" and "ethics" not merely in the narrow but also in the broad sense. For example, he classifies both duties of right and duties of virtue under the general heading of a "metaphysics of *morals*" (emphasis added). He writes in his Introduction to the *Metaphysics of Morals* that all duties, as duties, belong to "ethics" (*MM* 219). Early on in his Preface to the *Groundwork*, Kant identifies "ethics" or the "doctrine of morals" as the "science" of laws of freedom (387). He does not intend the terms "ethics" or the "doctrine of morals," in that context, to refer exclusively to what properly belongs within the sphere of the doctrine of virtue.

iii. Further clarification of the relation of the Groundwork to the Metaphysics of Morals

We now turn to the question of the relation of the two divisions of the *Metaphysics of Morals* to the *Groundwork*. As mentioned above, the *Groundwork* provides the foundational principle upon which both divisions of the *Metaphysics of Morals* rest. The *Metaphysics of Morals* specifies the general duties (of virtue and of right) that human beings have to themselves and to one another. The *Groundwork* provides the principle that justifies these duties as duties. The *Groundwork* "searches for" and "establishes" the supreme practical principle, the principle that governs or grounds both classes of duties. That supreme principle is the categorical imperative.[12]

Given the fact that the task of the *Groundwork* is to provide the principle that ultimately justifies both duties of virtue and of right, we might expect that work to devote equal time to both kinds of duties. Oddly enough, this is not the case. The *Groundwork* contains virtually no mention of the role of the supreme principle in determining whether or not an action is in conformity with right. Instead, Kant's focus is the role of the supreme principle in determining whether our intentions or motives conform to virtue. The examples he discusses in the *Groundwork* to illustrate the application of the supreme law, that is, belong properly within the sphere of the *Doctrine of Virtue*.[13]

3. SOME DISTINGUISHING FEATURES OF KANT'S APPROACH TO PRACTICAL PHILOSOPHY

3.1 *The substantial doctrine*

Kant argues that the categorical imperative is the fundamental law or principle by means of which we determine what is and is not practically required of us, what is and is not our duty. In our chapter

[12] Kant writes in the *MM* that the categorical imperative or supreme practical principle "affirms what obligation is" (225). Obligation or constraint can be merely internal (as in the case of duties of virtue) or external (as in the case of duties of right). In both cases, however, it is the categorical imperative that defines this constraint. For another passage in which Kant clearly identifies the categorical imperative as the supreme principle of both parts of the doctrine of morals [*Sittenlehre*], see his Introduction to *MM* (226). Manfred Baum explores the novelty of Kant's break with the natural rights tradition on the division of duties of right and of virtue in his "Recht und Ethik in Kants praktischer Philosophie," in Juergen Stolzenberg (ed.), *Kant in der Gegenwart* (Berlin/New York: Verlag Walter de Gruyter, forthcoming). See also Gregor's Introduction to her translation of *The Metaphysics of Morals*, pp. 7–10.

[13] At center stage of the *Groundwork* is the good will, and a good will is defined not with reference to its (externally coercible) actions, but rather with reference to its inner disposition or motives. For a helpful explanation for Kant's reasons for restricting his attention in the *Groundwork* to duties of virtue, see the beginning of Chapter II of M. J. Gregor *Laws of Freedom* (New York, NY: Barnes & Noble, Inc., 1963).

devoted to Section II of the *Groundwork*, we will consider in some detail his various formulations of the law. For present purposes, however, the following rough representation of it will suffice. In essence, what the categorical imperative commands is that we respect the dignity of all rational natures. On Kant's account, dignity is something all rational natures have. A being has dignity, for Kant, not because of its socio-economic status, religious beliefs, sex, or race. A being has a dignity because of its practical rationality; it possesses the faculty Kant calls "practical reason." These are technical terms, and we will eventually have to consider them with care. At this point we need merely point out that Kant does not equate practical reason with intelligence or cleverness. The capacity of practical reason refers, rather, to the faculty of free will or self-determination. To say that the categorical imperative commands us to respect the dignity of all rational natures, then, is to say that it commands us to respect and promote the expression of practical rationality or freedom. For Kant, the source of all practical value is freedom.

3.2 The universality of the supreme practical law

The supreme practical law or categorical imperative is universal in two respects:

i. The supreme practical law is universal with respect to the scope of its application.

The categorical imperative itself as well as the specific duties that derive from it require us to respect and treat with dignity *all* rational nature. Otherwise put, respect for dignity, on Kant's account, applies impartially to rational nature. No rational being is unworthy of respect, and no rational being deserves more respect than any other. Not surprisingly, Kant concentrates his attention on the duties we have toward *human* rational natures. He nonetheless asserts repeatedly that *all* rational natures, without exception, are worthy of respect.

ii. The supreme practical law is universal with respect to the scope of its validity.

Kant argues that the practical law is valid for – that is, binding on – all rational nature. It is the standard, for all rational nature, by means of which it is possible to determine whether a disposition or will is good and whether an action is right. Although valid for all rational nature, however, the law does not necessarily *command* all rational nature. Kant allows that there may be rational beings whose nature is in perfect conformity with duty and who therefore do not have to be commanded to respect duty. The supreme practical law must take the form of a command or imperative only for finite or imperfect rational natures such as human rational natures.[14]

3.3 *The necessity of the supreme practical law*

When the categorical imperative determines that we have a duty to perform some action, we are necessarily obligated to perform that action. It is not that we are only more or less obligated to perform it, or that we are obligated to perform it only if doing so strikes our fancy. Kant holds, for example, that we have a duty not to mutilate our bodies for pleasure or profit. Because we have this duty, we *necessarily* must comply. We are neither invited nor allowed to use our discretion in deciding whether we must comply. Although some may want to challenge the view that we have such a duty, the point about necessity is this: when something is determined to be a duty in a given case, it binds unconditionally, according to Kant.[15]

3.4 *The rational grounding of practical philosophy*

The precise implications of the rational grounding of Kant's practical philosophy are difficult to grasp and thus require more extensive introduction. Kant insists that his practical philosophy is grounded in (that is, justified by) reason. The supreme practical law or categorical imperative upon which his practical philosophy is based is itself a law of reason, in his view. As a law of reason (as a priori), it relies on experience neither for its origin nor for its justification.

---

[14] Kant discusses this point in Section II of the *Groundwork*, beginning at (413f.).

[15] Kant distinguishes the features of universality and necessity as I have done so here, but he does not always clearly distinguish them. When he insists upon the necessity of the supreme practical law at (389) of the *Groundwork*, for example, he goes on to characterize necessity in terms of universal validity. He distinguishes the two features, however, in his account of the forms of judgment in the *CPR* A 70/B 95. To characterize a judgment as universal is to specify its quantity; to characterize a judgment as necessary (or "apodictic") is to specify its modality. Earlier in the first *Critique*, Kant again claims that the two features are distinct, but he adds that they "belong together inseparably" (B 4).

In insisting upon an a priori grounding, Kant turns his back on centuries of efforts to justify a supreme practical principle. One popular approach he rejects seeks to ground morality in observed facts about human nature – facts, say, about what all humans desire. Since the third century BC, Epicureans have argued, for example, that all humans desire happiness and that we therefore have a duty to do what produces or promotes happiness. For reasons we will consider beginning in Section 5 below, Kant opposes any kind of empirical grounding. His view is that instead of trying to ground practical philosophy on what observation reveals to us about human nature, it is essential that we rely on an appeal to reason and its laws.

Kant is equally dismissive of the proposal to ground practical philosophy on appeals to divine authority. As we will see shortly, this does not mean that he awards religion no role whatsoever in his practical philosophy. It does mean, however, that religious authority, on his conception, is not the ground upon which practical philosophy rests. To put this point in another way, the categorical imperative, for Kant, has neither its source nor its warrant in religious authority.

The idea that practical philosophy must have reason as its basis might strike us as unusual. It is a fundamental feature of Kant's approach, but why does he insist upon it? I devote much of my attention in the remaining pages of this Introduction to answering this question. I begin with a brief review of two of Kant's reasons for rejecting a theological grounding of practical philosophy.

4. THE GROUNDING OF PRACTICAL PHILOSOPHY MUST BE REASON NOT RELIGION

In my biographical sketch, I noted Kant's Protestant upbringing. Although he did not always approve of the way in which Christianity was practiced in his time, and although he denied that the existence of God could be proved, Kant was nonetheless a believer. His religious background makes itself known in the *Groundwork*, although it is less evident there than in some of his other works. Kant's insistence upon the duty not to commit suicide and the duty to love one's neighbor, for example, calls to mind values of the Christian tradition (values that, of course, are not exclusively

Christian).[16] His language is sometimes borrowed from religion, for instance, when he contrasts the "kingdom" or "realm of nature" with the ideal "kingdom" or "realm of ends" (438). At other times he is quite explicit in insisting upon a role for religion in practical philosophy. This is especially the case in his works, the *Critique of Practical Reason* and *Religion Within the Boundaries of Mere Reason*, where he asserts that morality ineluctably leads to religion.[17] Kant's reasoning, very roughly, is that we need the notions of a life beyond this life and of a divine creator in order to adequately conceive or imagine the goal we seek to realize when we act from the moral law. Practical philosophy thus necessarily leads us to, as well as requires, these "practical postulates" or "rational beliefs," on his account.[18]

Yet Kant repeatedly underscores the point that practical philosophy cannot be based or grounded on these notions. Practical philosophy is grounded on reason – more precisely, on practical reason, the capacity of the agent to freely determine her own actions. We find a particularly clear expression of this position in his Preface to the 1793 edition of the *Religion*:

So far as morality is based upon the conception of man as a free agent who, just because he is free, binds himself through his reason to unconditional laws, it stands in need neither of the idea of another Being over him … nor of an incentive other than the law itself, for him to do his duty. (Paragraph 1)

Kant's reasons for insisting that morality cannot be grounded on religion could easily fill the pages of a separate commentary. For our purposes, it will suffice simply to mention the key claims of two of his arguments.[19]

---

[16] In a passage in the *CPrR*, Kant suggests that his own supreme principle of morality is essentially the same as the Christian principle of morals (129). For a summary of the Christian influence on Kant's practical philosophy see H. J. Paton, *The Categorical Imperative: A Study in Kant's Moral Philosophy* (Philadelphia, PA: University of Pennsylvania Press, 1971), p. 196. For a more scholarly treatment of this issue, see T. M. Greene, "The Historical Context and Religious Significance of Kant's Religion." In his translation of *Kant's Religion Within the Limits or Reason Alone*.

[17] See *CPrR* (124–132) and Kant's Preface to the 1793 edition of *Religion Within the Boundaries of Mere Reason*, esp. paragraph 2.

[18] *CPrR* (126). For a discussion of the practical postulates and relation of religion to morality in Kant, see Chapter XIV of L. W. Beck, *A Commentary on Kant's Critique of Practical Reason* (Chicago/London: University of Chicago Press, 1960).

[19] I return to this topic in my remarks on the final pages of the subject matter of the *Groundwork*. See my discussion in Chapter 4, section 18.6.

Kant rejects a "theological" grounding, first, because such a grounding, as he understands it, assumes not just that the source of all duties is God, but also that it is possible to demonstrate the existence or reality of God. Since Kant denies that such a demonstration can be provided, he also dismisses the effort to provide a theological grounding.[20] Kant's second reason for rejecting a theological grounding is tied to the implications he believes such an approach has for how we understand our motivation for respecting duty. To ground morality theologically is to derive it, as he puts it in the *Groundwork*, "from a divine all-perfect will" (443). Kant worries that, on this account, our motivation for respecting duty would be to answer the command of that divine will. We would do our duty in order to please God, and we would want to please God either from fear of punishment or in anticipation of some future reward. Ultimately, our incentive for acting from duty would be to secure our own happiness.[21] In Kant's view, however, morality is not a doctrine of how we are to make ourselves happy; it is instead a doctrine of how we are to become *worthy* of happiness.[22]

5. GROUNDING PRACTICAL PHILOSOPHY IN REASON VERSUS EXPERIENCE: ARGUMENT I

As mentioned back in Section 3.4, Kant in addition rejects efforts to ground practical philosophy in experience. In the *Groundwork* he is much more preoccupied with this particular strategy for grounding practical philosophy than with its theological counterpart. His opposition to this strategy is evident on virtually every page of the work. It is crucial, then, that we achieve a basic grasp of his reasons for dissatisfaction with this approach. To do so, we need to bring to the foreground some of Kant's more general philosophical commitments. I noted earlier that he is a systematic philosopher. In opposing an empirical grounding of practical philosophy, he helps himself to assumptions he

---

[20] See Kant's discussion of these points in the *MM II* (443f.), section 18, and beginning at (486).

[21] Kant makes this claim also in the *CPrR* (129). A theological grounding is unacceptable, he says, because the incentive to duty is, in effect, happiness (or wished for results). See also *CPrR* (147).

[22] *CPrR* (130). To put the point in more technical terms, a theological grounding of morality would be, for Kant, a "heteronomous" grounding. Kant makes this point explicitly in the final paragraphs of Section II of the *Groundwork* (442–445) and in the *CPrR* (39–41).

believes he has successfully defended in the context of his theoretical philosophy.

Kant provides two arguments in defense of the thesis that practical philosophy must be grounded in reason rather than experience. I consider the first here, and turn my attention to the second in Section 6 below. The first argument may be represented as follows:

  i. If we ground morality in experience, we give up universality and necessity.
 ii. We cannot give up universality and necessity.

Therefore, morality cannot be grounded in experience.

Passages expressing this argument are ubiquitous in the *Groundwork*. One such passage appears in Section II:[23]

> Empirical principles are not at all fit to be the ground of moral laws. For the universality with which these are to hold for all rational beings without distinction – the unconditional practical necessity which is thereby imposed upon them – comes to nothing if their ground is taken from the special constitution of human nature or the contingent circumstances in which it is placed. (442)

In sections 3.2 and 3.3, we considered Kant's commitment to the universality and necessity of the supreme practical law. We now need to determine why he was so convinced that universality and necessity cannot be derived from empirical principles. Why, in other words, did he hold premise "i" above?

Our first order of business is to clarify Kant's understanding of the effort to provide an empirical grounding of practical philosophy. As a grounding, it is intended to justify or warrant a practical standard. As an *empirical* grounding, it relies on evidence obtained from experience – evidence, for example, about human nature. This factual evidence is then taken to justify a supreme practical principle. The factual thesis Kant cites most often in the *Groundwork* is this: "All humans desire happiness."[24] From this factual thesis, proponents of this approach derive the principle that, "One *ought* to promote happiness."

---

[23] For further passages, see *Groundwork* (408, 411, 425, 441–445).

[24] Kant discusses this thesis in various places in the *Groundwork*, but see esp. (441–445). See also his discussion in the *CPrR* (34–41).

Kant does not dispute the fact upon which this derivation is based, the fact that all humans desire happiness.[25] Nor does he challenge the claim, even, that we each have a duty to promote happiness. He does, however, call into question the reasoning that is supposed to allow us to infer the supreme practical principle from the factual premise. He believes that if we reason in this way, the practical principle that is the conclusion of the argument cannot have the status of universality and necessity. On that basis alone the argument must be rejected, in his view.

Our question now has to be: Why was Kant convinced that any empirical grounding, even one supported by well-confirmed facts, is unable to secure for our moral principles the status of universality and necessity? If we are persuaded (as he is) that "all humans desire happiness," why is it not possible to derive from this factual premise the universally and necessarily valid duty to promote happiness?

We cannot answer this question without doing a bit of preparatory work. According to Kant, empirical judgments or judgments from experience can *never* be known to be universally and necessarily valid. In the *Critique of Practical Reason* he goes so far as to tell us that it "is an outright contradiction to want to extract necessity from an empirical proposition" (12). This remark reveals the influence on his thinking of the eighteenth-century Scottish philosopher David Hume. It will serve our purposes to briefly review that influence, with regard in particular to Hume's impact on Kant's understanding of the nature of empirical reasoning. To prepare the way, we first need to highlight a few features of empirical judgments.

5.1 Empirical versus non-empirical judgments

First, by "empirical judgment" in this discussion, I have in mind judgments such as the one just mentioned: "All humans desire happiness." Other examples include, "smoking causes cancer" or "Peter's bouillabaisse is delicious." Notice that these judgments are empirical *generalizations*. They are thus unlike another class of empirical judgments,

---

[25] Evidence that Kant agrees with the claim that humans necessarily desire happiness may be found, for example, at *Groundwork* (415), where he writes that happiness as a purpose "can be presupposed surely and a priori in the case of every human being."

judgments which merely report our past and present experiences. Examples of this second class of judgments include, "the apple tastes sweet to me now" or "the apple tasted sweet to me yesterday." These latter judgments report our experiences, but they do not reason or generalize from our experiences. My remarks here will pertain only to empirical generalizations.

What makes a generalization empirical? The answer to this question has to do with how we go about providing evidence in support of it. Simply put, we consult experience. Consider this example of an empirical judgment: "Smoking causes cancer." Researchers justify this claim with reference to tests they have performed that suggest a correlation between smoking and cancer. They notice that smokers are more likely than non-smokers to get cancer. They generalize from their case studies and assert with probability that "smoking causes cancer."

Contrast this kind of judgment with a typical example of a *non-*empirical judgment: "A = A" (the law of identity). Most philosophers do not classify this judgment as empirical. They argue that its truth does not rely on the evidence of the senses at all. They identify it as a conceptual truth – a truth of reason or "relation of ideas" (borrowing Hume's terminology). On this interpretation, the truth of "A = A" reflects nothing of what our senses disclose to us about the world. Instead, its truth reveals a law governing the nature of thought. Most would say of this law that it governs thought *necessarily*, that is, absolutely or unconditionally. Most would also say that since the law expresses a feature of *all* thought, regardless of the physical universe in which thought occurs, the law is valid for thought *universally*.

5.2 Reasons for doubting that we can know empirical judgments to be universally and necessarily valid

Remember that, in Kant's view, we are *never* warranted in attributing universality and necessity to empirical judgments. On his account, this is another way of saying that we are never warranted in awarding empirical judgments the status of law. If we again consider the generalization "all humans desire happiness," we can clarify his reasoning.

First, why might we be tempted to award a judgment like "all humans desire happiness" the status of law? One reason might have to do with the judgment's level of generality. The judgment predicates happiness not merely of some but of "all humans." It has the sweeping scope of judgments we identify as laws. Another reason might reflect the fact that we have abundant observational evidence in support of the generalization and have not yet encountered an exception to it. We might then consider ourselves warranted in asserting that we know the judgment with necessity.

Philosophers have offered a number of reasons for doubting that we can ever be justified in attributing universality and necessity to empirical judgments. An argument typically given for why we cannot know judgments such as "all humans desire happiness" to be universally valid is this: as an empirical generalization, the judgment derives a conclusion about "all humans" from observations of merely some humans. It shares with all empirical generalizations the property of going beyond the evidence of experience. An argument typically given for why we cannot know the judgment with necessity is that our perceptual tools and methods are imperfect. It may be that we "see" only what we want to see, or that what we see is a mere shadow or appearance of the real.

To these arguments, Hume added his own doubts about our claims to empirical knowledge. His doubts resulted in far more radical conclusions about the status of those claims, and as I mentioned, his conclusions had a powerful impact on Kant. Hume argued that we are not entitled to assert that our empirical generalizations are even contingently or probably true. Even were our observations perfectly complete and accurate – even were we to observe the behavior of every person who has lived up to now, and to control for all possible factors that might compromise the accuracy of our observations – experience, in his view, cannot provide the *least bit* of evidential support for these judgments. Hume pointed out that when we assert an empirical generalization such as "all humans desire happiness," we in effect assume that observed past regularities inform us with some degree of probability about future ones. We presuppose, then, that the future will resemble the past. He insisted, however, that observation warrants us only in making conclusions about correlations *up to now*. The uniquely Humean claim is this: we cannot rule out the possibility that the laws of nature could change, rendering past observations of no evidentiary import whatsoever. This is why our empirical general-izations cannot be said to have even probable warrant, in his view. And if they lack probable warrant, they lack necessity as well.

5.3 Kant accepted Hume's conclusion entirely

Kant was wholly persuaded by Hume's argument. If a judgment is empirical (derived from experience, or derived a posteriori), it cannot be known to be either universally or necessarily valid. Strictly speak-ing, as Hume pointed out, the judgment cannot be demonstrated to be even contingently true. Even if the judgment that "all humans desire happiness" accurately records our observations up to now, we have no grounds for predicting even with probability what humans will desire in the future. The most we can hope to get from empirical principles, principles based on observation, is what Kant refers to as "comparative universality" or universality "through induction." For judgments such as the generalization that all humans desire happiness, we are entitled to claim only that, "as far as we have yet perceived, there is no exception" to this rule.[26]

   This completes our discussion of one of Kant's reasons for insisting that the foundation of practical philosophy has to be reason rather than experience. Practical philosophy must rest on a rational or a priori basis, since this is its only hope of yielding commands that we can justify as universally and necessarily valid.[27]

6. GROUNDING PRACTICAL PHILOSOPHY IN REASON VERSUS EXPERIENCE: ARGUMENT 2

Kant offers a second argument in defense of his conclusion that we cannot ground practical philosophy in experience. This second argu-ment concerns his unique conception of human freedom. We can sketch the argument as follows:

---

[26] Kant discusses the distinction between "comparative" and "strict" universality in the *CPR* B 3f. A principle is strictly universal, he tells us there, if no exception to it is "allowed to be possible." The only class of judgments that have this property, on his account, are a priori judgments, judgments that derive from pure reason.

[27] For more on the topic of Kant's account of the status of empirical judgments, see H. J. Paton, *The Categorical Imperative*, pp. 82–84.

i. If we ground morality in experience, we cannot provide for the possibility of human freedom.
ii. Human freedom must be presupposed as a condition of the possibility of morality.
    Therefore, morality cannot be grounded in experience.

Neither of the above premises is self-evident. It is not obvious, for instance, why the appeal to experience in grounding practical philosophy should pose a threat to human freedom. We can best appreciate Kant's reasoning in this argument if we begin by considering his defense of the second premise.

6.1 Freedom must be presupposed as a condition of the possibility of morality

Recall what we said earlier about Kant's general task in the *Groundwork*. He writes in his Preface that he seeks to "search for" and "establish" the supreme principle of morality (392). For imperfectly rational natures, such as human nature, the supreme principle of morality or categorical imperative is formulated as a command. It does not describe how we *in fact* behave; it *requires* us to behave in a certain way. It expresses an *ought*. As noted above, it commands us to respect human dignity.

Kant often reminds us that we can only reasonably be *commanded* to do what we in fact *can* do. The requirement of the categorical imperative that we respect human dignity thus depends on the assumption that it is *possible* for us to act on its requirement. It depends, that is, on the assumption that we are free. Imagine for a moment that this were not so. Imagine that all our behavior, even our thoughts, were completely determined by forces over which we had no control. If this were the case, we would be like puppets on a string, merely reacting to the forces that govern us. In this situation, it would be inaccurate to claim that we had any real choice about which actions to undertake and which to avoid. It would be unreasonable to attribute to us responsibility for our actions. It would thus be unreasonable to say to someone, in light of his bad behavior, "You ought not to have done it." Were our thoughts and behaviors thoroughly determined, the moral "ought" would have no meaning.

The scenario just outlined is one in which we consider all human thought and action to be determined. It applies the thesis known as "universal determinism" to the realm of human behavior. According to the thesis of universal determinism, nothing happens in nature without being caused by some antecedent condition or conditions. More technically formulated, the thesis is this:

For every event y, there is an antecedent condition or set of conditions, x, such that given x, y had to happen.

Suppose that one day your car begins to emit black clouds of smoke. We would think it peculiar if the response of your mechanic was to say: "I cannot fix the problem because nothing is causing the black smoke to billow out of your tailpipe." We would find this response odd because we do not suppose that smoke simply comes into being spontaneously. We instead assume that something causes it to come into being. We set out in search of the antecedent condition or set of conditions without which it would not exist. We search, in other words, for the smoke's sufficient cause.

Kant never wavered in his adherence to the thesis of universal determinism. At the same time, he was deeply concerned about its implications for human freedom. He was aware that the truth of determinism implied that human behavior is nothing more than that of a biological machine. He was convinced that, on this account of human behavior, there is no way to defend the idea that we have genuine choice. Because Kant was as committed to the thesis of human freedom as he was to the thesis of universal determinism, he set out to establish that the two positions could both be true.

To appreciate what is unique about Kant's argument for reconciling freedom and determinism, we need to distinguish his argument from another such effort – an effort we would today identify as that of "compatibilism" or "soft-determinism." Kant rejected this approach because of its reliance on what, in his view, was a merely "comparative" or "psychological" conception of freedom.[28] Although it may not be apparent now, once we have grasped Kant's reasons for opposing the "comparative" or "psychological" conception of freedom, we will be in a better position to understand his commitment to assumption "i" above:

---

[28] Kant employs these labels in his discussion in the *CPrR* (96).

If we ground morality in experience, we cannot provide for the possibility of human freedom.

6.2 Kant's rejection of the thesis of "comparative" or "psychological" freedom

The proponent of "comparative" or "psychological" freedom embraces the thesis of determinism according to which nothing happens in nature that is not caused. She applies that thesis to human nature. At the same time, she asserts that even though determinism is true, it is also the case that we are capable of freedom. She believes, furthermore, that these two theses do not conflict.

On Kant's analysis, the price this approach pays for achieving the compatibility of determinism and freedom is a drastically weakened conception of human freedom. For this compatibilist or soft-determinist, freedom is simply the absence of external constraint. Take, for example, my decision at this moment to type this sentence. Nothing is preventing me from doing so; no one has tied my hands behind my back. I have given some thought to the words I will type, and I proceed to carry my decision out. According to this compatibilist, I engage in free activity. What Kant points out, however, is that it does follow from the absence of *external* constraint, as in the above case, that there is no constraint at all. Determinism holds that if some event, x, happens, there must be a sufficient cause without which x could not have happened. There must be a sufficient cause, even if the event in question is a choice or decision. For the consistent determinist, that is, even mental states are determined or caused. Thus, they are not free in any genuine sense; they are simply "caused from within," as Kant puts it.[29]

Kant urges us, then, to appreciate the full implications of the determinist's hypothesis. As he writes in the *Critique of Practical Reason*, it is a "wretched subterfuge" to identify as free those actions that are determined by an internal cause.[30] It is a "wretched subterfuge," because if determinism is true, then the behavior we seek to explain is not free – it certainly is not free in any sense that could warrant attributions of responsibility. Although the cause is internal,

[29] *CPrR* (96).   [30] *CPrR* (95f.).

we would nonetheless be mistaken in claiming that the agent could have acted otherwise. We would likewise be mistaken in judging that the agent ought not to have done what he did. For Kant, in short, "psychological" or "comparative" freedom is too weak to give the moral "ought" a point.

We now have our explanation for Kant's adherence to premise "i" above:

If we ground morality in experience, we cannot provide for the possibility of human freedom.

Kant holds that if we consider human nature just as we consider other objects of nature or experience, from the natural science point of view, then we have to admit that the only laws that govern it are deterministic laws of nature. We therefore must grant that we have no scientific basis for the assumption that human nature is free. This is why Kant was convinced that an empirical grounding is unable to provide for the possibility of human freedom. It is why he writes in the *Critique of Practical Reason* that freedom is the "stumbling block" of empiricism.[31]

7. KANT'S STRATEGY FOR SAVING FREEDOM

7.1 *Kant's determinism*

It is important that we bear in mind that Kant's critique of the above form of compatibilism did not lead him to a wholesale rejection of determinism. Following Newton, he was committed to the view that everything in nature is caused by mechanical forces.[32] He understood that the task of the natural sciences is to explain the behavior of phenomena, including human behavior, with reference to these forces. He granted, then, that in so far as we seek a scientific explanation of human behavior, we have to work within the deterministic framework.

---

[31] *CPrR* (7).
[32] Kant's determinism is explicit, for example, in his commitment to the following principle, the Second Analogy of experience: "All alterations occur in accordance with the law of the connection of cause and effect," *CPR* B 232.

7.2 Kant's conception of freedom

Given his commitment to determinism, Kant had a formidable problem to solve. He wanted to save freedom, and the freedom he wanted to save had to be something other than "psychological" or "comparative" freedom; it had to amount to more than the mere absence of external constraint. Kant thus set out to provide for the possibility of what he called "transcendental" freedom. On his definition, transcendental freedom is a special capacity of self-determination, a capacity that, as he puts it, involves "independence from everything empirical and so from nature generally" (*CPrR* 97). As I suggested earlier, Kant believed he had to save this more radical kind of freedom because doing so, in his view, was the only way to provide for the possibility of practical imputation. He also thought that saving freedom in the transcendental sense was necessary to secure a particular conception we have of ourselves, namely, as beings capable of genuine agency. This latter point deserves elaboration.

In the *Critique of Pure Reason*, Kant considers a case of a person who tells a malicious lie.[33] Kant first asks us to think about what it means to examine this case empirically, that is, from the standpoint of natural science. In doing so, we rely on the methods of the sciences of empirical psychology, sociology, perhaps even genetics, to explain how the lie came about. We give an account of its various possible causes such as the agent's defective upbringing, natural temperament, social circumstances, and so forth. But Kant goes on to emphasize the following point: even were our sciences able to supply a complete account of the causes of the lie, we would nonetheless blame the agent. We would insist that the agent *could have done otherwise*. We would do so because we think of ourselves as more than merely cogs in nature's machine; we assume we have the capacity of freedom.

Kant intended this example to illustrate what he took to be a *necessary* fact about human nature. In his view, we necessarily consider ourselves from two perspectives. On the one hand, we think of ourselves as creatures of nature, determined by laws of physics, biology, and psychology – laws over which we have no control. On the other hand, we attribute to ourselves the capacity of

---

[33] *CPR* A 554/B 582.

self-determination.[34] Again, by self-determination Kant has in mind more than simply the power to reflect and deliberate. Unless properly qualified, this latter account of human freedom is merely a version of the "psychological" or "comparative" freedom Kant dismisses as a "wretched subterfuge." For Kant, human freedom requires independence from the realm of nature. He insists upon this claim repeatedly, for example, when he tells us in the first *Critique* that when reason acts freely, it acts "without being determined ... by external or internal grounds temporally preceding it in the chain of natural causes" (*CPR* A 553/B 581).[35]

7.3 Kant's strategy for harmonizing freedom and nature

Kant recognized that he needed some way to defend the following position, set forth in the *Critique of Pure Reason*:

Causality according to the laws of nature is not the only form of causality from which all the appearances of the world can be derived ... [I]t is also necessary to assume a causality of freedom. (*CPR* A 444/B 473)

As we just saw, Kant held that we necessarily think of ourselves as free in the transcendental sense. What he needed was an argument demonstrating that it is *legitimate* for us to regard ourselves in this way. He needed to show that regarding ourselves in this way is more than just a case of flattering self-deception.

His strategy, in essence, was to argue that the scientific perspective is insufficient or limited in a significant way. It is insufficient not just because it is unable to provide for the possibility of human freedom but also with respect to its own aims. The aim of scientific or theoretical inquiry is to know nature. But it cannot succeed in this endeavor, Kant argues, by relying on its own resources alone. It depends on other forms of inquiry – in particular, practical inquiry – for its completion.

---

[34] Kant thus writes in the *Groundwork* (455) that, "[a]ll human beings think of themselves as having free will."

[35] A convincing defense of the point that Kant's concept of transcendental freedom implies independence from the realm of nature is provided in Chapter 11 of H. E. Allison, *Kant's Theory of Freedom* (Cambridge University Press, 1990), p. 207.

Kant devotes the third section of the *Groundwork* to the task of establishing that we are justified in thinking of ourselves as free. His arguments there essentially summarize the results of his discussion in the Third Antinomy section of the *Critique of Pure Reason*. I turn, now, to provide a brief sketch of two of his arguments.

7.4 Saving freedom: argument 1

In the 1787 Preface to the *Critique of Pure Reason*, Kant informs us that a central task of that text is to draw the precise boundaries of theoretical or scientific cognition. He notes that he will draw the limits of knowledge in order to "make room for *faith*."[36] He claims that a considerable advantage of this limitation is that it provides for the possibility of human freedom.

Kant draws the limits of our theoretical or scientific knowledge by restricting the scope of the possible objects of this kind of knowledge. On his account, objects of theoretical or scientific cognition are what he calls "appearances." This a technical term, for Kant. He does not use it as we might – to designate illusions or phantoms. On his definition, an appearance is a possible object of inner or outer sensation. Objects of inner sensation (such as my awareness, now, of the progression of my thoughts) are necessarily experienced by us in time. Objects of outer sensation (such as the chair upon which I am sitting) are necessarily experienced by us in space as well as in time.

Kant argues that space and time are "a priori forms of intuition." They are "a priori" in that we bring them to, rather than abstract them from, experience. They are part of what we might call our cognitive hardwiring. They are forms of "intuition" in that they condition how objects must be given to us in sensation. Kant distinguishes a priori forms of intuition from a priori forms of understanding. The latter are concepts ("categories") without which we could not *think* objects. The former are conditions by means of which we *sense* or *intuit* objects.

But how does this thesis that space and time are a priori forms of intuition imply a limitation on the scope of our knowledge? The answer is that space and time, on Kant's conception, are necessary

[36] *CPR* B xxx.

constraints on what can be possible objects of experience for us. If we remove the conditions of space and time, he says, what remain are "things in themselves." While things in themselves are *thinkable* without contradiction, they are non-empirical or "transcendent" objects in that they cannot be given in space and time. Because they cannot be given in space and time, we can have no empirical cognition of them; they are thus wholly unknowable from a scientific or theoretical point of view. This means that for our form of cognition, "transcendent" objects such as God, freedom, and immortality are not possible objects of scientific knowledge.

Not only does Kant limit the scope of our theoretical or scientific cognition in this way, he also acknowledges that there may be other finite beings whose forms of intuition are unlike our own. *We* have to experience objects of nature in space and time. But – and this is the crucial point – we have no grounds for assuming that our form of experience is the only form there is.[37] In denying that we can know things in themselves, Kant thus "makes room" for speculation about a causality of freedom. Freedom is not a possible object of our scientific knowledge, but this is no reason to dogmatically deny its reality for other forms of experience. Theoretical considerations about the limits of our knowledge thus permit speculation about the idea of freedom as an alternative form of causality. Although we cannot know that we are free, we may legitimately think of ourselves as free. In light of the fact that freedom is a condition of the possibility of morality, there are obvious practical advantages of doing so.

7.5 Saving freedom: argument 2

If we take a second look at the passage quoted above in Section 7.3, this time including the phrase I omitted, we discover a clue to a further Kantian argument for saving freedom:

---

[37] Kant makes this point in the Transcendental Aesthetic section of the *CPR* B 72. In his words: "It is not necessary that we limit the kind of intuition in space and time to the sensibility of human beings; it may well be that all finite thinking beings must necessarily agree with humans in this respect (*though we cannot decide this*)" (emphasis added). He reminds us of this point in Section III of the *Groundwork* at (451). The "*world of sense*," he writes there, can be "very different according to the difference of sensibility in various observers of the world."

Causality according to the laws of nature is not the only form of causality from which all the appearances of the world can be derived. In order to explain appearances it is also necessary to assume a causality of freedom. (*CPR* A 444/B 473)

Notice Kant's observation that it is "in order to explain appearances" that we need to assume a causality of freedom. As in the case of the first argument, he once again seeks to convince us that freedom must be presupposed not just on practical but also on theoretical grounds. Whereas the first argument depends on restricting the scope of the objects of our theoretical or scientific knowledge, the strategy of the second argument is to persuade us that scientific inquiry rests on assumptions it is unable to justify. Scientific inquiry is in this sense not self-sufficient.

To appreciate one respect in which scientific inquiry is not self-sufficient, consider the assumption that the causality of nature is the only form of causality there is. Kant tells us that the rule expressing the causality of nature is that "nothing happens without a cause sufficiently determined a priori" (*CPR* A 446/B 474). Departing from Hume, he insists that this rule is an a priori law of nature rather than merely an empirical generalization. As a priori, it is universally and necessarily valid, in his view. Anything that is an object of nature must conform to it.

But Kant is also convinced that scientific inquiry is ultimately unable to justify the assumption that the causality of nature is the only form of causality there is. He argues this point by drawing our attention to all that the above-mentioned law of nature implies. As we have seen, the claim that "nothing happens without a cause sufficiently determined a priori" is equivalent to the claim that for any event, y, there is some condition or set of conditions, x, such that given x, y had to happen. Now, in searching for the sufficient condition for an event y, our inquiry regresses from conditioned to condition. Like the child who is curious, first, about the cause of her existence, and then about the cause of her parents' existence, and so forth, we push our inquiry back in search of that point at which our questions can finally cease. This is what is involved in seeking the sufficient condition for an event. Ultimately, we search for an "unconditioned condition," a cause that is itself uncaused. But given that what we seek is an unconditioned condition, Kant points out, we have to grant that the object of our inquiry is not itself a possible object of scientific knowledge. A genuinely sufficient cause or unconditioned condition cannot be an object of scientific knowledge because objects of scientific knowledge are governed by the causality of nature. The law of the causality of nature, as we have seen, is that nothing in nature "happens without a cause sufficiently determined a priori." The law of nature implies, in effect, that an unconditioned condition, or a cause that is truly sufficient, is not to be discovered in nature. Although the law of nature posits the idea of a cause that is sufficient or uncaused, this idea refers to an object that is not itself a possible object of scientific knowledge.

The law expressing the causality of nature thus requires us to think of an object that science itself can never know. Kant refers to this idea as that of an "absolute beginning." It is a beginning that is "spontaneous" or not in time. Kant identifies this idea of an absolute or spontaneous beginning as that of "transcendental freedom" (*CPR* A 446/B 474). He thus argues that for the sake not just of practical but also of theoretical inquiry, we have no option but to presuppose in addition to a causality of nature, a causality of transcendental freedom.

CHAPTER 2

Kant's Preface

I. INTRODUCTION

Kant's task in his Preface to the *Groundwork* is threefold: First, he sets out to clarify his main objectives in the text. Second, he provides clues to the method he will use to accomplish his objectives. Third, he indicates how he intends to organize the work. He devotes his first paragraphs to clarifying the title of the book, a title even he admits is "intimidating" (391). The *Groundwork*, he says, is not a work in physics or logic but a work in the area he refers to as "morals" [*Sitten*] or "ethics" [*Ethik*]. Kant notes that the book is a special kind of treatise in morals or ethics: it is a "groundwork" of the "metaphysics" of morals. These latter terms are technical; we will have to consider what he means by them.

1.1 The objectives of the Groundwork

As I noted in my Introduction, Kant describes the chief task of the *Groundwork* in the following passage:

The present groundwork is ... nothing more than the search for and establishment of the *supreme principle of morality*. (392)

To "search for" the supreme principle is to set out to discover the principle that is appropriate and adequate as the ultimate or fundamental moral standard. To "establish" the principle is to justify or ground it. Clearly, then, Kant aims to offer an argument in the *Groundwork* for why the principle he identifies as supreme is, indeed, just that. He emphasizes in the Preface that this task of searching for and establishing the principle is different in important respects from that of actually applying the principle. He admits that application of the principle to particular cases would be useful in demonstrating the principle's adequacy, but he also tells us that application is not his concern here (392).

Kant provides a preliminary expression of the supreme principle of morality in Section I (at (402)). In Section II, he gives us his first official formulation of the principle and identifies it as the "categorical imperative" (416). He "establishes" the principle by arguing that it has its ground as well as its source in pure reason. The fact that the principle has its ground as well as its source in pure reason means, for Kant, that the principle is a priori. We should not conclude from the fact that the principle is a priori, however, that his ethics contains no empirical elements whatsoever. In the Preface, Kant addresses the issue of what is and is not empirical in his practical philosophy. As we will see, he urges the importance of keeping separate the a priori and a posteriori or empirical components of practical philosophy. He stresses this point in his Preface and reminds us of it frequently in all three sections of the text.

1.2 On the need for a supreme principle

Practical philosophy is in need of a supreme principle, Kant says, because "as long as we are without that clue and supreme norm by which to appraise" morals correctly, morals "remain subject to all sorts of corruption" (390). The context in which this remark appears makes it clear that Kant seeks to insure that when we assess the moral worth of actions or persons, we have at our disposal the *right* standard and not some seemingly adequate substitute. He is aware that philosophers through the ages have proposed various principles as the supreme standard. His bold claim, however, is that only *his* principle gives us the supreme moral law in its "purity and genuineness."

1.3 On the need for a grounding or justification

A grounding of the categorical imperative is necessary, according to Kant, because we should not be satisfied with the mere assertion that the categorical imperative is the supreme principle of morality. The *Groundwork* provides an argument in support of that assertion. Kant considers it his philosophical mission to convince us that his supreme law – as well as his general approach to practical philosophy – is the only adequate one. He sets out to convince us of this in good philosophical fashion: not by deploying sophistical tricks or persuasive fallacies, but by supporting his claims with good reasons and solid evidence. He believes the reasons he supplies in favor of his theory are reasons each of us will find compelling.

1.4 Kant's method for searching for and establishing the supreme principle

We can derive clues to Kant's method from the fact that he is convinced that the supreme principle of morality has its source as well as its justification in reason. This allows us to anticipate that his grounding of the categorical imperative will not involve an appeal to empirical evidence. Although he occasionally points out that people as a matter of fact already do at least implicitly acknowledge the validity of the supreme moral law, he also insists that the validity of the law is not established by means of empirically derived facts about how people actually behave or about beliefs they happen to have. In grounding the law, Kant's argument will be more conceptual in nature. It will involve the analysis of key concepts, such as that of a good will, duty, and practical reason. Ultimately, it will also require reflection on the a priori conditions and limits of human knowledge.

2. ETHICS, PHYSICS, LOGIC (387F.)

Because one of Kant's objectives in the Preface is to clarify his subject matter, he announces in his opening sentences his intention to first consider the principle responsible for distinguishing the sciences of ethics (or morals), physics, and logic. He will compare ethics to logic and to physics in two respects: First, his comparison will be based on the kinds of objects proper to each of these sciences. Second, he will relate the sciences with regard to the source of their fundamental laws. Although as Kant notes, the division of the sciences of physics, ethics, and logic may be traced all the way back to the ancient Greeks, he intends to offer his own account of the basis of their division. He begins by separating all "rational knowledge" into the categories of "material" and "formal." Of the three sciences, he says, only logic is, strictly speaking, formal.

2.1 The "formal" nature of logic

Logic is formal, according to Kant, because of the kind of object with which it deals. Its object, he says, is the "form of the understanding and reason," the "universal and necessary laws of thinking." Simply put, its object is thought itself. A material science, in contrast, "has to do with determinate objects and the laws to which they are subject" (387). The determinate object of physics is nature (or objects of nature). The determinate object of ethics is the "human being's will."

Kant expands on the formal nature of logic in the *Critique of Pure Reason*.[1] There he writes that (general) logic "has to do with nothing further than itself and its own form." It abstracts "from all objects of cognition and all the distinctions between them" (*CPR* B ix). Logic lays down the functions of thought, without regard to the particular objects or content of thought. It specifies, on the one hand, rules of reasoning or inference. We learn from logic, for example, that if we assume that all men are mortal, and further assume that Socrates is a man, then we are warranted in concluding with necessity that Socrates is mortal. Logic in addition compares and classifies judgments with respect to what Kant calls their "logical form" – with respect, that is, to the various ways in which concepts may be brought into combination with each other. Kant includes among the various logical forms of judgment, for example, the form of *quantity*. We distinguish universal judgments ("All S is P"), for instance, from particular judgments ("Some S is P"). Judgments necessarily have some *quality* as well: a judgment expresses either "reality" ("S is P"), "negation" ("S is not-P"), or "limitation" ("S is non-P"). Kant holds that these logical forms are valid for all thought in general, irrespective of the particular objects of thought. The logical forms and rules of reasoning apply, then, whether or not the object we are thinking about is a number, an object of nature, or God.

---

[1] What Kant calls "formal" logic in the *Groundwork* is equivalent to "pure general logic" in the *CPR*. See B 78f./A 54f.

2.2 The "material" nature of physics and ethics

Physics and ethics are material because both fields of inquiry restrict their attention to "determinate objects" and the special laws that govern them. The objects of physics are objects of nature. An object of nature, on Kant's account, is an object given in space and time; it is what he calls an "appearance." Appearances (or, as we might also refer to them, empirical objects or objects of experience) are governed by natural laws or forces. The science that investigates these objects and the laws specific to them is physics, a "doctrine of nature."

The object of ethics is the human will (387). Kant labels the laws that govern the will "laws of freedom," and he tells us that the science of such laws is ethics [*Ethik*] – also known, he says, as the "doctrine of morals" [*Sittenlehre*].[2] Whereas laws of nature describe how objects of nature *in fact* behave, laws of freedom dictate how we *ought* to behave.

Two remarks are in order here about the way in which Kant identifies the object of ethics in this passage. Note, first, that he says not just that ethics determines the laws of the human will, but that it determines laws of the human will "insofar as that will is affected by nature" (387). Kant thereby acknowledges the fact that, even though human beings are capable of freedom, they at the same time exist in nature and are therefore also determined by laws of nature. He focuses our attention, then, on one of the great challenges of his discussion. He needs to provide an argument demonstrating that these two seemingly contradictory features of human nature – as both free and as "affected by nature" – can coexist. In stating early on in the Preface that the object of ethics is the human will "insofar as that will is affected by nature," he informs us of his view that, although we are entitled to think of ourselves as free, we are not capable of casting off the determinations of nature entirely.

Note, second, that Kant sometimes broadens the scope of the object of the *Groundwork*. Although at (387) he tells us that the object of ethics is the human will, he states elsewhere that the validity of the practical principles he is concerned to establish extends not just to the

---

[2] Here we have examples of what I referred to in my Introduction (2.3, ii) as Kant's use of the terms "ethics" and "morality" in the broad sense.

human will, but to "every rational being as such" (412).[3] He thus shifts back and forth between the claim that the object of his inquiry is human rational nature and the claim that his object is rational nature in general.

2.3 Logic is not just formal but also "pure"

Logic is "pure" with respect to the source of its laws. Its laws derive without exception from reason rather than experience. Given that its laws derive from reason, they are a priori versus empirical or a posteriori. Logic is an instance of pure philosophy, Kant says, because any science that "sets forth its teachings simply from a priori principles" is an instance of "pure philosophy" (388).[4]

2.4 Physics and ethics, although "material," both have a "pure" (and hence "metaphysical") part

As we saw, Kant holds that physics and ethics are material sciences because each deals with a particular kind of object rather than with the form and rules of thought in general. In adding to this characterization the claim that each has a pure part, Kant means to draw our attention to the fact that each of these domains of inquiry rests entirely on a priori principles. This is a feature physics and ethics share with logic. I drew attention to this aspect of Kant's ethics in my Introduction. I singled out as one of the substantive doctrines of his practical philosophy his claim that the supreme moral law has its source in reason (and is thus a priori).

In these early paragraphs of the Preface, Kant furthermore clarifies what he means by the "metaphysical" part of a science. He tells us that only a material science can have a metaphysical part. The

---

[3] At (410n) of the *Groundwork*, Kant writes that the moral principles he defends "are not based on what is peculiar to human nature." From such principles, he continues, "it must be possible to derive practical rules for every rational nature." See also *Groundwork* (408, 425, 442) and *CPrR* (32).

[4] Although laws of logic are without exception pure, Kant recognizes that experience plays a role in how we actually apply them. Distraction and forgetfulness, for example, can interfere with our ability to reason well. It is the business of "applied" logic, he tells us in the *CPR*, to study the "empirical conditions under which our understanding is exercized," B 77/A 53. See also A 54f./B 79.

metaphysical part of a material science is its pure part.[5] Since only a material science can have a metaphysical part, there can thus be a metaphysics of physics and of ethics but not of logic (388).

2.5 Unlike logic, physics and ethics both have an "empirical" part

Physics rests on pure or a priori laws, but it also has an empirical part in that the objects governed by its laws are objects of experience ("appearances"). As Kant remarks here, laws of physics "must determine laws of nature as an object of experience." We would be mistaken, he implies, were we to assume that laws of physics in addition legislate over objects *not* discoverable in the realm of experience, objects such as God or the immortal soul.

Ethics has an empirical part in this very same sense. Its object, the human will, is likewise an object of experience. This is the message Kant intends to convey when he writes that ethics has to do with "laws of the human being's will insofar as it is affected by nature" (387). The human will "affected by nature" is the will of an object in space and time, governed by natural forces, and motivated in its conduct by incentives that derive from its empirical nature. Of course, we know from our remarks above (at Section 2.2) that Kant believes we are warranted in thinking of ourselves not merely as objects of nature, determined by laws of nature, but also as free. As free, our will has the capacity to rise above the forces of nature; it can initiate actions from a standpoint outside time. Properly speaking, then, the object of ethics, according to Kant, is a will that is *both* empirical and non-empirical; it is both an object of nature and capable of transcending nature. More precisely, the object of Kant's ethics is the human will considered from each of these two points of view.

Kant draws our attention to a second respect in which ethics has an empirical part. This second respect is worth considering in some detail. He alludes to it in passing at (388) and expands upon it at (389) as well as elsewhere in the text.[6] At (388) he says that moral philosophy has an empirical part in that it "takes into account"

---

[5] Kant provides this characterization of metaphysics in the *CPR* as well. See, for example, A 841/B 869.

[6] For example, in Section II at (412).

conditions under which the moral law "very often" does not successfully determine the will. His suggestion seems to be that moral
philosophy has an empirical part insofar as it is concerned with factors
that can interfere with our motivation to act from duty. Obviously,
the moral law does not always sufficiently determine our will. Most of
us, at least on occasion, behave badly or entertain immoral thoughts.
In some cases, environmental conditions tempt us away from respecting duty (we succumb, for instance, to peer pressure). In other cases,
our behavior is in part caused by a genetic predisposition (a "bad gene"
inclines us to violence). The part of moral philosophy that considers
the many contingent empirical factors that play a role in determining
the effect of the moral law on our will is the part Kant refers to as
"anthropology" (389).

As already noted, Kant gives us a more expansive account of this
empirical part of ethics at (389). In a passage there he assigns to
anthropology not merely the role just outlined, but a further role.
The passage merits quoting at length:

[A]ll moral philosophy is based entirely on its pure part; and when it is
applied to the human being it does not borrow the least thing from acquaintance with him (from anthropology) but gives to him, as a rational being,
laws a priori, which no doubt still require a judgement sharpened by
experience, partly to distinguish in what cases they are applicable and partly
to provide them with access to the will of the human being and efficacy for
his fulfilment of them; for the human being is affected by so many inclinations that, though capable of the idea of a practical pure reason, he is not so
easily able to make it effective *in concreto* in the conduct of his life.

One remark in this passage is potentially misleading. Kant writes that
moral philosophy "does not borrow the least thing" from anthropology. As subsequent sentences of this passage reveal, the remark is an
overstatement and thus should not be taken literally. Very likely, Kant
overstates his point because he wants us to bear in mind that moral
philosophy borrows nothing from anthropology *for its grounding*.
There is nothing empirical, in his view, about the *origin* or *justification*
of the supreme law.

The quoted passage indicates two roles for anthropology. One is
the role we just reviewed. A "judgement sharpened by experience" is
needed, Kant tells us, in order to provide moral laws "access to the will
of the human being and efficacy for his fulfilment of them." Here

again, Kant highlights the service anthropology can perform in illuminating the conditions that must be in place for moral laws to actually motivate us. As he argues elsewhere, anthropology teaches us that social institutions such as education can awaken in us the right kind of attitudes toward the moral law and inspire us to act from it.[7]

But anthropology performs a further role. It can also assist us in the application of the moral law to concrete cases. As essential as it is that we be motivated to act from the law, we also need to know how to apply the law. For this we require, among other things, knowledge of human nature. I cannot effectively carry out my duty to develop my talents, for example, if I am unable to realistically identify them. Nor can I act from the duty to help my neighbor if I am ignorant of her particular needs and of the kind of aid that would benefit her. Without knowledge of human nature, our good intentions are liable to result in deeds that are ineffective or even counterproductive.

Notice that if practical philosophy had no empirical part in the first sense – were its object not the human will "affected by nature" – it would not require the empirical part in the second sense. Practical philosophy would have no need, that is, for anthropology.[8]

3. THE "METAPHYSICS" OF MORALS (388)

We now know that the metaphysical part of morals and of physics, for Kant, is their "pure" or (as he sometimes calls it) "rational" part. Their "pure" or "rational" part is that part of their teachings that is a priori. The metaphysical part of morals, then, refers to its a priori laws or principles.

---

[7] Kant provides a helpful elaboration of this point in the Introduction to his *MM*. Moral anthropology deals, he says, "with the subjective conditions in human nature that hinder people or help them in fulfilling the laws of a metaphysics of morals. It would deal with the development, spreading, and strengthening of moral principles (in education in schools and in popular instruction), and with other similar teachings and precepts based on experience. It cannot be dispensed with, but must not precede a metaphysics of morals or be mixed with it" (217).

[8] At (412), Kant writes that while moral laws "are to hold for every rational being as such," anthropology is needed for the "application" of moral laws to human beings in particular. For discussion of the role of anthropology in Kant's practical philosophy, see R. Louden, *Kant's Impure Ethics: From Rational Beings to Human Beings*, C. M. Schmidt, "The anthropological dimension of Kant's Metaphysics of Morals." *Kant-Studien* 96 (2005), 42–62; A. Wood, *Kant's Ethical Thought*, Part II.

Kant argues that the supreme a priori principle of practical philosophy is the categorical imperative. In my Introduction, I provided a
preliminary representation of this law. I said that it essentially commands
us to respect the dignity of all rational nature. The law itself is quite
general, but Kant believes it is capable of yielding more specific commands. He contends that, when applied to human nature, it justifies a
number of moral imperatives. These more specific imperatives require
us, for example, to be truthful, to be benevolent, to respect the property
of others, and so forth. On Kant's account, these imperatives are also
metaphysical laws or principles. Like the supreme moral law itself, they
have their ground and source in reason. They are thus also a priori.

We are now in a better position to understand the title of the work
we are considering. The *Groundwork* lays the ground of the metaphysical part of morals. Its task is to search for and establish the a priori
law that lies at the basis of practical philosophy, the law Kant names
the "categorical imperative."

3.1 *Ambiguities in Kant's use of the term "metaphysics"*

In the first paragraphs of the *Groundwork*, Kant uses the term "metaphysical" to refer to that part of the teachings of a science that derives a
priori. In other contexts, however, he uses the term "metaphysical" to
mean something else. In the *Critique of Pure Reason*, for example, he
occasionally uses it to refer to a particular form of inquiry, a form of
inquiry devoted to the consideration of objects he designates as "super-
sensible."[9] As I mentioned in my Introduction, Kant argues in the first
Critique that these objects cannot be cognized or known by us. The
metaphysician who assumes that objects such as God, freedom, and the
immortal soul are knowable is guilty, in his view, of "dogmatism" (*CPR*
A xiv). But Kant also argues that our ideas of the traditional objects of
metaphysics can have a valuable – even indispensable – use.

This latter point is central not just to Kant's theoretical philosophy
but to his practical philosophy as well. At the basis of his practical

---

[9] See, for example, B xiv of the first *CPR*, where Kant defines metaphysics as a "speculative
cognition of reason that elevates itself entirely above all instruction from experience." At B
395n, he identifies as the "proper end" of metaphysics the three ideas of God, freedom, and
immortality.

philosophy is the assumption that even though we cannot know we are free, we must nonetheless think of ourselves as free. This suggests that there is a second sense in which the *Groundwork* may be said to contain a metaphysical component. Its approach to practical philosophy is metaphysical not just because it is based on a priori laws. The work is also metaphysical in that it investigates the "idea and the principles" of an object that is not to be discovered in the realm of experience, namely, the "*pure* will" (390). Although the main task of the *Groundwork* is to "lay the ground," that is, to search for and establish the categorical imperative and in so doing provide an a priori foundation for practical philosophy, the entire enterprise depends on the idea that we are more than merely cogs in nature's machine. The project of the *Groundwork* depends on the fact that we necessarily think of ourselves as having a will that is pure. It furthermore rests on establishing that we are entitled to think of ourselves in this way.

4. ON KEEPING SEPARATE THE PURE AND EMPIRICAL PARTS OF PRACTICAL PHILOSOPHY (388F.)

One of the main messages of Kant's Preface, a message to which he frequently returns in the text, concerns the importance of not conflating the pure and empirical parts of practical philosophy. The pure part, we now know, is the part that is metaphysical in both senses discussed above. It refers, on the one hand, to the a priori laws at the basis of practical philosophy, and, on the other, to an object with which the work is principally concerned: the pure will. The empirical part of practical philosophy, on Kant's account, refers both to the fact that its laws govern a human will that is not *merely* pure but also "affected by nature," and to the role played by anthropology.

4.1 On the importance of dividing labor (388–390)

Kant's insistence upon the necessity of keeping the pure and empirical parts of practical philosophy separate is already apparent in the sixth paragraph of his Preface. He notes there the benefits for "trades, crafts, and arts" of a division of labor, benefits also awarded those who resist the temptation to become a "jack of all trades." He suggests in this passage that philosophy would be well advised to follow suit. Those involved in the empirical part of philosophy should stick to their business, and those involved in the pure part should stick to theirs. He thus urges:

> that the empirical part always be carefully separated from the rational part, and that a metaphysics of nature be put before physics proper (empirical physics) and a metaphysics of morals before practical anthropology, with metaphysics carefully cleansed of everything empirical so that we may know how much pure reason can accomplish in both cases and from what sources it draws this a priori teaching of its own. (388f.)

This is a recurring theme of the *Groundwork*. Kant returns to it a few paragraphs later when he claims that any investigation that "mixes" "pure principles with empirical ones does not even deserve the name of philosophy" (390). Since this point is of great importance for him, we need to be clear about its meaning.

In the passage just quoted in which he writes of the necessity of keeping pure philosophy "cleansed" of "everything that may be only empirical," Kant is warning us not to forget the metaphysical or pure grounding of ethics. Obviously, he thinks that if we rest ethics on an *empirical* ground, we lose something important. I discussed this point at length in my Introduction. I suggested there that Kant provides two arguments for why morality cannot rest on an empirical ground. It will be useful to recall those arguments briefly.

The first argument is expressed in this important passage:[10]

> Everyone must grant that a law, if it is to hold morally, that is, as a ground of obligation, must carry with it absolute necessity; that, for example, the command, 'thou shalt not lie,' does not hold only for human beings, as if other rational beings did not have to heed it, and so with all other moral laws properly so called; that, therefore, the ground of obligation here must not be sought in the nature of the human being or in the circumstances of the world in which he is placed, but a priori simply in concepts of pure reason. (389)

Kant assumes in this passage that we will all agree that moral laws are universally valid. They are valid, as he says, not just for human rational natures, but for rational nature as such. He implies that we will also agree that moral laws bind with necessity. If I have a duty to be

---

[10] For similar passages, see *Groundwork* (408, 411, 425, 441–445).

truthful in a certain instance, I am bound to act from that duty unconditionally. My obligation is neither partial nor negotiable. For reasons mentioned in my Introduction, Kant is convinced that if we give practical philosophy an empirical grounding, we lose its universal and necessary validity. That is why he insists that "a metaphysics of morals is indispensably necessary" (389).

Kant's second argument in support of the claim that practical philosophy must be "cleansed" of "everything" "empirical" has to do with the role of freedom. He holds that if we have no justification for attributing to ourselves the capacity of freedom, the whole enterprise of practical philosophy is undermined. This second argument is nowhere explicitly mentioned in the Preface, but it is hinted at in the following remark:

[T]he metaphysics of morals has to examine the idea and the principles of a possible pure will and not the actions and conditions of human volition generally, which for the most part are drawn from psychology. (390f.)

Practical philosophy must be grounded in reason in order to insure that its principles are universally and necessarily valid. But practical philosophy in addition requires as a condition of its possibility the presupposition of a will that is pure or free. If we consider human nature merely from an empirical standpoint – if we take the human will to be nothing more than a will "affected by nature" – we in effect deny our capacity to act from motives that are non-empirical or pure. We leave ourselves no way to defend the thesis, then, that we have freedom. If we cannot defend that thesis, our attributions of responsibility and agency are empty.

5. BREAKING INTO A NEW FIELD: THE PURE WILL (390F.)

Given the centrality of the idea of a pure will to Kant's entire project in the *Groundwork*, it is odd that he says so little about it in his Preface. He thus hardly prepares us for what is the focus of much of his discussion in Section I. The main task of that discussion is to outline features of a special kind of motivation, one whose source is not nature but freedom. Otherwise put, Kant's main objective in Section I is to clarify what it means to be motivated by a pure will.

The one indication Kant gives us in the Preface of the importance of this idea is his remark that, with the idea of the pure will, he is breaking "into an entirely new field." What is new, he writes, is the notion of a will "completely determined from a priori principles without any empirical motives." Here Kant alerts us to the fact that his practical philosophy relies on an account of human motivation that is unprecedented in the history of philosophy. The pure will, as he intends it, cannot be examined or explained from the standpoint of "psychology." It cannot, because it is not the kind of object susceptible to empirical or scientific study. The pure will is a "metaphysical" object, an object nowhere to be found in the realm of experience. It is capable of moving us to act, but it does so, remarkably, from a standpoint outside space and time.

Kant thus puts us on notice here that his idea of the pure will requires us to think of human freedom in a radically new way. His conception of freedom is not reducible to that of the ordinary compatibilist, for whom freedom is merely the absence of external constraint. Nor is it adequately identified simply as the capacity of self-determination, or of deliberative action, or of action governed by reasons we give to ourselves. These descriptions gesture at, but do not adequately capture, the conception of freedom Kant considers necessary for the grounding of practical philosophy. They leave out of account an essential component of what is metaphysical about his "metaphysics of morals," namely, the idea of a will that is pure.[11]

6. THE ORGANIZATION OF THE *GROUNDWORK* (392)

Kant divides the *Groundwork* into three sections following the Preface:

First section: "Transition from common rational to philosophic moral cognition."

Second section: "Transition from popular moral philosophy to metaphysics of morals."

Third section: "Final step from metaphysics of morals to the critique of pure practical reason."

---

[11] I thus agree with Henry Allison, who writes in *Kant's Theory of Freedom* that "Kant's moral theory rests ultimately on a 'thick' conception of freedom and not on a 'thin', relatively unproblematic conception of rational agency."

All that Kant tells us in his Preface about the organization of the work is that he will "proceed analytically from common cognition to the determination of its supreme principle, and in turn synthetically from the examination of this principle and its sources back to the common cognition in which we find it used" (392). In the last paragraph of Section II, he claims that *both* sections I and II are "analytic." Sections I and II are "analytic," then, and Section III is "synthetic" (or "proceeds synthetically"). What do these terms mean?

For clarification, we can benefit from clues Kant provides in other works. In his 1783 *Prolegomena to Any Future Metaphysics that Will be Able to Come Forward as Science*, he writes that to proceed analytically is to begin from an uncontroversial or generally accepted concept, and then inquire into the conditions of its possibility.[12] Both in the *Prolegomena* and in §117 of his 1800 *Jäsche Logic*, Kant describes this form of inquiry as "regressive:" we "regress" from a concept back to the principles or assumptions that must be presupposed in order to explain as well as ground or condition it. The point of this endeavor is to gain a better understanding of the concept in question as well as of the conditions upon which it rests.

Since Kant claims that both sections I and II of the *Groundwork* are "analytic," we can first treat them as a unit. What is the concept he subjects to analysis in both sections? The final paragraph of Section II is informative. There Kant takes stock of what he has so far accomplished in the text. He writes that, at this point in his discussion, he has explicated the "generally received concept of morality" and revealed that autonomy of the will "lies at its basis" (445).[13] Section I of the *Groundwork* begins with the "generally received concept of morality"

---

[12] Kant writes in the *Prolegomena* that he will begin with "something already known to be dependable, from which we can go forward with confidence and ascend to the sources which are not yet known, and whose discovery not only will explain what is known already, but will also exhibit an area with many cognitions that all arise from these same sources" §4 (275). A few paragraphs later, he describes the analytic procedure in this way: "one proceeds from that which is sought as if it were given, and ascends to the conditions under which alone it is possible" §5 (276n).

[13] Gregor translates the passage to read: "By explicating the generally received concept of morality we showed only that an autonomy of the will unavoidably depends [*anhänge*] upon it, or much rather lies at its basis [*zum Grunde liege*]." In a footnote to this passage she suggests that "*anhänge*" should perhaps be translated as "is attached to it." The translation "is attached to it" seems to me to better capture Kant's meaning, for how could an autonomy of the will both depend on and lie at the basis of the generally received concept of morality?

(this is the "common rational ... moral cognition" referred to in its title). Kant applies his analytical procedure and thereby determines by the end of Section II that at the basis of that generally received concept is the assumption that human nature is endowed with autonomy or freedom of the will. By the time he has reached the end of Section II, then, he has completed the transition from the "common" concept of duty to the "metaphysics of morals" mentioned in the title of Section II. We can therefore say that Sections I and II together constitute the two parts of an analytical inquiry that begins with the common cognition of morality and regresses to an idea upon which that common cognition ultimately rests: the idea of an autonomous or free will.

Sections I and II, however, each cover different ground. The analytical regress in each section thus unfolds by way of different steps. The title of Section I announces that there will be a "transition," in that section, from "common rational" to "philosophic moral cognition." As already mentioned, Section I opens with an examination of the common concept of morality, the concept of a good will. The movement of the discussion is a regression to the "philosophical" cognition of the concept. By this Kant means that, thanks to his examination of the common concept, he is able to reveal assumptions that lie at its basis. In so doing, he deepens our understanding of the concept. We learn, for instance, that when we judge that a will is good, we imply that it acts from duty rather than from inclination. Pushing our analysis back further, we also learn that when we claim that a person acts from duty, we imply that she is motivated by an a priori practical law, namely, the categorical imperative.

The title of Section II indicates that we are to expect a different transition there, this time from "popular moral philosophy" to a "metaphysics of morals." Contrary to what we might expect, the concept of "popular moral philosophy" is not identical to the concept of "common rational cognition" with which Kant begins Section I. In fact, Kant's view is that the popular concept of morality is unreliable. He introduces it at the beginning of Section II only in order to warn us not to confuse it with "common moral appraisal" which, in his words, is "very worthy of respect" (412). The popular conception makes a brief appearance in Section II, but then disappears from Kant's discussion.

So one step in the transition in Section II from "popular moral philosophy" to a "metaphysics of morals" disqualifies the former as a dependable guide to the concept of morality. Once Kant disqualifies the "popular" approach in the early paragraphs of Section II, he returns to the work he began in Section I: he further carries out his analysis of the "common" cognition. The regress culminates in an approach to morality that is "metaphysical" in two senses: (i) It reveals, as a result of the analytical work of Section I, that the law that expresses duty is a priori rather than empirical; and (ii) it reveals, as a result of the analysis of Section II, that the very possibility of duty or of practical obligation, has "at its basis" the idea of a will that is autonomous or free.

We have yet to comment on the contrast Kant draws between the first two ("analytic") sections of the *Groundwork* and the third ("synthetic") section. The title of Section III is, "Final step from metaphysics of morals to the critique of pure practical reason." Kant indicates elsewhere that a "synthetic" investigation is "progressive" or forward-moving rather than "regressive."[14] His brief description of his synthetic method in the Preface, however, seems to imply just the reverse. What he tells us is that he will proceed "synthetically from the examination of ... [the supreme moral] principle and its sources *back* to the common cognition in which we find it used" (392; emphasis added). In what way, then, is the movement of the discussion in Section III synthetic or progressive?

Because the nature of Kant's argument in Section III is particularly difficult to grasp, it is best to postpone a detailed treatment of it until we are further along in our commentary.[15] A few brief observations are nevertheless in order here. By the end of Section II, Kant believes he has persuaded us that the common concept of duty depends on the idea of a will that is autonomous. He believes he has demonstrated this by making explicit, by means of his analytical procedure, what is already thought in the common cognition of morality. The task of Section III is different. It is not that of making explicit the assumptions implied by a given concept. Instead, its role is justificatory. By the end of Section II, Kant has revealed that we necessarily think of ourselves as autonomous. In Section III, he moves on to demonstrate that this self-conception is warranted. He sets out to establish that we can legitimately consider ourselves to be determined to act not merely

---

[14] *Prolegomena* §5 (276n).
[15] I begin consideration of this issue in the final section of my discussion of Section II.

by laws of nature but also by laws of freedom. He seeks to show that this self-conception is more than just a self-serving illusion.

The only hint Kant gives us regarding his method of argumentation in Section III – other than to say that it is not analytic – is contained in the section's title. The title indicates that a transition will be made from "metaphysics" (from the idea of a pure will) to a "critique of practical reason." Kant does not prepare us for the phrase "critique of practical reason." It refers to his effort to demonstrate that pure reason can be the source of laws that govern our behavior – that pure reason can be practical.[16] Expressed in another way, the phrase refers to Kant's project of establishing that we are entitled to think of ourselves as determined to act by laws of the pure will.[17] As for the method he deploys in securing this entitlement, for now it suffices to say that the proof consists in arguing that our view of ourselves as merely empirical creatures, as determined in all that we do by laws of nature, is critically incomplete. As I observed in my Introduction, Kant borrows from arguments he has defended in the *Critique of Pure Reason* in claiming that scientific knowledge, including scientific knowledge of human nature, must ultimately and necessarily rely on ideas it cannot itself justify.

As we saw, Kant suggests that the argument of Section III is not just forward-moving but also involves a step back. He indicates this when he writes that his discussion will take us from the "examination of [the supreme moral] principle and its sources back to the common cognition in which we find it used" (392). He does not explain how Section III takes us back to the common cognition of morality, but we can venture a guess. When Kant reaches the end of Section III, he believes he has successfully established our warrant in thinking of ourselves as autonomous or free. Having established this, he can reflect back on his starting point and satisfy himself that his work is done. He can claim that, thanks to his efforts, the common cognition of morality with which his investigation began is now securely grounded.

---

[16] In the Preface to his *CPrR*, Kant writes that the task of a "critique of practical reason" is to demonstrate "that there is pure practical reason" (3). Otherwise put, its task is to establish that "freedom is real" (4).

[17] Kant identifies the (pure) will and practical reason in the *Groundwork* at (412).

CHAPTER 3

Section I: Transition from common rational to philosophic moral cognition

I. INTRODUCTION

1.1 The title of Section I

We saw in the final paragraphs of our previous chapter that Kant indicates that he will "proceed analytically" in Section I from a "common rational moral cognition" to the "determination of its supreme principle" (392). The "transition" Kant refers to in the title of Section I, then, is a transition from what he supposes is a commonly accepted concept – in this case, the concept of a good will – to the assumptions upon which that concept is grounded or based. The movement is regressive: from a conditioned concept to its conditions.[1]

But what qualifies a cognition as "common," on Kant's account? This question is especially pressing in light of the fact that, in Section II, he will insist upon distinguishing the "common" from the "popular" cognition of a good will. In our discussion of the Preface we learned that Kant is convinced that only the common cognition furnishes reliable insight into the concept of a good will. We will examine his reasons for this view in some detail when we turn, in the next chapter, to our discussion of the first paragraphs of Section II. For now, we need merely note that Kant seems to identify "common moral cognition" with something akin to moral insight or intuition.[2] The

---

[1] For an explanation of what it means for a concept to be conditioned, see my discussion in Section 6 of Chapter 2, including note 12.

[2] This is confirmed by the first sentence of Section II where Kant says emphatically that the "common" concept of duty is not a concept of experience (406). As he notes a few paragraphs later, the origin of the common concept of duty lies "prior to all experience" in reason (408).

popular concept of the good will is unreliable, in his view, because it derives its concept of duty from a different source, namely, from experience.

As we will discover, the *Groundwork* contains a number of references to common cognition. Kant very likely has common cognition in mind, for instance, when he writes in his Preface that:

Everyone must grant that a law, if it is to hold morally, that is, as a ground of obligation, must carry with it absolute necessity. (389)

Kant repeatedly tells us in the *Groundwork* that common human reason (or "natural sound understanding," as he sometimes calls it[3]) is in agreement about the nature of duty and its underlying principle.[4] In setting out in Section I with the common concept of the good will, then, he clearly thinks of himself as beginning his discussion with a concept that is uncontroversial. Common reason knows how to distinguish good from bad conduct, he tells us at the end of Section I (404). It knows this without the aid of science or philosophy or even worldly experience (403f.). Common human reason is in agreement about what one must do to be "honest and good, and even wise and virtuous" (404).

As already indicated, Kant asserts that we make the transition from the common to the philosophical concept of a good will by employing the method of analysis. By reflecting upon and analyzing the concept, we are supposed to be able to discover the assumptions upon which it rests. As the discussion of Section I progresses, Kant gradually brings these assumptions to light. We learn from his analysis of the common cognition of the good will that:

  i. The goodness of a good will has to do with its motivation, not with what it actually achieves (394).
 ii. A good will is motivated by duty (398).
iii. Duty "is the necessity of an action from respect for law" (400).
 iv. The practical law worthy of our respect is the categorical imperative (402).

---

[3] See *Groundwork* (397).   [4] Kant makes this kind of claim at A 807/B 835 of the *CPR* as well.

It is not until Section II that Kant explicitly labels as the "categorical imperative" the law that is worthy of our respect. He does, however, provide his first formulation of the law in Section I:

I ought never to act except in such a way that I could also will that my maxim should become a universal law. (402)

By the end of Section I, Kant claims to have completed the transition from "common rational" moral cognition to "philosophical moral cognition." He has analyzed the common cognition of a good will and thereby deepened our understanding of the meaning of that concept. He has revealed the principal assumptions that lie at its basis. As he points out in the final paragraphs of the section, a "transition" from the common to the philosophical understanding of the concept is necessary because common or pre-philosophical human reason is easily led astray (404f.). Although it knows the difference between good and bad conduct, common human reason is sometimes tempted to act contrary to duty. When it succumbs to this temptation, it looks for ways to rationalize its actions. It is prone to deceive itself about what duty requires. A transition to philosophical moral cognition is necessary, Kant argues, in order to guard the concept of duty against corruption. A philosophical understanding keeps us honest about the meaning or "correct determination" of the concept (405).

1.2 The opening paragraphs of Section I: The common cognition of a good will

The "common rational moral cognition" with which Section I begins is the idea of a good will. As we saw, Kant's only mention of the will in his Preface is his comment that:

the metaphysics of morals has to examine the idea and the principles of a possible *pure* will. (390)

Of course, this remark refers to a pure will, not a good will. But Kant intends to establish a connection between these two concepts; indeed, one of his principal tasks in both sections I and II is to establish that connection. As noted above, he argues in Section I that a good will is good because of its motivation. A good will acts "from duty," he says, and out of "respect" for law. When he tells us that a good will acts from duty and out of respect for law, he means to distinguish this kind of motivation from other kinds of motivation. In particular, he is concerned to contrast the motive of duty with that of happiness. I discussed his reasons for this in my Introduction. I drew attention there to the fact that when we act from happiness, according to Kant, we are motivated by incentives that are empirical. Although we have the freedom to decide whether to allow these incentives to govern our actions, we cannot, strictly speaking, choose these incentives. Nature determines us to have them. Moreover, incentives that are empirical versus pure, in Kant's view, cannot support commands that have the status of law, commands that are universally and necessarily valid.[5]

2. NOTHING IS GOOD WITHOUT LIMITATION BUT THE GOOD WILL (393–396)

The discussion begins with this sentence:

It is impossible to think of anything at all in the world, or indeed even beyond it, that could be considered good without limitation except a good will.

Here Kant indicates that the identifying mark of a good will is that it is good "without limitation." By itself, this characterization is not terribly informative; it does not indicate the precise respect in which the good will, on his account, enjoys no limitation. Kant introduces the following contrast to explain: All other goods, he tells us, are good only relatively. He mentions three sets of relative or conditional goods and classifies the first two under the heading "gifts of nature." Among the many gifts of nature are those he refers to as "talents of mind." Understanding, wit, and judgment count as gifts

---

[5] My characterization of incentives here as "empirical" might seem redundant in light of Kant's remark in Section II (427) that he uses the term "incentive" [*Triebfeder*] to refer to "subjective" (that is, empirical or contingent) ends. But Kant is not perfectly consistent in his use of this term. At (440), for example, he identifies "respect" for the moral law as an "incentive." As for Kant's use of the term "motive" [*Bewegungsgund*], he tells us at (427) that he reserves this term for ends that are objective. I depart from Kant, in my discussion, and use "motive" to refer to ends or purposes in general, whether subjective (contingent) or objective (necessary). For a discussion of the importance of the distinction between motive and incentive in Kant, see Chapter 10 of Henry Allison's *Kant's Theory of Freedom*, pp. 186ff.

of nature, presumably, because we owe our possession of them, at least in part, to some inborn capacity. They are goods insofar as they provide some benefit either to those who have them or to others. Kant likewise categorizes "qualities of temperament" as gifts of nature. These include character traits such as "courage, resolution, and perseverance in one's plans."

Kant refers to the second kind of relative good as "gifts of fortune." These gifts are bestowed upon us not by nature but by circumstance. Some of us, at some point in our lives, are fortunate enough to enjoy goods such as power, riches, honor, health, and happiness. But not even happiness, which Kant defines here as the "complete well-being and satisfaction with one's condition," is an unconditional good, on his account.

Why does Kant characterize the above goods as only relatively or conditionally good? It is tempting to derive the answer to this question from his remark that although these goods may be "good and desirable for many purposes," they can also become "extremely evil and harmful" (393). We might interpret this remark to imply that the merely relative worth of these goods is tied to the fact that they can lead to bad effects. It is always possible, for example, that a person fortunate enough to possess great power will use that power to oppress others. Likewise, a person of great natural intelligence might decide to devote her gifts to destructive ends. We misunderstand Kant, however, if we take his point to be that gifts of nature and of fortune are merely conditionally good because they sometimes result in bad consequences. Were this his view, he would then have to say about the unconditionally good will that it always produces good effects. But this is not Kant's view. Instead, he claims that the goodness of a good will has nothing to do with "what it effects or accomplishes" (394).

To get a better grasp of what Kant has in mind in claiming that some goods are only conditionally good, it will help to return to the remark with which we began, this time quoting it more fully. He says of conditional or relative goods that they can become "extremely evil and harmful" if the will which is to make use of them "is not good." His claim here is that these goods are only conditionally good because they are not necessarily accompanied by a good "character" or will. Unless they are accompanied by a good will, they can become "extremely evil." Even goods that are "conducive" to the good will and "make its work easier" (goods such as "moderation in affects and passions" and "self-control") lack unconditional worth, on this account. They lack unconditional worth because it may happen that these traits are accompanied by a will that is *not* good. As Kant observes, a "scoundrel" may possess qualities of self-control and calmness of reflection, qualities that aid him in achieving his ends. But these qualities are only relatively good. Far from necessarily attaching to a will that is good, they attach to the will of a scoundrel (394).

Clearly, Kant holds that the unconditional goodness of a good will is a function of what motivates it. He is explicit about this point when he writes that a good will is unconditionally good not because of "what it effects or accomplishes ... but only because of its volition" (394). Kant is worried about situations in which gifts of nature or circumstance are not accompanied by good character or guided by the right "basic principles." This is why he claims that not even happiness is unconditionally good; even happiness can be achieved by persons of bad character. What *is* unconditionally good, in Kant's view, is the person who, because of her admirable character, is *worthy* of happiness (393). Such a person is motivated in the right kind of way.

We might have questions at this point about Kant's treatment of the effects of our actions. Based on the passages we just reviewed, it is undeniable that he is committed to the assumption that the effects of our actions are of no relevance in our assessments of character. In his words, the worth of a good will has to do "only" with its volition. A good will's "usefulness or fruitlessness" can neither add nor subtract from its worth. Even should it "wholly lack the capacity to carry out its purpose," he writes, the good will continues to "shine" "like a jewel" (394). This feature of Kant's position might strike us as puzzling, for it is not difficult to imagine a person who is pure of heart – whose intentions are always good – but "all thumbs" when it comes to realizing those intentions. Instead of spreading her inner goodness around, this person seems to cause nothing but harm. She is like the person who cherishes plants but consistently kills them, or who loves children but always makes them cry. Would we think it appropriate to characterize the will of such a person as unconditionally good? Kant seems to have no doubt that we would. After all, the problem in such cases is not the agent's volition or willing, but rather her inability to effectively realize the ends of her willing. What she lacks is not a good will but good judgment.[6]

Kant concedes that even though "common understanding" accepts this idea of a will whose goodness has nothing to do with its usefulness, the idea itself is nonetheless "strange" (394). He is aware that he needs to tell us more about what motivates a good will. In his next three paragraphs he moves in the direction of doing so, although in a roundabout way. Indeed, the next paragraphs seem at first glance to bear no connection at all to his immediately preceding discussion. Kant calls our attention to the unique powers of our faculties of instinct and of reason, and of their specific functions. Although it is hardly apparent at first, these comments are part of his effort to further clarify the motivation of a good will. He inserts these remarks about the respective roles of reason and instinct, because he will eventually assert that what motivates a good will is reason.

2.1 The "true vocation" of reason (395–396)

These paragraphs contain a number of assumptions about our faculties of reason and instinct, and the role nature has assigned them. Kant does not go to the trouble of defending these assumptions here since he has done the work of defending them in other texts. As just mentioned, he concludes these paragraphs with the claim that the good will is motivated by reason. To prepare the way for that conclusion, he introduces us to his conception of reason's nature and function.[7]

Kant begins with the claim that nature has assigned purposes to our various faculties, purposes for which each faculty is best adapted. Nature did not assign to our faculty of reason the task of securing our happiness (our "preservation" and "welfare"). If it had, this would have been a "very bad arrangement." As Kant puts the point here,

---

[6] In fact, it would not be incorrect to characterize the willing of a good will, on Kant's account, as necessarily good. Strictly speaking, good will cannot have bad effects; only bad judgment can produce bad effects. Again, the problem is not with the willing, but with the implementation of what is willed. On this point, see H. Paton, *The Categorical Imperative*, p. 40, and Stephen Engstrom, "Kant's conception of practical wisdom," *Kant-Studien* 88 (1997), 16–43.
[7] Paton provides a helpful discussion of these paragraphs in *The Categorical Imperative*, p. 44.

reason's "insight" is too weak to formulate a plan for attaining happiness or to determine the means of attaining happiness.

By "reason," in these paragraphs, Kant has in mind not the theoretical faculty of knowledge but a "practical" faculty, a faculty capable of influencing our conduct. But the fact that he is describing the function of *practical* reason here makes it even more mysterious that he thinks this faculty is poorly suited to secure our happiness. If reason can determine us to act, why is it unable to determine us to act in a way that satisfies our interest in our welfare? Why is Kant so keen to convince us that "instinct" (or what he also refers to as "inclination") is better-suited to the job?

Again, these paragraphs contain mere assertions without defense or even much explanation. Kant simply contends that reason is not fit to concern itself with happiness. When a "cultivated" reason strives after the "enjoyment of life" and "happiness," he observes, it is apt to miss its mark. Not only is reason ill-equipped to satisfy these needs, it is preoccupied with needs of its own. It adds to or "multiplies" the needs or ends set by instinct, and the ends it adds are different from those of happiness. This is one of the principal messages Kant wishes us to take away from this discussion: The ends or purposes set by practical reason are distinct from ends set by instinct or inclination.

Kant expands on these issues in two essays that appeared in the years immediately preceding and following the publication of the *Groundwork*: his 1784 essay "Idea for a Universal History from a Cosmopolitan Point of View" and his 1786 "Conjectural Beginning of Human History." In the "Idea for a Universal History," Kant describes reason as "a faculty of widening the rules and purposes of the use of all its powers beyond natural instinct."[8] Had nature not given us reason, he suggests, we would never have advanced from the "lowest barbarity to the highest skill and mental perfection."[9] The faculty of reason is thus responsible for the progress humanity has made beyond its natural animality.

But, as Kant goes on to argue, this progress comes at a price. Creatures governed by instinct satisfy their needs by answering the call of nature (by securing food and shelter and so forth). Their ends

---

[8] In *On History: Immanuel Kant*, trans. and ed. L. W. Beck, IN, second thesis.
[9] *Ibid.*, third thesis.

or purposes are given by nature and are not products of choice. Creatures in possession of reason, however, are capable of imagining and creating ends. These created or "artificial" ends (such as the desire for esteem) are both more complicated and more difficult to satisfy.[10] The gift of choice and self-determination that comes with the possession of reason thus brings with it a new set of burdens and responsibilities. Kant notes in the *Groundwork* that many respond to these added burdens, and to the inability of reason to secure our happiness, with an attitude of "misology," a hatred of reason (395).

When Kant moves on in the next paragraph of the *Groundwork* to spell out his view of the particular end nature has assigned the faculty of practical reason, what he tells us is this: The function of practical reason is not to secure happiness or produce a will that is good merely as a means to happiness. Instead, the function of practical reason is to produce a will that is *"good in itself."* This, he says, is reason's "true vocation." As for what Kant means by a will that is good in itself, we so far know only that its goodness has nothing to do with the effort to secure ends set by inclination or instinct. Not only is the end set by practical reason different from the ends set by inclination or instinct, the end set by practical reason sometimes requires us to sacrifice those latter ends. A will that is good in itself, in other words, must in some instances act in ways that limit or interfere with the attainment of happiness.[11]

2.2 *Actual versus intended effects of willing (395–397)*

Let us quickly take stock of the ground we have covered in these last few pages. We began Section 2 by introducing Kant's account of the good will. We learned that the unlimited goodness of a good will has to do with its willing or motivation, not with "what it effects or

---

[10] The conception of the ends of practical reason Kant discusses in his 1786 "Conjectural Beginning of Human History" is borrowed from Rousseau, as Kant notes. As we will see, he offers us his own variation on Rousseau's account in the *Groundwork*.

[11] For further discussion of these passages in the *Groundwork*, see Christoph Horn's essay "Kant on Ends in Nature and in Human Agency," in Christoph Horn and Dieter Schönecker, eds. *Groundwork for the Metaphysics of Morals*, pp. 45–71.

accomplishes" (394). We noted that this account implies that a will can be good without qualification or limitation even if the effects of its willing are "evil" or "harmful." We then went on to explore the first hints Kant gives us of the motivation of a good will. We determined that, on his definition, a good will is motivated by ends of practical reason, not by ends of instinct or inclination.

It is important that we do not lose sight of the fact that when Kant claims that the good will shines "like a jewel" regardless of the effects of its willing, he is referring to the *actual* effects of its willing (394). He means to acknowledge that the best of intentions can sometimes misfire, due to no fault on the part of the agent. In escorting the elderly person across the street, the good neighbor could not possibly have predicted that she would be moving him right into the sniper's line of fire.

But Kant's insistence that the *actual* effects of an agent's willing are irrelevant in assessing the goodness of an agent's will should not be interpreted to imply that *intended* effects are irrelevant in the assessing an agent's will. Kant sometimes seems to give the impression that not even intended effects are morally significant. In the passages we considered above at Section 2.1, for example, he contrasts a will that is good "in itself" with a will that is good "as a means to other purposes" (396). We might take this comment to imply that, for Kant, a will that is good in itself is good independently of its aims or purposes. We might even be tempted by the more extreme view that a will that is good in itself *has* no aims or purposes, on his account.

But each of these interpretations is mistaken. If we read these passages more carefully we discover that what Kant in fact says is that a will that is good in itself is good not "*as a means* to *other* purposes" (396; second emphasis added). He makes this same qualification in the next paragraph. He writes there that a good will is good apart from any "*further* purpose" (emphasis added). It is not Kant's view, therefore, that a good will acts for no purposes at all. Nor is it his view that the goodness of a good will is independent of its purposes. He urges only that a certain *class* of purposes is irrelevant to the goodness of a good will, namely, purposes set by instinct or inclination. What motivates a good will, in other words, is something other than the desire to achieve happiness.

2.3 Deontological and teleological elements of Kant's practical philosophy

Moral theories are commonly classified as either "teleological" or "deontological." A teleological theory (sometimes also referred to as "consequentialist") defines the good with reference to actually attained ends or purposes. An action is good, according to this kind of theory, if it produces the right kind of consequences. One example of such a theory is utilitarianism. For the utilitarian, an action is good if it maximizes happiness for the greatest number of people. A deontological theory, on the other hand, measures the goodness of at least some acts with reference to something other than their actual consequences. Acts are judged good because they conform to or instantiate some rule or moral principle.

In light of Kant's claim that the goodness of a good will derives not from what it "effects or accomplishes" but from its "volition," it is easy to understand why his moral theory is often classified as deontological. It is indeed accurate to attribute to him the view that the actual consequences of an agent's willing are irrelevant in determining the goodness of that agent's willing. As we have just seen, however, it is a mistake to conclude from this feature of Kant's moral theory that consequences are of no importance for his practical philosophy whatsoever. A few points are worth bearing in mind here. First, remember that Kant's practical philosophy has two divisions, a doctrine of virtue (or a "moral theory" in the narrow sense) and a doctrine of right. In the context of the doctrine of virtue, the object of moral assessment is the agent's will or principle of volition. In the context of the doctrine of right, however, the object of assessment is an agent's behavior. The doctrine of right thus abstracts from any consideration of the principle of volition underlying a given piece of conduct. Its task is to determine whether our "external actions" are in conformity with right and thus do not infringe upon the freedom of others.[12] In light of the specific concern of the doctrine of right, it would be inaccurate to characterize Kant's practical theory as a whole as uninterested in judging the actual effects of our actions.

---

[12] Kant expresses the "universal principle of right" as follows: " 'Any action is *right* if it can coexist with everyone's freedom in accordance with a universal law' " (*MM* I 231).

But even if we restrict our attention to his doctrine of virtue where the objective is to assess volitions rather than actions or behaviors, it would be a mistake to attribute to Kant the view that the good will has no interest in the actual effects of its willing. Kant's concept of the good will is sometimes portrayed in just this way. Since its goodness is linked not to what it "effects or accomplishes" but only to its willing, the goodness of a good will is supposed by some critics to consist in its mere obedience to a rule or principle. On this reading, a good will, for Kant, is nothing more than a competent rule follower. A good will is not concerned about the consequences of its willing; its only aim is to do what practical reason requires. It acts from duty for duty's sake.

It should by now be obvious that this reading is no better than a caricature of Kant's view. For from the fact that the goodness of a good will is not tied to the actual effects of its willing, it does not follow that a good will does not *care* about the actual effects of its willing. A good will, on Kant's account, acts with purposes in mind; it acts to realize certain ends. As we have seen, the ends it seeks to realize are set by practical reason. Kant has not yet specified or filled in the content of those ends; but the fact that he has not yet specified them should not mislead us into thinking that the good will *has* no ends or purposes. Otherwise put, it should not mislead us into thinking that the good will strives for nothing more than to bring its volition into compliance with a rule.[13]

2.4 The "highest" versus the "sole and complete" good (396)

Note Kant's remark that although a good will is the "highest good," it is not the "sole and complete good." He does not explain this distinction here; he says only that the "highest good" is "the condition of every other [good]."[14] The highest good is the condition of other goods in the sense we have already considered. While the scoundrel

---

[13] For further discussion of the teleological elements of Kant's approach, see H. Paton, *The Categorical Imperative*, Chapter X, Section 5; Barbara Herman, "Leaving Deontology Behind," in *The Practice of Moral Judgment* (Cambridge, MA/London: Harvard University Press, 1993), pp. 208–240; Allen Wood, *Kant's Ethical Thought*, p. 114. See also the now classic account of what Kant means by a will that is "good in itself" in Christine Korsgaard's essay, "Two Distinctions in Goodness," in her collection *Creating the Kingdom of Ends*, pp. 249–274.

[14] As Kant puts it in the *CPrR*, virtue "(as worthiness to be happy) is the supreme condition of whatever can even seem to us desirable and hence of all our pursuit of happiness" (110).

may possess many good qualities (self-control, a cool head), these are at best conditional or relative goods, morally speaking. They are accompanied by a will that is not good (by a bad character). The good will, in contrast, is the only good that is good in itself. It requires no other good as a condition of its goodness. In this sense it is the "highest good."

Kant clarifies the distinction between the "highest" and the "sole and complete" good in the *Critique of Practical Reason*. He observes there that it is an unfortunate fact about human existence that having a good or virtuous will is no guarantee of happiness. Just like everyone else, the virtuous get sick, suffer losses, are victims of immorality and injustice. For this reason, a will that is good is not the "sole and complete good." The latter kind of good contains as a necessary ingredient happiness as well as virtue. Not only does it contain both, but in the sole and complete good, happiness is "distributed in exact proportion" to virtue (110).[15]

3. FURTHER EXPLICATION OF THE NATURE OF A GOOD WILL: FOUR MOTIVATIONAL TYPES (397–399)

Kant begins this discussion by reminding us that the concept of a will that is good in itself is not his invention. As a common cognition, he says, the concept "already dwells in natural sound understanding" (397). He has already asserted that a good will is good because of its volition. He has also told us that a will is good only if it wills an end set by practical reason. Kant now moves on to provide a first indication of what this end is. The end of practical reason, he says, is duty. A good will, then, is a will that acts *from duty*.

In the next three paragraphs, Kant distinguishes a will that acts from duty from a will that is motivated in other ways. He provides examples of four kinds of motivational grounds of action. Only the fourth describes a will that acts from duty. Only the fourth, then, is an example of the motivation of a good will. Kant discusses the other three kinds of cases for purposes of contrast.

[15] There is a vocabulary change in the *CPrR*, at (110). Kant does not refer to virtue as the "highest good" there as he does in the *Groundwork*. Virtue is the "supreme" good, but not the "highest good," which is "happiness distributed in exact proportion to morality."

3.1 Case 1: Acting in a way that is obviously contrary to duty (397)

Kant writes that he will "pass over" actions that are "already recognized as contrary to duty." He will pass over these cases, because they are the most obvious cases of what a good will is *not*. Although Kant provides no examples, he probably has something like the following in mind: Suppose that, while taking an exam, you notice a classmate engaged in an act of cheating. Presumably, she does so because she believes this may help her get a good grade. In cheating, she is clearly not much bothered by the fact that she is stealing the work of another and very likely upsetting the fair distribution of grades. In a case like this, Kant says, the question "never arises" whether the action is performed from duty. The question never arises, because no one would for a moment consider it appropriate to characterize the cheater's will as good. Her cheating behavior is clear evidence that she acts contrary to duty.

3.2 Case 2: Acting in conformity with duty but not from immediate inclination (397)

Kant claims that in this second kind of case it is once again "easy" to determine that the agent does not act from duty. Although these actions are not performed from duty, they are nevertheless "in conformity with duty" [*pflichtmässig*], on his account.

Let us look straightaway at his example:

> [I]t certainly conforms with duty that a shopkeeper not overcharge an inexperienced customer, and where there is a good deal of trade a prudent merchant does not overcharge but keeps a fixed general price for everyone, so that a child can buy from him as well as everyone else. People are thus served *honestly*; but this is not nearly enough for us to believe that the merchant acted in this way from duty and basic principles of honesty. (397)

In what sense does the merchant's action conform with duty? Only in this sense: he keeps a "fixed general price for everyone" and does not overcharge. His customers are thus "served *honestly*," as Kant says.

Notice that what Kant identifies as conforming with duty here is not the merchant's intention or principle of volition but rather his behavior – his action considered apart from his intention. Kant's main objective in his discussion of these cases, however, is to determine what it is for a person to have a good *will*. To determine whether the merchant has a good will, we need to look beyond mere behavior to what *motivates* it, to the principle of volition. This is why Kant goes on to point out that the reason the merchant keeps a "fixed general price for everyone" is because "his advantage required it." The merchant has established that honesty pays. He calculates that, should it become public knowledge that he overcharges his inexperienced customers, he risks damaging his reputation and thus also his business. He charges a fair price not because he is committed to "principles of honesty," but "merely for purposes of self-interest." Had he no reason to fear that he might be exposed for overcharging, he would overcharge.

How are the first two kinds of case different? Kant says of the second but not of the first case that the action is "in conformity with duty." The action of the prudent merchant conforms with duty because he charges a fair price. As just noted, what conforms with duty is his conduct – his behavior considered in isolation from his intention. Considered in isolation from the intention, the merchant's action is not a violation of duty. In this respect, the merchant case is different from the cheating case. Kant says of the first class of cases that they are "already recognized as contrary to duty." In the example I gave, we already recognize in the classmate's act of peering furtively at her neighbor's work that she does not act in conformity with duty. In cases like this, we can confidently infer from the agent's behavior a less than honorable intention. This is most likely why Kant remarks that, in this first kind of case, the question "never arises" whether the agent acts from duty.

Kant associates a further feature with the second class of actions. He tells us that these are actions "to which human beings have *no inclination* immediately and which they still perform because they are impelled to do so through another inclination." What does he mean in saying that human beings have "*no inclination* immediately?" The merchant in Kant's example receives *no immediate gratification* from treating his customers honestly. He does not really *want* to serve them honestly; he is not at this point in time particularly *inclined* to do so. He certainly is not honest, Kant says, "from love" for his customers. He acts honestly only because he is "impelled to do so through another inclination." By this Kant means that the merchant expects some reward down the line. He performs a prudential calculation to determine that his good behavior will eventually benefit him. He will sell more cars, make big profits, and perhaps get to retire early. He acts from inclination, but the inclination that motivates him is for a future reward. In this sense, the inclination is not "immediate." Kant turns his attention to examples of acting from immediate inclination in Case 3.

3.3 Case 3: Acting in conformity with duty and from immediate inclination (397–398)

At least most of the time, everyone has an "immediate inclination," Kant says, to preserve his own life (397). In calling this inclination "immediate," Kant means to suggest that, at least most of the time, we preserve or take care of ourselves in order to gratify the interest we now have in doing so. This serves our interests now, not just down the line (as in the prudent merchant case). Kant's chief concern in his discussion of this third kind of case is to stress that there is an important difference between preserving one's life from immediate inclination and doing so from duty. He wants to convince us that the person who preserves his life from immediate inclination has "no inner worth," and his maxim or principle of intention has "no moral content." Why not? Kant asks us to contrast the case of a person who preserves his life because he enjoys it, with that of a person who preserves his life even though he suffers from "adversity and hopeless grief." If this second person preserves his life "without loving it," he does so for some reason other than to gratify immediate inclination. What motivates him, Kant says, is duty.

To further clarify the contrast between acting from duty and acting from immediate inclination, Kant describes a sympathetic soul who, "without any other motive of vanity or self-interest" finds "inner satisfaction in spreading joy." In spreading joy, this "philanthropist" indeed acts in conformity with duty. His behavior is certainly in line with what duty demands. Nonetheless, his beneficent actions have "no true moral worth," on Kant's account.

Kant's judgment is likely to seem harsh to us if we do not understand the ground upon which it rests. His reasoning here is essentially the same as in Case 2. As in the example of the merchant, what motivates the beneficent philanthropist is not duty but inclination.

The only difference is that the philanthropist acts from *immediate* inclination. The philanthropist genuinely enjoys spreading joy. He derives gratification from doing so now; unlike the merchant, he is not merely counting on some eventual reward. Kant grants that the philanthropist's kindness and generosity deserve "praise and encouragement"; but Kant also thinks we will all agree that actions of this kind are not worthy of "esteem."

What is Kant's point here? The philanthropist's actions are not worthy of esteem because of the way in which their motivational ground is identical to that of both the cheater and the merchant: he acts from inclination. Clearly, Kant does not give significant weight to the important respect in which the philanthropist case *differs* from the other two cases. It differs in that only in this third case are we tempted to characterize the agent's will as good. Unlike the cheater and the merchant, the philanthropist derives pleasure from spreading joy. Although it is true that he acts in order to gratify inclination, his inclination (in contrast to that of the cheater and the merchant) seems thoroughly admirable from a moral point of view.

What could possibly be morally deficient, then, about the motivation of the philanthropist? To pose this question in another way: What does Kant believe is morally objectionable about the desire to spread joy? Kant gives us some indication of his answer to this question when he turns in Section II to discuss different kinds of commands or imperatives. In the present context, however, he says almost nothing to clarify his view.

We can somewhat demystify Kant's treatment of Case 3 by drawing out a few implications of the position he is rejecting. Suppose we take on the role of his opponent and define moral worth as follows: An agent has moral worth if she acts from inclinations of a particular kind, inclinations such as those of the philanthropist. On this proposal, a good will is a will that desires to spread joy. Now, the first thing to notice is that this definition of moral worth is not likely to be compelling to those who do not share the inclinations of the philanthropist. It will have little appeal, for instance, to the prudent merchants and cheaters of the world. Such persons have no desire to spread joy. Given that they lack that inclination, they also lack any reason to endorse this account of moral worth. As far as they are concerned, the proposed definition of a good will does not apply to them.

From Kant's point of view, this kind of outcome is unacceptable. As we know from his Preface, he insists that moral requirements are valid not just for some, but for all rational natures (389). Duty cannot consist in acting from the desire to spread joy, on his account, because not all of us have the inclination to spread joy. Not all of us would, therefore, accept this conception of duty as valid.

One point we must not overlook here is that the moral deficiency Kant discovers in Case 3 has nothing to do with the inclination to spread joy in particular. Kant discovers a problem in the philanthropist case only because he is convinced that moral worth cannot derive from acting on inclinations of *any* kind. This is a point he alerted us to earlier in Section I. He characterized the good will, remember, as a will that acts to realize ends set by reason, not ends set by inclination or instinct. Again and again in the *Groundwork*, he reminds us that the appeal to inclinations – or to that in which they "unite in one sum," namely, happiness – cannot serve to ground morality. As I stressed in my Introduction, this is a central theme of the text.

Although Kant is more expansive on this topic in Section II, it will aid our present understanding of his treatment of Case 3 if we say something now about his particular account of the nature and origin of inclinations. As just mentioned, his view is that no appeal to inclinations of any kind can ground moral rules that have universal and necessary validity. For Kant, then, the problem is not just that there is no basis for the assumption that each of us in fact desires to spread joy. The problem is rather that *no* inclination can be attributed to rational natures universally and necessarily. This is because inclinations, on his conception, reflect our particularity. Inclinations are the desires and preferences we have in virtue of who we are as empirical natures. Each of us has a unique personal history and inhabits a unique place in space and time. No two of us enter the world exactly alike, and no two of us have exactly the same experiences. Although there may be partial agreement among persons at a given time about what is desirable and what is not, there will never be total agreement. No two of us ever has precisely the same set of inclinations.

Not only do inclinations reflect our particularity and thus distinguish us from one another, our inclinations, in addition, are subject to change. Today the philanthropist feels sympathy for his neighbors; tomorrow that feeling may be crowded out by another. The desires and preferences that derive from our empirical natures are not fixed – nor is our conception of their fulfillment, that is, our idea of happiness. If we were to base our moral obligations on inclination, our obligations would come and go. They would be as variable as our moods.

To summarize these points: Since inclinations are not the kind of thing about which there can be universal agreement, they cannot serve to ground moral rules that have universal validity. Since inclinations are variable, they furthermore cannot support rules that have the status of necessity.

There is, however, a further problem with the effort to ground morality on an appeal to inclination, a problem Kant alludes to at (399). Suppose that by some remarkable circumstance we all happened to accept as valid the command to act from a particular desire. Even were this to happen, it would not be *possible* for each of us to obey that command, in Kant's view. The reason for this is that inclinations are not the kind of thing that can be commanded. We cannot, simply by an act of will, cause ourselves to want or desire something. (We may be able to cause ourselves to strive to attain something, but we cannot cause ourselves to desire that thing.) So even if each of us did accept the validity of the command to desire to spread joy, for example, only those already in possession of philanthropic inclinations could actually answer the command. Our capacity to act from duty would depend, then, on the inclinations nature happened to give us. Our moral worth would ultimately be decided by luck.

This is not our final occasion for considering these difficult issues. We will return to them again in Section II when we consider Kant's claim that moral rules must command "categorically" rather than merely "hypothetically." (See my comments in Chapter 4, Section 5.)

3.4 Case 4: Acting from duty (398)

Kant finally introduces us to examples of actions performed from duty. In the second part of (398), he asks us to imagine that the philanthropist's circumstances change and he is overcome with grief. Because the philanthropist is now preoccupied with his own troubles, he no longer has the inclination to sympathize with the plight of others. Kant asks us to suppose that, even though the philanthropist now lacks the desire to do so, he nonetheless "tears himself out of this deadly insensibility" and reaches out to help others. Here, for the first time, Kant says, we have an example of what is involved in acting "simply from duty." Here, finally, is an instance of "genuine moral worth."

Notice that in describing this as a case of "genuine moral worth," Kant refers to the philanthropist's will. Clearly, the man's helpful acts are in conformity with what duty demands. In this respect, the case is identical to Kant's example of Case 3. But Kant is concerned to emphasize the sense in which this fourth case *differs* from the other cases. What is different is the grieving philanthropist's will – the fact that he is motivated by duty. This is likewise true of the example Kant next considers. In this example, a man is "by temperament cold and indifferent to the sufferings of others." If he nonetheless finds "within himself a source from which to give himself a far higher worth than what a mere good-natured temperament might have," then, in being beneficent from duty, the man demonstrates his good character. Like the grieving philanthropist, this man has a good will.

3.5 A common objection to Case 4

Of the various kinds of cases Kant considers, only the fourth, in his view, qualifies as a case in which the agent has a good will and thus "genuine moral worth." Kant therefore seems to give us grounds for concluding that, on his account, having moral worth necessarily requires us to *oppose* inclination, to do what we do not want to do. In both versions of Case 4, the agents have no desire to act from duty. One is preoccupied with his troubles, the other is cold by temperament. In acting from duty, each agent resists the pull of his inclinations. These examples appear to suggest, then, that the person who acts from duty – the good will – must at the same time oppose inclination, according to Kant. The examples, in other words, seem to suggest that if our inclinations are in any way gratified in what we do, it must be the case that we lack moral worth.

This criticism has a long history. It appears in satirical form in the following two epigrams by Kant's contemporary Friedrich Schiller:

> Gladly I serve my friends, but regrettably I do so with pleasure.
> Thus I am often troubled by the fact that I am not virtuous.

(To which the following response is given:)
The only advice for you is to try to despise them.
And thus do with repugnance what duty commands.[16]

Schiller's objection, however, misrepresents Kant's position.[17] If we look back to our review of Kant's discussion of the different motivational types, we can see why. The main lesson Kant wishes us to derive from his discussion is that a person has moral worth when she is motivated by duty, not by inclination. This definition of moral worth does not imply that a will is good only if it *opposes* inclination. The philanthropist derives pleasure from spreading joy. Kant does not intend to suggest that, if the philanthropist is to have moral worth, he must act contrary to his generous inclinations. Instead, Kant's view is that, if the philanthropist is to have moral worth, he must be kind to others because he knows that duty requires it. He must recognize the validity of the obligation to care, and that recognition must be what ultimately moves him to act.

So a good will, on Kant's definition, need not oppose inclination.[18] It is not even the case that a good will's *sole* motivation must be duty, according to Kant. A will is good if it would act from duty even if it did not also possess the desire to do so. A good will's goodness is not compromised should it happen that the inclination to act from duty is also present. The presence of the inclination merely aids the good will in doing what morality requires. In cases like this, moral worth is easier to achieve because the good will does not have to engage in battle with its desires.[19]

How can we explain the fact that Kant's examples indeed seem to suggest that the will that acts from duty must at the same time oppose

---

[16]   This epigram, attributed to Schiller, is from a collection of short satirical epigrams by Goethe and Schiller that appeared in the Musen-Almanach of 1879, *Xenien*. An English selection and translation is provided in Paul Carus, *Goethe and Schiller's Xenions*, p. 114. The translation I have provided here of the Schiller epigram is my own.

[17]   The same could be said, I believe, of a relatively recent expression of Schiller's critique. See Bernard Williams's essay, "Persons, Character and Morality," in his collection *Moral Luck: Philosophical Papers 1973–1980.*

[18]   Kant is explicit about this point in the *CPrR*. He tells us there that there is no necessary "opposition" between the "principle of happiness" and that of morality (93).

[19]   For two excellent discussions of Kant's account of moral motivation, see chapters 4 and 5 of Marcia Baron's *Kantian Ethics Almost Without Apology* (Ithaca, NY: Cornell University Press, 1995), and Chapter 1 of Barbara Herman's *The Practice of Moral Judgment.*

inclination? Kant gives us a clue in Section II. He tells us there that we can most confidently determine that an agent acts from duty when his action obviously opposes his inclinations. These are the cases, Kant says, in which the motive of duty is "more manifest" (425).[20] When a man whose temperament is cold and indifferent helps his neighbor, we have good reason to believe that he does so not from inclination but from duty. But when another man acts from duty and at the same time possesses the inclination to do so – when a philanthropist, for example, reaches out to his neighbor – his motive is more difficult to discern. As Kant points out, we can with greater confidence identify cases in which duty is the motive when inclination is pulling in the opposite direction. He relies on such cases in his examples in Section I, because his aim there is to illustrate in the clearest possible terms the motivation of a good will.[21]

4. THE INDIRECT DUTY TO SECURE OUR OWN HAPPINESS (399)

As we have seen, Kant defines happiness as the state of "complete well-being" or as "the sum of satisfaction of all inclinations" (393, 399). We achieve happiness (that is, perfect happiness) when all our inclinations (the desires and preferences we have as empirical natures) are gratified. Kant has just told us that a good will acts from duty, not from inclination. Again, this does not mean that he holds that the good will is a will that necessarily always *opposes* its inclinations. Nor does it mean that a will is only good if it *eliminates* its inclinations. Kant's view instead is that a will is good only when duty and not inclination is the force that ultimately moves it to act.

After cautioning us against thinking that inclination or happiness can serve as the principal motive of a good will, Kant goes on to insist that we have an "at least indirect" duty to secure our own happiness. He indicates his reason for this claim when he notes that dissatisfaction with one's own condition can "easily become a great *temptation to*

---

[20] For further evidence that this is Kant's view, see *CPrR* (156).
[21] Paton describes Kant's use of these kinds of examples to illustrate the motive of duty as his "method of isolation." See *The Categorical Imperative*, p. 49. For further discussion of this issue, see Korsgaard's essay, "Kant's Analysis of Obligation: The Argument of Groundwork I," in her *Creating the Kingdom of Ends*.

transgression of duty." His point, very simply, is that unhappiness can hinder us from acting from duty. If I am starving from hunger, I will be tempted to steal for food. If I am grieving or depressed, I will probably be unresponsive to the needs of others. We have an indirect duty to secure our own happiness, then, because unhappiness interferes with the motivation to act from duty. Were happiness not a condition of acting from duty, we would have no obligation to secure it. Presumably, this is why Kant characterizes the duty to secure our own happiness as indirect.

4.1 The "precept" versus the "inclination" of happiness (399)

After announcing that we have an indirect duty to secure our own happiness, Kant adds the remark that "all people have already, of themselves, the strongest and deepest inclinations to happiness." This comment is curious. If each of us is in fact inclined to secure our own happiness, why should we need to be commanded to do so? Kant's insistence upon the duty to secure our happiness is even more puzzling in light of his further claim that inclinations are not the kind of things that *can* be commanded. Inclinations are attributes we are determined to have. As we noted back at Section 3.3, they derive from our natural constitution and its interaction with social and environmental conditions. They cannot be called up by an act of will. In Kant's view, we can no more be commanded to have inclinations than we can be commanded to have a particular eye color or IQ.[22]

But if inclinations or feelings cannot be commanded, then happiness cannot be commanded either. What can Kant mean, then, in asserting that we have a duty to secure our own happiness? His answer to this question is that the duty or "precept" to be happy does not legislate over our feelings. On his account, duty commands the will, and the will (as he understands it here) is distinct from the faculty of inclination or feeling. In his foregoing discussion, Kant made it clear that he thinks that inclination or feeling is not the only force that moves us to act. The grieving philanthropist is able to respond to duty even though he has no inclination to do so. Even though his mind is

---

[22] Kant argues these points also in the *CPrR* (37). It would be "foolish," he tells us there, to command happiness.

overclouded by grief, he can choose to care about the suffering of others. In choosing to care, he responds not to the command to feel what Kant calls "pathological" love, which lies "in the propensity of feeling;" rather, he responds to the command that requires of him "practical" love, which "lies in the will." Likewise, a man with gout can respond to the duty to look after his own wellbeing even though he prefers to "enjoy what he likes" and indulge his appetite for fine wines and rich foods.[23] Although it is not possible for him to will away his desire to live well, he is nonetheless capable of acting from the duty to take care of himself. He can decide to put himself on a healthy diet.[24]

5. THE THREE PROPOSITIONS OF MORALITY (399–401)

Kant explicitly formulates only a second and third "proposition of morality," leaving us to fill in the first. His mention of the second proposition occurs just a few paragraphs following his discussion of the four motivational types. It is reasonable to assume that by the first proposition of morality he has in mind the general point he wishes us to derive from that discussion. If this assumption is correct, then the first proposition is very likely something like the following:

First proposition
A good will acts from duty, not from inclination.

Second proposition

Fortunately, we do not need to guess about the second proposition. Kant formulates it at (399):

[A]n action from duty has its moral worth *not in the purpose* to be attained by it but in the maxim in accordance with which it is decided upon.

Obviously, the distinction Kant wishes to emphasize in this second proposition is between the maxim of an action and its purpose. He

[23] Gout is a disease resulting from excess uric acid in the blood. It causes inflammation of the smaller joints, especially in the feet and hands. Flare-ups can be precipitated by the consumption of alcohol and high-purine foods.
[24] For a more extensive treatment of Kant's argument that we have a duty to secure our own happiness, see Paul Guyer's essay, "The Form and Matter of the Categorical Imperative," in *Kant und die Berliner Aufklärung: Akten des IX. Internationalen Kant-Kongresses I*, ed. Volker Gerhardt, Rolf-Peter Horstmann, and Ralph Schumacher (Berlin/New York, NY: Verlag Walter de Gruyter, 2001), esp. pp. 148ff.

goes on to characterize a "maxim" as an action's "principle of volition." This definition of a maxim is consistent with his remarks in
notes both at (401) and in Section II, where he describes a maxim as
"the subjective principle of acting" or the "principle in accordance
with which the subject *acts*." (420n).[25]

There is something odd, however, about Kant's insistence here that
the moral worth of an action has to do with its maxim but not with its
purpose. It is odd, because he elsewhere seems to imply that a maxim
or principle of volition is nothing other than the *expression* of an
agent's purpose. The maxim of the prudent merchant, remember, is
to keep a general price for everyone "for purposes of self-interest"
(397). This maxim certainly seems to express the merchant's purpose.
The grieving philanthropist sympathizes with the fate of others
because he knows it is his duty to do so. Here, too, his maxim
seems to express his purpose. It is therefore difficult to understand
why Kant's second proposition of morality warns us against conflating
the maxim and the purpose of an action.

One possible explanation of Kant's meaning is this: Perhaps the
distinction he wishes us to bear in mind is not between an agent's
maxim and her *intended* purpose, but between her maxim and its
attained purpose (its *actual* consequences). If we look at Kant's fuller
expression of the second proposition, this reading appears to have
some basis:

[A]n action from duty has its moral worth *not in the purpose* to be attained by
it but in the maxim in accordance with which it is decided upon, and
therefore does not depend upon the realisation of the object of the action
but merely upon the *principle of volition* in accordance with which the action
is done. (399)

Note Kant's remark here that moral worth "does not depend upon the
realization of the object of the action." This remark underscores the
fact that intentions and realized intentions are not the same thing.
Perhaps the second proposition of morality is supposed to remind us,
then, that Kant's concern in the *Groundwork* is to assess intentions
rather than realized intentions. He seeks to identify the disposition of

[25] See also in Kant's Introduction to the *MM* (225). He writes there that a "*maxim* is a *subjective*
principle of action, a principle which the subject himself makes his rule (how he wills to act)."

a good will, and a good will's goodness has nothing to do with its actual effects.

The problem with this line of interpretation, however, is that it is not supported by the first sentence of the proposition. In the first sentence, Kant refers to the purpose "to be attained." He surely means by this the *intended* purpose or aim. In this paragraph, moreover, he enlists the language not of actual or realized purposes, but of "hoped for" effects. In what can the worth of a good will lie, he asks, if not in the "hoped for effect" of its actions? So the distinction mentioned in his second proposition of morality is indeed the distinction between our maxims and our hoped for or intended purposes.

In what sense, then, is moral worth tied to our maxims but not to our hoped for purposes, according to Kant? He writes at (400) that it is "clear from what has gone before" that the "purposes we may have for our actions" are not what gives a will moral worth. What has gone before? Kant has just told us that we have an indirect duty to secure our own happiness. Prior to that, he provided examples of the four motivational types. The point of that discussion, in his words, was to "explicate the concept of a will that is to be esteemed in itself and that is good *apart from any further purpose*" (397; emphasis added). We learned from his discussion that such a will acts "not from inclination but *from duty*" (398). Together, these latter points contain a clue to what Kant has in mind when he tells us, in his second proposition, that an action performed from duty does not have its worth in the purpose to be attained by it. He means that an action does not have its worth in any purpose *other than duty*, in any "further purpose." He means, in other words, that an action does not have its worth in any purpose or end set by desire or inclination.

It is thus not Kant's aim to persuade us that a good will acts from no purposes at all. As I suggested back at Section 2.2, his meaning is rather that a good will is motivated by a *certain class* of purposes or ends. If we return once more to our quoted passage and expand it one last time, this point becomes difficult to overlook:

[A]n action from duty has its moral worth *not in the purpose* to be attained by it but in the maxim in accordance with which it is decided upon, and therefore does not depend upon the realisation of the object of the action but merely upon the *principle of volition* in accordance with which the action is done *without regard for any object of the faculty of desire.* (399f.; final emphasis added)

The last ten words here are crucial: a good will is not motivated by objects of the faculty of desire. Its worth does not lie in the "hoped for" or "expected" realization of these objects. Its motivation does not derive, then, from its empirical nature; it is governed by something other than what Kant in this paragraph refers to as "a posteriori" or "material" incentives. A good will acts to realize some end, but the principle that determines it to act is "formal" or "a priori" rather than material or empirical.[26]

We now see that it would be a mistake to interpret the second proposition of morality as implying that when a will acts from duty, on Kant's account, it does not act to realize an aim or purpose. *Every* volition or act of willing has some object, in his view.[27] A will has moral worth, however, only when it wills to realize a certain kind of object – only when its principle of volition is formal rather than material. This point is fully consistent with the main lesson of Kant's discussion of the four motivational types, namely, that a good will acts from duty, not from inclination.

Third proposition
"[D]uty is the necessity of an action from respect for law" (400).

Kant tells us that this third proposition is "a consequence of" the preceding two. According to the first proposition (on my proposal), a good will is motivated by duty. According to the second, the moral worth of a good will derives from its maxim or principle of volition, and that principle of volition, we now know, must be formal or a priori. The third proposition asserts that a will that is good acts "from respect for law" (400). Kant says no more at this point about the nature or content of the law that is the object of the good will's respect. He does, however, give us some indication of what he means by the concept of respect.

On the basis of what Kant has so far revealed about the motivation of the good will, we can infer that action grounded on respect for law is significantly different from action grounded on empirical incentives or ends of inclination. In his brief discussion at (400–401) and his two

---

[26] Kant elaborates on this distinction between material and formal ends in Section II at (427f.).
[27] See also *CPrR* (34).

notes at (401), Kant further clarifies the distinction between these two kinds of motivational grounds. He insists that objects of inclination can *never* be objects of respect. If something either satisfies or is likely to satisfy my inclinations, I will approve of and perhaps even feel ("pathological") love for it, but it will not be for me an object of respect. The key reason for this, Kant indicates here, is that objects of inclination are not products of free choice; they do not reflect the "activity of the will." Instead, they are given to me as "effects" of nature's programming. Kant clearly reserves the notion of respect for objects that are caused by the will.

When I act from duty, Kant writes, I "put aside . . . every object of the will." By "object of the will," in this context, he means objects of desire or inclination. As we saw earlier, it is not his view that the will that acts from duty *has* no object and thus acts with no purpose or aim in mind. Instead, he holds that the aim or end of a good will is ultimately something other than an end of inclination. Kant is explicit about this point in the following passage:

> [A]n action from duty is to put aside entirely the influence of inclination and with it every object of the will; hence there is left for the will nothing that could determine it except objectively the *law* and subjectively *pure respect* for this practical law. (400f.)

The goodness of a good will thus depends on its being motivated by something other than objects of inclination; such objects are not possible objects of respect. But now we need to understand what Kant has in mind in this passage by the claim that nothing can determine or motivate the good will except "objectively the *law*" and "subjectively *pure respect* for this practical law." He gives us some help in the note in which he explains the meaning of the term "maxim." There he identifies the "objective principle" with the "practical *law*" (the law he will eventually refer to as the categorical imperative). The will that acts from duty, then, is determined or motivated by the objective principle or categorical imperative. At the same time, however, Kant suggests that it is also correct to characterize the will that acts from duty as determined or motivated "subjectively [by] *pure respect*" for the law. He perhaps intends the word "subjectively" in this context to capture an idea he discusses at length in his second note at (401), namely, that respect is a special kind of feeling. Kant seems to hold, then, that the will that acts from duty is motivated both by the objective law as well as, subjectively, by feeling. What we learn from the note on respect is that these are not distinct motivations, for Kant. As we will see in a moment, they are two ways of describing the same motivational ground.

6. RESPECT AS A SPECIAL KIND OF FEELING (401N)

Kant is not inconsistent when he describes the good will in each of these two ways: as motivated by the supreme practical law and as motivated by the feeling of respect. As we saw, respect on his account can have only one thing as its object: the supreme practical law (the objective principle of morality). The will that acts from respect, then, is equivalent to the will that acts from the objective moral principle.

The fact that Kant identifies respect as a feeling, however, might confuse us. Normally when he describes actions motivated by feeling, he means to refer to the responses we have to forces governing us as empirical natures, responses that come to be as effects of nature's laws on us. Nature stirs up my hunger for food; food then becomes the object of my desire or inclination. My desire is a feeling "*received* by means of influence," as Kant says; it is "pathologically" effected – effected, that is, by a sensible condition (in this case, my pangs of hunger).[28] As we know, Kant insists that desires and inclinations (feelings whose origin is empirical) can never provide the motivational ground for a good will.

It turns out, however, that respect is a feeling quite different from this. On his account, respect is a feeling awakened in us by the idea of a law we "impose upon" ourselves. I have the capacity to impose law on myself thanks to the fact that I am more than merely an empirical nature. I am not just "influenced" or determined by laws of nature; I also have free will or practical rationality. The feeling of respect, then, results from the "activity" of my will. Respect is caused by my practical rationality; it comes to be (is "self-wrought") in response to an idea or "rational concept" I give myself as a practically rational being, namely, the idea of the moral law. As Kant writes in

---

[28] See also *CPrR* (75).

the *Critique of Practical Reason*, respect is a feeling, but it is a feeling "produced solely by reason" (75f.).[29]

7. THE FIRST APPEARANCE OF THE SUPREME PRACTICAL PRINCIPLE (402–403)

We know from the third proposition of morality that duty is "the necessity of an action from respect for law." We know, furthermore, that the special feeling of respect is a feeling we have in response to a law that is the product of our will. But what *is* this law that is the object of respect? So far Kant has provided no clues. What kind of law is capable of motivating me to "put aside entirely the influence of inclination" or to "infringe upon" my self-love? In posing this question, Kant is in effect demanding a more complete answer to the question with which Section I began, the question "What is a good will?" He expresses this demand at (402) in the following way:

But what kind of law can that be, the representation of which must determine the will, even without regard for the effect expected from it, in order for the will to be called good absolutely and without limitation?

Kant anticipated his answer back at (400) in his discussion of the second proposition of morality. He told us there that a good will is determined not by some a posteriori or material incentive, but by a formal or a priori principle. Now he is asking: What *is* that formal principle or formal ground of determination? For the first time, he gives us an answer. The principle of the good will, he says, is "the conformity of actions as such with universal law" (402). He formulates this principle as the following requirement:

I ought never to act except in such a way that I could also will that my maxim should become a universal law. (402)

When a will is good or acts from duty, it is determined or motivated by this principle. Although Kant does not identify it as such here, this principle is the first expression in the *Groundwork* of the supreme law of morality, the categorical imperative.

---

[29] For a careful examination of Kant's notion of respect see Andrews Reath, "Kant's Theory of Moral Sensibility." *Kant-Studien* 80 (1989), 284–301.

What can we say, at this point, about the meaning of the principle? We know that, for Kant, common human reason "agrees completely" with it. "Common human reason," he says, "always has this principle before its eyes." Kant therefore implies that this is a principle we already use in testing our maxims or intentions for their moral worth (even though we might not be aware that we do). In effect, the principle says that a good will acts only on maxims it can will as universal law. But what is meant by this phrase "universal law?" What law does Kant have in mind? A partial answer to this question is suggested in his remark that what serves the will as its principle is "mere conformity to law as such." Kant does not expand on this comment here, but we eventually learn that he means something like this: The maxims of a good will conform to the *form* of law. To say that a maxim conforms to the form of law is to say that it possesses the following properties of law: it is universally as well as necessarily valid.

Of course, a number of questions remain unanswered. How are we to know, for example, *which* maxims qualify as universally and necessarily valid? Although Kant does not address this question in Section I, he argues in Section II that a maxim is universally and necessarily valid if it could be willed by all rational natures.

8. THE LYING PROMISE EXAMPLE (402F.)

Kant now provides a concrete example of what is involved in testing for the morality of a maxim. He asks us to imagine whether, in order to escape hardship, it is morally permissible to make a promise with the intention of not keeping it. (He will return to this kind of case twice in Section II (at (422 and 429f.)). Kant notes that we can approach this question in two ways. We can try to determine whether it would be *prudent* to make the false promise, that is, whether the promise would serve the interests of inclination and thus be conducive to happiness. Alternatively, we can ask whether the false promise would be consistent with *duty*. Kant's chief objective in this paragraph is to emphasize that these two approaches are not the same.

To evaluate the maxim from the standpoint of prudence is to consider the consequences for happiness of acting on it. The agent in Kant's example performs a prudential calculation and decides not to tell the lying promise. Although he believes the act might benefit him in the short-term, he worries that in the long-term it could cause him great inconvenience. The lying promise might be found out; if it were, he might never again be trusted. The agent thus chooses to be truthful. What motivates him is his concern for his own happiness or welfare.

Kant insists, however, that we can also test our maxims in an "entirely different" way; we can ask whether we ought to be truthful "from duty." Applying this reasoning, our test is whether the maxim could hold as universal law. On Kant's analysis, the maxim fails this moral test. If the maxim to tell a lying promise were to hold as universal law, he says, it would "destroy itself."

Unfortunately, Kant's remarks in these paragraphs do little to clarify the distinction he wishes us to bear in mind between the moral and prudential approaches to this case. Indeed, his explanation for why the maxim fails the *moral* test sounds entirely *prudential*. Were the maxim to tell the lying promise to become universal law, he tells us, it would hold not just for the agent in question but for others as well. Everyone, then, would make a false promise when in difficulty. But if everyone were to make a false promise in cases like this, the agent's maxim would "destroy itself." The maxim would destroy itself, because universalization would interfere with the achievement of the maxim's aim. The maxim expresses the agent's intention to tell a false promise in order to extricate himself from difficulty. If everyone were to tell false promises in cases of difficulty, however, the practice of telling false promises would become commonplace. If this were to happen, then any particular lying promise would probably not be believed. The agent in Kant's example would be unable to achieve his aim.

Since Kant's remarks here do not help us understand how the moral test (the test for universalization) is different from the pruden-tial test, we need to provide that explanation for him. Fortunately, we have the resources to do so based on what we have learned about his moral theory so far. As we know, the prudential decision procedure considers the consequences of breaking the promise with regard to ends of inclination or happiness. In the lying promise example, the agent asks whether lying is the best course of action from the stand-point of avoiding some difficulty. Here his concern is happiness – in this case, his own happiness. When we reason morally, however, we ask a different kind of question. On Kant's account, we ask whether our maxim could be universally willed. The question I ask, then, is whether my maxim could be valid "for myself as well as others." This time my concern is not with my own desires and interests, my own happiness. Nor is my concern, even, with the happiness of others. Rather, in asking whether the maxim could be universally willed, I am concerned with a different kind of end – an end I share with others universally and necessarily. I indeed care about the consequences of my willing, but now my focus is on the consequences of my willing for an end that is universally and necessarily shared by all rational natures.

The key point to bear in mind here is one we stressed earlier: on Kant's account, ends of happiness or prudence are not ends that can be universally and necessarily shared. This point is especially obvious when the happiness I am concerned to realize is merely my own. In cases like this, I am preoccupied with my own particular needs and desires; I am indifferent to whether my needs and desires are valid for others. But even should I be motivated to promote the happiness of others (or the happiness of everyone), my maxim will still fail to be universally and necessarily valid. This is for reasons we reviewed back in Section 3.3 of this chapter. Ends of happiness, as we saw, lack the status of universal and necessary validity, according to Kant. No two of us share exactly the same conception of happiness. Even did we happen to agree today on the ingredients of happiness, we might not agree tomorrow. For each of us, moreover, the idea of happiness is variable over time. Testing a maxim for its prudential consequences, then, is significantly different from testing a maxim for whether it can be made universal law. Ends of happiness or inclination, on Kant's definition, can *never* ground rules that are universally and necessarily valid.

Returning to the lying promise example, how can we now explain why the agent's maxim fails the moral test? In performing the moral test, the question we must ask is why the universal permissibility of the maxim would be incompatible with a universal and necessary end. If made universal law, the maxim would undeniably threaten the practice of making promises. No doubt, this would interfere with the effectiveness of any particular lying promise. And no doubt, this outcome would be detrimental from the standpoint of happiness. The *moral* point, however, is that this consequence would also interfere with an end shared universally and necessarily by all rational natures. Kant has so far given us very little indication of what that end is. He has told us only that it is an end of practical reason, not of inclination, and that it is the object of the special feeling he calls respect. As he admits here, he has not yet made explicit "what this respect is based upon." We have to wait until Section II for further specification of this universal and necessary end. (See my discussion beginning at Section 9.2 of Chapter 4.)

In Section II, Kant provides further examples of applying the supreme moral principle to test the moral worth of maxims. When we consider those examples, we will have the opportunity to deepen our understanding of his account.

9. FROM "COMMON RATIONAL MORAL COGNITION" TO "PHILOSOPHIC MORAL COGNITION" (403–405)

Recall the question Kant asked at the beginning of (402):

But what kind of law can that be, the representation of which must determine the will, even without regard for the effect expected from it, in order for the will to be called good absolutely and without limitation?

The answer Kant has provided up to this point is that the maxims of a good will conform to law. They have the form of law, in other words, and are therefore universally and necessarily valid. This is so far a fairly thin account of the motivation of the good will, but Kant will expand upon it in Section II. So far, however, we know that he thinks that "common human reason agrees completely" with this conception of duty, and "always has this principle before its eyes." He repeats this point beginning at (403). It takes no "penetrating acuteness," he says, to grasp what the law governing moral assessment is. Common human reason "uses the norm for its appraisals" as a kind of "compass" for distinguishing what is good from what is evil.[30]

In these final paragraphs, Kant reminds us of what he set out to accomplish in this first section of the *Groundwork*. His task has been

---

[30] See also *CPrR* (36): "So distinctly and sharply drawn are the boundaries of morality and self-love that even the most common eye cannot fail to distinguish whether something belongs to the one or the other." What duty requires is "plain of itself to everyone." For further passages from the *CPrR*, see (27) and (155).

to make "common human reason" "attentive to its own principle" (404). As I stressed early on in this chapter, Kant never suggests that the concept of duty is his own invention. His contribution has merely been to make the concept explicit. He has analyzed the concept of the good will in order to heighten our awareness of what duty requires. Of the many points he intended to call to our attention by means of this analysis, perhaps the most important is that the concept of duty, or the supreme law of morality, has its origin in reason.

It is noteworthy that Kant mentions the name of Socrates in this context. He comments that it would be "easy to show" how common human reason, with its "compass" in hand, is able to distinguish between good and evil. It would be easy to show this, he continues, "as did Socrates." Very likely, Kant has in mind here Plato's Dialogue, the *Meno*. In that Dialogue, Socrates draws a few lines in the sand and poses questions to an uneducated slave boy. He does so in order to demonstrate that the boy is capable of knowing geometric truths without instruction from a teacher. The knowledge the uneducated boy already possesses merely needs to be activated or awakened with the help of probing questions. No doubt, Kant mentions Socrates in this passage, because he sees himself as likewise engaged in the enterprise of bringing to the surface knowledge each of us, as rational natures, already possesses.[31]

These final paragraphs reveal Kant's conception of the role of the moral philosopher involved in the project of grounding a metaphysics of morals. Common human reason, not philosophy, is the author of the supreme moral principle. But common human reason is easily led astray; it has the tendency to forget or even deceive itself about what it already knows. As we have seen, the demands of duty have to compete with the demands of happiness for our attention, and very often happiness wins the upper hand. On such occasions, common human reason is prone to deceive itself about its motives. It makes excuses for itself; it looks for ways, even, to distort the meaning of the moral law. There exists the constant danger, then, not just that

---

[31] Kant has more to say about this topic in the "Doctrine of Method" section of the *CPrR*. Common human reason, he says there, has long known the answer to the question, "What is *pure* morality?" It knows the answer to this question, just as it knows the difference between the right and left hand (155).

common cognition will ignore the guidance of its inner compass, but that it will lose the ability to recognize that guidance for what it is.

Philosophy, however, can help common human reason stay on track. It can describe with precision the nature of a good will. It can carefully draw the distinction between actions performed from duty and actions performed from inclination. Philosophy can thereby make it more difficult for us either to forget or to fool ourselves about what morality requires.[32]

---

[32] For a more extensive treatment of Kant's point that a task of the moral philosopher is to guard against the tendency of human reason to lead itself astray about what morality requires, see Paul Guyer's essay, "The Strategy of Kant's *Groundwork*," in his *Kant on Freedom, Law, and Happiness* (Cambridge University Press, 2000).

CHAPTER 4

Section II: Transition from popular moral philosophy to metaphysics of morals[1]

I. INTRODUCTION: THE MAIN TOPICS OF SECTION II

Of the three sections of the *Groundwork*, Section II is by far the longest and most sweeping in scope. It is in this Section that Kant finally identifies the categorical imperative as the supreme law of morality. He discusses a number of different formulations of the law, and he explains the sense in which the law commands categorically. In addition, he considers various applications of the moral law. He indicates in a preliminary way how particular duties may be derived from it. Kant also sets out to deepen our understanding of the central character of Section I, the good will. He further clarifies the way in which the motivational ground of the good will differs from other motivational grounds. As we know, the good will acts from duty. In acting from duty, it allows the categorical imperative to govern its will. We learn in Section II that the categorical imperative is a law rational agents give themselves. Kant argues that rational agents are able to give themselves law in virtue of their remarkable capacity of self-determination or autonomy.

2. DUTY IS NOT A CONCEPT OF EXPERIENCE (406–412)

The first sentence of Section II reminds us of a central claim of the *Groundwork*, namely, that the concept of duty is not a concept of experience. We first encountered this claim in Kant's Preface. A "metaphysics" of morals is "indispensably necessary," he asserted

---

[1] The German for what Mary Gregor has translated as "popular moral philosophy" is "*populären sittlichen Weltweisheit.*" "*Weltweisheit*" literally means "world wisdom."

there, precisely because morality cannot rest on anything empirical (389). Now, in the first ten paragraphs of Section II, he provides a number of reasons in favor of this view.

2.1 *Experience provides no evidence that there is such a thing as a moral disposition (407–408)*

The effort to ground morality in experience can take a variety of forms. For example, it can take the form of appealing to experience for evidence that people can actually be motivated by duty. According to this view, the observation of human nature provides justification for the assumption that duty really does function as a determining ground of the will.

What Kant argues in these first paragraphs of Section II, however, is that this appeal to experience for proof is in vain. It is in vain, because the principles governing human motivation are ultimately unavailable to us empirically. As he writes:

> it is absolutely impossible by means of experience to make out with complete certainty a single case in which the maxim of an action otherwise in conformity with duty rested simply on moral grounds.

Even when our behavior clearly *conforms* to duty, we can never be certain it is actually *motivated* by duty. The problem is that, in attempting to know our motives, we seek access to something "unseen" – to the "inner principles" determining our actions. Of course, we like to "flatter ourselves" that we at least on occasion act from a motive more "noble" than that of self-interest or self-love. But it is always possible that what really moves us is what Kant refers to here as the "dear self."

Kant notes that if we insist that experience is our only source of evidence for the reality of the moral disposition, we play into the hands of the skeptic. The skeptic "ridicules" all morality as a mere "phantom" of the imagination; she doubts whether "true virtue is to be found in the world" (407). Kant, of course, does not share the skeptic's doubts. Even though we cannot rely on experience to support the thesis that people are capable of acting from noble motives, this is no reason, in his view, to call into question the validity of the idea of duty itself, the validity of the command of morality. Even if "up to now" experience has furnished no proof that there ever has been a sincere friend, pure sincerity in friendship is nonetheless required of us (409).

Kant's point here is that the conclusion that morality is a mere "phantom" does not necessarily follow from the fact that we have no certainty "up to now" that anyone has ever acted from duty. In a passage further on in Section II, his language is even stronger. In practical philosophy, he writes, "we have to do not with assuming grounds for what *happens* but rather laws for what *ought to happen* even if it never does" (427). So even if no one *ever* acts on practical laws, Kant seems to imply, those laws still obligate us.

Does Kant take seriously the possibility that none of us will ever act from duty? This view is not implied by his discussion at (407–408). The message he conveys there is merely that experience can never establish with certainty that a person's motivation is duty. As it turns out, this is the message of (427) as well. When he writes that his concern is not with "grounds for what *happens*" but with laws for "what *ought to happen*," he is not asserting that none of us will ever act from duty. Rather, he once again means to emphasize the futility of the attempt to derive evidence of the motivating role of duty from "what happens," from our observations of actual human conduct.

2.2 We cannot derive from experience laws that are apodictically valid for all rational natures (408)

Kant moves on to provide additional reasons for calling into question the assumption that morality has its ground in experience. One reason has to do with the *scope* of the validity of moral laws. Kant simply asserts here, as he does elsewhere, that the idea of duty is valid not just for human nature but for "all *rational beings as such*" (408). Since we have no experience of non-human rational nature, we of course cannot rely on experience to support the assumption that duty is valid for all rational nature. (Kant insists upon this point also at (389), (410*), and (442).)

A further reason for doubting that morality can be derived from experience concerns the *modality* of moral laws. On Kant's account, moral laws command apodictically, that is, necessarily.[2] For reasons I discussed at length in Section 5 of my Introduction, Kant holds that empirical evidence can never support judgments with this kind of validity. In light of the nature both of their scope and modality, then, moral laws must have their origin "completely" in pure practical reason.

2.3 We cannot derive the concept of duty from examples (408–409)

Kant next turns his attention to the proposal that we derive our idea of duty from concrete examples of moral conduct. The proposal takes its point of departure from the fact that we use examples to illustrate cases of moral conduct. From this fact, it then infers that such examples can supply our *standard* of moral assessment.

On Kant's analysis, this reasoning fails to appreciate that we can only single out someone (say, the "Holy One") as our moral example if we are already in possession of some "ideal of moral perfection." It is not that our standard for judging derives from our examples; rather, we identify a piece of conduct as exemplary only by means of applying a prior standard. Kant grants that examples have an important role to play in practical philosophy. They can inspire and encourage us, as well as "make intuitive" what the moral law requires of us. But he considers it naïve to suppose that our concept of duty derives from examples.

2.4 Morality cannot be grounded on popular opinion (409–412)

The discussion of this subsection begins with the following rather indecipherable sentence:

If there is … no genuine supreme basic principle of morality that does not have to rest only on pure reason independently of all experience, I believe it unnecessary even to ask whether it is a good thing to set forth in their generality … these concepts.

---

[2] In the B-edition "Transcendental exposition of the concept of space," Kant tells us that apodictic judgments are "combined with consciousness of their necessity," *CPR* A 25/B 41. He contrasts apodictic judgments both with those that are accompanied by consciousness of mere possibility ("problematic" judgments) and with "assertoric" judgments that are true (actual) but not necessary. He writes that apodictic judgments "cannot be empirical or judgments of experience, nor inferred from them." An example of an apodictic judgment is "space has only three dimensions," A 25/B 41. See his remarks also in the *Jäsche Logic* Section 30.

Note, first, that by "these concepts," Kant refers us back to the previous paragraph and his references there to the concepts of "moral perfection," of "God as the highest good," and of a "free will." Bearing this in mind, we can rewrite and simplify the above-cited remark as follows: "Given that the supreme principle of morality rests on pure reason, we should not need to ask whether it is necessary to set forth in their generality concepts such as that of moral perfection and of a free will."

Why does it follow, for Kant, that from the fact that the supreme principle of morality rests on reason, concepts such as that of moral perfection need to be "set forth in their generality?" Fortunately, his answer to this question is less mysterious than the question itself. His answer is that, "in our day," the preferred practical philosophy is *not* the "pure rational" variety which is "separated from anything empirical" (a "metaphysics of morals"), but rather "popular" practical philosophy. The concepts of morality need to be "set forth in their generality," then, because they are distinct from, and must not be confused with, their preferred popular counterpart.

Kant has no objection to the effort to "descend to popular concepts" if by this we mean the effort to make practical philosophy generally accessible. He does, however, object to those who would make popular approval the *standard* of the correctness of our moral principles. That is, he opposes the attempt to *ground* morality on popular opinion. Kant writes here that popular opinion produces a "disgusting hodgepodge of patchwork observations and half-rationalized principles, in which shallow pates revel because it is something useful for everyday chit-chat" (409). Clearly, he thinks that popular opinion is unreflective and unscientific. It suffers from sloppy reasoning and lacks a solid philosophical basis. All that popular opinion is able to supply is a wide assortment of poorly supported theories of human nature and of the nature of morality. Popular opinion offers us nothing upon which to ground principles that have universal and necessary validity.

Precisely because moral principles must have universal and necessary validity, in Kant's view, popular philosophy has to be kept separate from a metaphysics of morals. This is why he argues in the *Groundwork* for the necessity of progressing *beyond* popular moral philosophy. It is why his title for Section II announces that he will provide a "transition" from "popular moral philosophy" to a "metaphysics of morals."

Not only is popular opinion incapable of providing universal and necessary moral principles, it is also unable to motivate us as effectively as the "pure thought of duty:"

> For, the pure thought of duty and in general of the moral law, mixed with no foreign addition of empirical inducements, has by way of reason alone … an influence on the human heart so much more powerful than other incentives, which may be summoned from the empirical field. (410f.)

Kant explains what he has in mind here in his note at (411). We are more likely to be inspired by the person whose motivation is duty alone than by the person who is in part also moved to achieve her own happiness. For this reason, the person who acts from the "pure thought of duty" has a greater "influence on the human heart."

2.5 Popular opinion versus "common reason" (409–412)

As we just saw, Kant has no quarrel with the effort to make practical philosophy popular, if by this we mean the effort to make the concept of duty inspiring as well as "commonly understandable." For the reasons we just reviewed, however, he firmly resists any attempt to *ground* morality on popular opinion. It is important that we bear in mind that the popular approach to moral philosophy he has been sketching in these opening paragraphs of Section II is not to be confused with the "common rational moral cognition" he referred to back in Section I. To see this, consider the following passage from (411):

> [I]t is clear that all moral concepts have their seat and origin completely a priori in reason, and *indeed in the most common reason* [emphasis added].

Here Kant identifies moral concepts that have their origin "completely a priori in reason" with those that have their origin in "the most common reason." In the next paragraph, he says of "common moral appraisal" that it is "very worthy of respect" (412).

Given our discussion in Section I of Kant's characterization of "common human reason" or "common human understanding," these remarks should come as no surprise. Remember that in Section I the progression of his discussion was from "common rational moral cognition" to "philosophic moral cognition." He relied on common human reason as his starting point, since common human reason "always" has the principle of morality "before its eyes."[3] In the progression to "philosophic moral cognition," he made explicit the principle common human reason already applies or acknowledges. Common rational moral cognition was the starting point from which he extracted his philosophical account of the nature of a good will. In Kant's estimation, then, common rational moral cognition is a source of reliable insight into the concept of duty; popular opinion is not. [4]

3. ADVANCE FROM POPULAR PHILOSOPHY TO A METAPHYSICS OF MORALS (412)

Up to this point in Section II, Kant has focussed his attention on how *not* to ground morality. We make a mistake, in his view, if we try to ground morality in experience, whether by seeking our standard of conduct in popular opinion or by appealing to examples. Of course, the fact that morality cannot be grounded in experience does not imply, in his view, that morality *has* no ground. Kant does not hold, in other words, that we have *no* way to demonstrate that moral laws are binding for all rational natures. He has already asserted that the ground of morality is to be discovered in principles or laws that are a priori. He now proceeds to draw out the implications of this claim.

To say of a law or principle that it is a priori is to say that it has its origin as well as its justification in pure reason. Since the supreme law of morality is a *practical law* – a law that legislates over actions – its source, according to Kant, is pure practical reason. In the paragraph at (412) in which he signals the transition or "advance" he will now make to a metaphysics of morals, he indicates his argumentative strategy. He will examine the "practical faculty of reason" and then explain how the "concept of duty arises from it."

---

[3] *Groundwork* (403).
[4] Further references to "common human reason" or "common understanding" may be found in *Groundwork* (394) and (397). See also *CPrR* (36): "What is to be done in accordance with the principle of the autonomy of choice is seen quite easily and without hesitation by the most common understanding." See also *CPrR*, (27) and (155).

4. THE WILL AS PURE PRACTICAL REASON (412–414)

Kant's discussion of the nature of practical reason begins with this important assertion:

Everything in nature works in accordance with laws. Only a rational being has the capacity to act *in accordance with the representation of laws*, that is, in accordance with principles, or has a *will*.

In order to understand the point of the first sentence of this passage, we need to recall our discussion beginning at Section 6 of my Introduction. Remember that Kant holds that when we identify something as an object of nature (an "appearance"), we imply that it is given in space and time and governed by laws of nature. Objects of nature lack the power to move or determine themselves. Their behavior is entirely caused or conditioned by, and hence explainable with reference to, laws of nature. If we consider human behavior solely from standpoint of nature, we therefore must accept the implication that it is determined by laws of nature as well. Considered from this point of view, human beings no more have the capacity of self-determination or freedom than do plants or planets. Nor are they any more responsible for their actions.

It is significant that in the above-quoted passage Kant *contrasts* objects of nature with "rational beings." Rational beings possess a "will," a faculty Kant characterizes here as "nothing other than practical reason." A being that is "rational," he says, has the capacity to act "in accordance with the representation of laws." He will go on to argue that, thanks to that capacity, such a being enjoys genuine freedom.

Two observations are in order at this point. First, we might be tempted to interpret the phrase "rational being" to refer to a being that has the capacity to think and who uses that capacity in its efforts to know. But Kant's interest in the *Groundwork* is to elucidate the nature and role of *practical* reason. He has in mind not the faculty of thinking and knowing but the faculty that determines or influences our actions. Practical reason, on his account, is a faculty of willing, of translating ideas into action. As we will see, practical reason has a special kind of causal power. In his Preface, Kant alerted us to the fact that he would be examining the possibility of this very special faculty. He claimed that he would be breaking into an "entirely new field," in that he would be examining the "idea and principles" of a "possible *pure* will" (390). When Kant refers to "rational being" in the *Groundwork*, then, he usually has in mind a being that is practically rational, a being that possesses a pure will.

Note, secondly, that Kant has so far made no effort to defend the view that there *is* such a faculty of practical rationality (or that we are in fact endowed with a pure will). He reserves that task for Section III. His objective in the paragraphs we are presently considering is instead to introduce us to his account of practical reason. So far, he has told us only that a practically rational being has the capacity to act in accordance with the representation of laws.

Kant's next move is to point out that reason can be practical in either of two ways. Reason, he says, can determine the will either "infallibly" or "fallibly." To put this point differently, there are two kinds of practically rational beings, in Kant's view: those for whom reason determines the will infallibly and those for whom it determines the will fallibly. In due course, Kant will inform us that the human will is a fallible will and that practical reason thus determines our will merely fallibly.

4.1 A will that is "infallibly" determined by reason (412–414)

If reason infallibly determines the will, the actions of such a being that are cognized as objectively necessary are also subjectively necessary, that is, the will is a capacity to choose *only that* which reason independently of inclination cognizes as practically necessary, that is, as good.

Kant provides no explanation here of the technical terms "objectively necessary" and "subjectively necessary." We eventually learn, however, that "objectively necessary" actions, on his definition, are those that are universally and necessarily valid. In the context of practical philosophy, these are actions all rational natures can recognize as obligatory from a practical or moral point of view. Alternatively put, these are actions all rational natures can agree are required by duty. "Subjectively necessary" actions, in contrast, are actions an agent is actually motivated to perform. These actions may or may not also be objectively necessary.

In the passage quoted above, Kant writes that the actions of an infallible will are *both* objectively and subjectively necessary. He means by this that the infallible will is always motivated to respect duty. As he puts it, the infallible will "can be determined only through the representation of the good" (414). This is why there is, for it, a necessary conformity between what it wills and duty. The infallible will is "perfectly good" or "holy" (414, 439). It is never even "tempted" to break the law.[5] Not only does it always choose to act from duty, it does so "gladly," as Kant says.[6]

Given that the infallible will is "necessarily obedient" to reason, on Kant's account – given that, as he tells us in the *Critique of Practical Reason*, the infallible will is *incapable* of acting on maxims that conflict with duty – we might wonder whether he really means to attribute to such a being a faculty of choice. Kant does, however, define the infallible will as capable of choice.[7] It differs from the fallible will not because it is less free, but because it always chooses duty; it chooses "only that which reason … cognizes … as good" (412). The reason the infallible will always chooses duty is because, unlike the fallible will, it lacks the "incentives" or "sensible impulses" that compete with duty for its attention.[8]

4.2 A will that is "fallibly" determined by reason (412f.)

As we might expect, there is in the case of a fallible will *no* necessary conformity between what it wills and duty, on Kant's account. Unlike its infallible counterpart, the fallible will is not "solely" determined by practical reason. It is susceptible to other motivational impulses; it sometimes allows itself to act, for example, from inclination or feeling. Imagine a person who gratifies his ego by wielding power over others. One day, he is feeling particularly deflated and proceeds to bully his employees. In doing so, he is motivated by the desire to feel powerful. This desire is "subjectively necessary" for him in that it is in fact what determines his action. But the man's bullying behavior has no "objective validity." It surely would not be consented to or agreed upon by all

---

[5] *MM II* (396f.).
[6] *MM II* (405). See also Kant's discussion in *CPrR* (32). For an examination of the distinction between the holy will and the fallible will, see Marcus Willaschek's essay "Practical Reason," in *Groundwork for the Metaphysics of Morals*, eds. Christoph Horn and Dieter Schönecker, pp. 130–132.
[7] For more evidence, see *MM II* (405) and *CPrR* (32).   [8] *CPrR* (32).

rational natures (certainly not by his unfortunate employees). In this case, then, his will is obviously not "*in itself* completely in conformity with reason."

Cases in which our actions are not in complete conformity with reason are all too common for human rational natures. Such cases reveal the reality of the human condition, the condition of wills that are fallible and, as such, affected by "sensible motives."[9] It would nonetheless be a mistake to read Kant as committed to the view that fallible wills such as ours are *never* able to act from motives that are objectively necessary. On the contrary, he is convinced that we do in fact have the capacity to act in this way and that some of us, to some extent, realize this capacity. He does not try to justify this view here. Instead, his aim in these paragraphs of Section II is simply to draw attention to the respect in which our will is fallible and thus distinct from a will that is always and completely determined by reason.

4.3 For the fallible will, duty is expressed in the form of an imperative (413–414)

Kant claims that the will that is infallibly determined by reason does not have to be commanded to obey what reason requires. Given the points we have just reviewed, it should be obvious why this is so. The infallible will is always in fact motivated to respect duty. As Kant puts it, the infallible will's "subjective constitution" is "necessarily determined" by the "objective law of reason." For such a "perfect" will, he says, the "ought" is "out of place" (414). In the case of the fallible will, however, the situation is different. The fallible will can heed the call of reason because it possesses the capacity of practical reason. But, as our above example illustrates, the fallible will is also susceptible to other motivational forces. It can allow those other motivational forces to govern its will. This is why Kant claims that, for the fallible will, the law of practical reason must be expressed as an "ought."

---

[9] *CPrR* (32).

5. IMPERATIVES: HYPOTHETICAL VERSUS CATEGORICAL (414–421)

It would be natural at this place in our discussion to be curious about the law of reason that, in Kant's view, necessarily determines the infallible will and must, for the fallible will, appear in the form of a command. Up to now, he has said very little about it. We know that one of its features is that it is an "objective" law and as such "valid for every rational being." We also know that it is not an objectively valid law of logic or physics but rather an objective *practical* law. In our discussion of Section I of the *Groundwork*, we determined that the law of reason that commands our will, according to Kant, is the law that expresses our duty. But this still does not inform us about the *content* of the law. That is, it tells us nothing about what the law specifically requires.

In the paragraphs we are presently considering, Kant prepares the way for the account he will eventually provide of the content or meaning of the supreme law of practical reason, the law he comes to identify as the "categorical imperative." As a first step, he introduces a distinction between imperatives that are "categorical" and those that are "hypothetical."

All imperatives command actions in the service of achieving some purpose or end. In Kant's more technical terms, an imperative is a "practical law" that "represents a possible action as good and thus as necessary for a subject practically determinable by reason" (414).[10] Suppose I hold that vegetarianism is a good and decide to live the life of a vegetarian. Assuming both that this is really my end and that I am rational, I thus take myself to be obligated to live according to the principles of vegetarianism. I allow the following imperative to govern my actions: "In order to observe the principles of vegetarianism, I ought not to eat meat."

Kant acknowledges that actions may be determined to be good in a variety of ways, and the distinction he draws between kinds of imperatives turns on this fact. A categorical imperative, he tells us, represents an action as "objectively necessary of itself," that is, as "*in*

---

[10] In the *CPrR*, Kant defines an imperative as "a rule indicated by an 'ought' which expresses objective necessitation to the action" (20).

itself good." A hypothetical imperative, on the other hand, represents an action as "a means to achieving something else that one wills" (414). Obviously, we cannot understand Kant's distinction between the two kinds of imperatives without first exploring his distinction between these two kinds of goods.

We can begin by considering Kant's description of hypothetical imperatives. He writes that:

> the hypothetical imperative says only that the action is good for some *possible* or *actual* purpose. (414f.)

This remark might strike us as curious for the following reason. Kant characterizes the goods that are the concern of hypothetical imperatives as either "possible" or "actual." These would seem to exhaust the available options. From this comment about the goods of hypothetical imperatives, we might reasonably draw the implication that categorical imperatives command actions that aim at no good at all – they command actions, in other words, that *have* no end or purpose. Kant even seems to explicitly commit himself to such a view at the beginning of (415) where he writes that the categorical imperative "declares the action to be of itself objectively necessary *without reference to some purpose*" (emphasis added). Is it really Kant's intention to suggest here that the categorical imperative commands actions without reference to any end or purpose? The answer to this question is "no," but we need to cover more ground before we can explain his reasoning. We first need to review his classification of kinds of hypothetical imperatives.

5.1 Problematic hypothetical imperatives: commanding means to the achievement of possible ends (415)

On Kant's account, problematic hypothetical imperatives are imperatives that command actions that are good for some "possible" end or purpose. He labels these imperatives "rules of skill" or "technical imperatives" (416f.). We can best clarify what he has in mind with the help of his own examples. A physician wishes to look after his patient's health. To serve that end, he ought to follow a number of rules or procedures. He ought to perform certain tests, familiarize himself with his patient's medical history, and so forth. A poisoner aims to kill his victim. He likewise ought to follow certain rules if he is to achieve his goal. Minimally, he ought to be certain he has chosen a truly lethal poison. Parents wish to prepare their children for life. To serve that end, they ought to teach them the requisite skills. Kant tells us that he is not concerned here to evaluate the goodness or rationality of the ends referred to in these examples. He merely wishes to illustrate possible ends persons might have. Problematic hypothetical imperatives take the possible ends of persons and command the means for achieving them: "Given that my aim is to poison my victim, I ought to choose a poison that is sufficiently lethal." (Kant in addition describes problematic hypothetical imperatives as "analytic," but I will hold off discussion of this feature until Section 5.6 below.)

Why does Kant characterize the ends of problematic hypothetical imperatives as merely "possible" if they are ends that persons *actually* have? The reason is that, in the case of this class of hypothetical imperatives, there is no implication that a person's end is an end shared by all rational natures – not even by all human rational natures. The ends of the physician are relative to his specific objectives. Likewise for the poisoner and the parent. These are ends that particular individuals happen to have given their unique desires and circumstances. It would be a mistake to suppose that the ends of these individuals must also be actual for others.

5.2 Assertoric hypothetical imperatives: commanding means to the achievement of actual ends (415–416)

To characterize a purpose as "actual" versus merely "possible," in the sense Kant intends, is to imply that it commands ends or purposes that not merely some but *all* persons have. Kant holds that there is one end that can indeed be presupposed to be actual in all dependent or finite rational beings, an end that all such beings have by what he refers to as "natural necessity." That end or purpose is happiness (415). This is the end he described back in Section I as the "sum of satisfaction of all inclinations" (399). Assertoric hypothetical imperatives, then, command as practically necessary some action as a means to the achievement of happiness. Because the end of happiness belongs to the "essence" of human nature, Kant tells us, it is an end shared by all human nature.

The perceptive reader will notice that in the space of this single paragraph at (415), Kant changes the subject of his discussion from "all rational beings" to "every human being." We might wonder whether this change reflects an inconsistency on his part, or perhaps a bit of carelessness. In fact, however, he quickly qualifies the phrase "all rational beings" with the reminder that, in this context, he really means to refer only to those rational beings that are subject to imperatives, namely, *fallible* rational beings.[11] We need not take his reference to "human beings" later in the paragraph, then, as evidence of confusion or error. After all, the fallible rational will Kant is chiefly concerned to describe in the *Groundwork* is the *human* fallible will.

Remember that Kant is preparing us in these paragraphs for his introduction of the supreme practical law (the categorical imperative). As we have seen, he claims that, for fallible wills such as ours, that law must be expressed in the form of a command or imperative. He has also indicated that the supreme practical law is "objective." It has objective versus merely subjective validity, on his account, because it binds or is valid for "every rational being as such" (413). This raises the following question: Given that the objectivity of the supreme practical law is a function of its validity for all rational wills (its universal validity), why does Kant insist that assertoric hypothetical imperatives cannot qualify as objective? We know "surely and a priori," he has told us, that assertoric hypothetical imperatives command ends or purposes shared by "every human being" (415f.).[12] These imperatives would thus seem to have universal validity at least for human nature. But Kant insists that assertoric hypothetical imperatives necessitate our will only conditionally. He says that they command actions not "absolutely but only as a means to another purpose." (At one point, he even warns us against classifying these imperatives as "laws." Strictly speaking, he says, they are merely "counsels" (416)).[13] On what basis, then, are assertoric hypothetical imperatives conditional, in Kant's

---

[11] Kant is clear about this in the *CPrR* as well. "To be happy is necessarily the demand of every rational but finite being" (25).

[12] In claiming that we know "a priori" that every human desires happiness, Kant is asserting that this is a special kind of fact, a fact we know with necessity. An example of another fact we know a priori, on his account, is that objects of nature must be given to us in experience through our forms of intuition, space, and time.

[13] See also Kant's Preface at (389).

view? Why do they not qualify as laws? The answer to this question will become evident once we have further explored his contrast between hypothetical and categorical imperatives.

5.3 The categorical imperative: commanding means to unconditional ends (416)

Recall that in his Preface to the *Groundwork*, Kant informed us of his chief objective: to "search for and establish" the supreme principle of morality (392). Finally, at (416), he explicitly identifies that principle. He tells us that there is only "one" imperative that qualifies as the "imperative of morality," namely, the "categorical" imperative. This imperative is categorical, he says, because its command is "unconditional." In contrast to imperatives that command merely hypothetically, the command of the categorical imperative is "limited by no condition" (416).

We now need to determine the precise sense in which the categorical imperative is unconditional, on Kant's account. Perhaps by "unconditional" he means that the categorical imperative commands without reference to specific ends or purposes. As noted earlier, his language sometimes seems to suggest this. At the beginning of (415), for instance, he writes that the categorical imperative "declares the action to be of itself objectively necessary *without reference to some purpose*" (emphasis added).

In fact, however, Kant's view is not that the categorical imperative makes no reference whatsoever to purposes. Consider his remark at (414):

The categorical imperative would be that which represented an action as objectively necessary in itself, without reference to another end.

Note the equation here of the phrases "objectively necessary in itself" and "without reference to another end." Kant does not claim in this passage that an action that is "objectively necessary in itself" *has* no end or purpose; he merely claims that it represents an action as objectively necessary without reference to "another" end. This is the message conveyed in a comment he makes at (416) as well. The categorical imperative commands some conduct "immediately," he says, "without being based upon and having as its condition any *other purpose* to be attained by certain conduct" (emphasis added). So to say that an action is "objectively necessary in itself," according to Kant, is not to imply that it has *no* end or purpose. Instead, Kant means to exclude from actions that are objectively necessary only *some* ends or purposes, or only *a particular class* of ends or purposes.[14]

We encountered a version of this ambiguity earlier when we considered Kant's account of the good will in Section I (at 2.2). As we saw there, the good will is good "in itself" or "unconditionally," and Kant sometimes appears to imply by this that such a will acts with no regard for an end or purpose. When we inspected the text more closely, however, we discovered that his point is not that a good will acts from no purposes whatsoever. Rather, the will that is good "in itself," on his characterization, is "good *apart from any further purpose*" (397; emphasis added). Such a will, he goes on to tell us, acts "not from inclination but *from duty*" (398). Clearly, Kant's message is that a good will does not have its worth in any purpose *other than duty* – in any "further purpose." At (400) he is explicit about the kind of purposes that do *not* motivate a good will. A good will is not motivated by objects of the faculty of inclination or desire.

Just as it is a mistake, then, to suppose that Kant is committed to the view that a good will acts without regard to any end or purpose, so it is a mistake to suppose that the categorical imperative, on his account, commands actions that have no end or purpose. A good will acts to achieve some end; its answers to the call of duty rather than of ends set by desire or inclination. The categorical imperative commands actions that refer to some purpose as well, a purpose likewise set by something other than desire or inclination.

5.4 On the merely conditional validity of assertoric hypothetical imperatives

We have now identified one obvious difference between the categorical imperative and assertoric hypothetical imperatives. The difference has

---

[14] This interpretation is consistent with a passage we considered earlier from (414), where Kant writes that, "all imperatives are formulae for the determination of action that is necessary in accordance with the principle of a will which is good in some way." See also *CPrR* (34): "every volition must also have an object and hence a matter."

to do with the ends or purposes to which each kind of imperative refers. Assertoric hypothetical imperatives command actions as means to the achievement of happiness; the categorical imperative commands actions that serve some other end.

What remains unclear, however, is whether this difference suggests an answer to the question we raised in our final paragraph of Section 5.2. We wondered there about the basis for Kant's insistence that assertoric hypothetical imperatives have merely conditional validity. Given that these imperatives command the means to an end shared by every finite will (namely, happiness), why are they not unconditionally or absolutely valid? Why are they at best "counsels" but not "laws?"

As it turns out, the conditional character of assertoric hypothetical imperatives, on Kant's account, is tied to the fact that the end they serve – happiness – is an end set by inclination. Happiness is an end or purpose we have due to our empirical nature, or due to our nature empirically considered. As Kant says, we have this end by "*natural necessity*" (emphasis added). So in attributing the end of happiness to human beings, we treat humanity as an object of nature and hence as an object of empirical investigation.

The fact that happiness is an end set by inclination is significant for reasons we reviewed in our Introduction. In that discussion we identified two reasons for Kant's insistence that the grounding of morality cannot be empirical. One reason is that, if we treat human nature merely as an object of nature – as an appearance – we have no way to account for its capacity to rise above the laws of nature and act from freedom. As we saw, this leaves us no genuine basis for moral imputation. A second reason, for Kant, is that it is not possible to derive principles that are universally and necessarily valid from a merely empirical account of human behavior. Kant explicitly reminds us of this point later in Section II where he writes that, "empirical principles are not at all fit to be the ground of moral laws" (442). It is this second point he has in mind when he insists upon the conditional character of hypothetical imperatives.

The conditioned character of hypothetical imperatives is relatively obvious in the case of problematic hypothetical imperatives. It is a contingent fact about me at this particular time in my life that I wish to become a vegetarian and thus take myself to be bound by the command not to eat meat. This is a fact that singles out one of the ways in which I am a unique individual; its validity for me has to do with my present psychological state and circumstances. But given that the command reflects facts that are unique to me, there is no reason to assume that it is necessarily valid for everyone.

The conditional character of assertoric hypothetical imperatives is less obvious precisely because, on Kant's definition, these imperatives command means to an end that is universally shared. But even though Kant insists that it can be "presupposed surely and a priori" that every human desires happiness as an end (415f.), he also holds that we can only determine what individuals mean by happiness by consulting experience. When we do so, we discover that the concept of happiness admits of great variety. Not only that, it changes over time. In these passages, Kant returns to a claim he made back in Section I (399), namely, that it follows from the empirical nature of the concept of happiness that the concept is "indeterminate."

5.5 The indeterminacy of the concept of happiness (418–419)

Kant defines happiness in this paragraph as "a maximum of well-being in [one's] present condition and in every future condition" (418). But even though the concept of happiness admits of definition, it is nonetheless "indeterminate":

[T]he concept of happiness is such an indeterminate concept that, although every human being wishes to attain this, he can still never say determinately and consistently with himself what he really wishes and wills. (418)

Kant considers an example of a man who wills riches because he has convinced himself that wealth is the key to happiness. This man is blind to the fact that wealth can sometimes be the cause of "anxiety, envy and intrigue" and other ills. For another man, happiness consists in knowledge and insight. But this man fails to appreciate that knowledge can reveal to us the less as well as more pleasant sides of life.

Kant's general point here seems to be that our knowledge of the ingredients of happiness is invariably imperfect and incomplete. When each of us tries to specify what we mean by happiness, we consult our own experience. We know what has pleased us in the past, and rely on that knowledge to predict what will please us in the future.

But our desires as well as our circumstances change; our predictions are thus bound to be unreliable. Moreover, our insight into even our present desires is highly fallible. We err, then, if we suppose that experience can ever provide us certain knowledge of ourselves.

Kant thus concludes this discussion in the *Groundwork* with the remark that no one can frame with "complete certainty" a principle by which to determine what would make him happy. If my principle is to accumulate wealth, I can have no guarantee that this end will indeed produce the happiness I seek. I cannot really know that wealth is a means to my happiness. For this reason, Kant tells us that imperatives commanding the means of happiness (imperatives of prudence) cannot "present actions as practically *necessary*."[15]

5.6 The analytic character of hypothetical imperatives (415–421)

In our discussion above of imperatives of skill (problematic hypothetical imperatives), we passed over Kant's mysterious remark that, in the case of these imperatives, there is a conceptual or "analytic" connection between the object willed and what was willed as the means of achieving it (417). It will be useful to recall our earlier example to illustrate what he has in mind. If the object of my volition is to live the life of a vegetarian, then assuming I am rational, I necessarily also will the means to attaining that end: I will to no longer eat meat. It is "one and the same thing," Kant says, to represent something as an effect or aim that I wish to bring about (in this case, the aim of becoming a vegetarian), and to will to act in ways necessary to actually achieving that end (to will not to eat meat). The idea that

---

[15] In the *CPrR* (36), Kant specifies the indeterminacy of the concept of happiness in the following way: First, there is indeterminacy in an individual's concept of happiness over time. Today I am convinced that my happiness consists in achieving success as a rock star; tomorrow I decide I want more than anything to become a monk. As Kant notes, our judgments about happiness depend on our opinions that are "very changeable." Second, even though we all desire happiness, there is no interpersonal agreement about the ingredients of happiness. There is no reason to think, then, that my conception of happiness is identical to or even resembles yours. Instead, there is "endless" "variety of judgment" about happiness. For this reason, Kant concludes that we get from the principle of happiness "general rules but never universal rules, that is, … rules that must hold always and necessarily." In another passage in the *CPrR*, Kant tells us that even if it were the case that finite rational beings "were thoroughly agreed" regarding the ingredients of happiness, this "unanimity itself would still be only contingent." It would still lack the necessity of objective laws, laws derived a priori (26).

I have to give up eating meat is "already thought" in my desire to become a vegetarian. Did I *not* will to give up eating meat, we would have to conclude either that: (i) My professed desire to become a vegetarian is not sincere; (ii) I do not understand the meaning of the concept "vegetarian"; or (iii) I am irrational.

The analytic status of imperatives of prudence (assertoric hypothetical imperatives) is less straightforward. At the conclusion of his discussion of the indeterminacy of the concept of happiness, and after he has told us that imperatives of prudence can never command actions as practically necessary, Kant writes this:

> This imperative of prudence would … be an analytic proposition if it is supposed that the means to happiness can be assigned with certainty. (419)

In light of the fact that Kant has just argued that the means to happiness cannot be assigned with certainty, we might reasonably expect him to go on to tell us that imperatives of prudence are *not* analytic. Curiously, however, he concludes this paragraph with the remark that *both* imperatives of prudence *and* imperatives with skill are analytic propositions. How are we to make sense of this conclusion?

The implication of the above-quoted passage certainly seems to be that assertoric hypothetic imperatives are not analytic. Given that we can never know the means to happiness with certainty, it would seem to follow that our end – to achieve happiness – can never contain as "already thought" the necessary means of achieving it. As just noted, however, Kant asserts later in this same paragraph that assertoric as well as problematic hypothetical imperatives are analytic:

> [S]ince both merely command the means to what it is presupposed one wills as an end, the imperative that commands volition of the means for him who wills the end is in both cases analytic. (419)

Perhaps Kant has in mind something like this: It follows from the fact that the concept of happiness is indeterminate that we can never have a complete understanding of its meaning or ingredients. Nonetheless, each of us actually wills happiness as an end. In doing so, each of us presupposes some particular conception of it. To borrow again from one of Kant's examples, perhaps we believe that happiness consists in wealth. If we happen to be committed to this conception of happiness and set out to realize it, then "already thought" in this conception is the means for realizing it (that is, already thought is the idea that we need to acquire capital). As in the case of imperatives of skill, there is a conceptual or analytic connection, not between the general and indeterminate end of happiness and the means of achieving it, but between the *particular* account of happiness a person seeks to achieve and the means of achieving it.

5.7 Review: On why hypothetical imperatives are conditional and categorical imperatives are unconditional

Recall, first, Kant's characterization of imperatives in general: All imperatives, he says, "are formulae for the determination of action that is necessary in accordance with the principle of a will which is good in some way" (414). I consider some object good, and will an action that is necessary in order to bring that object about. I tell myself: "In order to achieve object X, I must will action Y." I am interested in willing Y because I consider X to be good. My willing of Y, then, is dependent on the aim or objective I express in my antecedent.

If we narrow our focus to hypothetical imperatives, we notice not just that the willed means is dependent on the willed object or end, but that the willed object or end posited in the antecedent of the command is *also* conditional or contingent, on Kant's account. As we just saw, hypothetical imperatives specify ends that derive from our empirical natures, ends that therefore cannot have the status of universal and necessary validity. Hypothetical imperatives thus command actions in the service of some contingent or "discretionary" purpose (420). In this sense, their validity rests on a "presupposition," as Kant says (419). Because hypothetical imperatives have merely conditional validity, they prescribe "principles" of the will but not, strictly speaking, "laws." Since their ends vary from person to person, they moreover cannot be stated in advance. In Kant's words, "When I think of a *hypothetical* imperative in general I do not know beforehand what it will contain; I do not know this until I am given the condition" (420). Not everyone seeks to become a vegetarian, and not everyone is convinced that wealth is the key to happiness. The mere idea of a hypothetical imperative therefore itself specifies no particular end.

There can be an infinite variety of such ends, given the infinitely diverse desires of persons.

Like all imperatives, the categorical imperative expresses a command "for the determination of action that is necessary in accordance with the principle of a will which is good in some way." It, too, may be expressed in the form: "In order to achieve X, I ought to will Y." But in the case of the categorical imperative – and of the specific practical rules or categorical imperatives grounded upon it – the object or end that appears in the antecedent is *un*conditional. It is unconditional because it specifies an end that is necessarily willed by *all rational natures*. In that a categorical imperative specifies an end that is universally and necessarily valid, a categorical imperative is properly a "practical law"; it brings with it the "necessity which we require of law" (420). Because the end specified by a categorical imperative does not derive from our empirical nature, that end is moreover determinate rather than indeterminate. When we think of a categorical imperative, Kant says, we "know at once what it contains" (420).[16]

5.8 How are categorical imperatives possible? (419–421)

Kant has asserted that the end or object of a categorical imperative is unconditionally valid, but how do we know that there *is* such an end? How do we know, in other words, that we ever in fact act on, or even merely recognize as valid, an end that determines our will more than conditionally or hypothetically? Kant identifies the categorical imperative as the supreme law of morality. He tells us that it is the imperative that motivates a good will. But what reasons are there for supposing that there *is* such a law? What evidence is there that the duty commanded by the categorical imperative is anything more than an "empty concept," having no validity for us at all (421)?

Kant raises these questions, but he does not undertake to answer them here. At this point in the text, he says, these questions must remain "undecided." He reminds us that we cannot rely on experience to establish the reality of the categorical imperative. We cannot, merely by inspecting our own motives or by observing the behaviors

[16] As Kant writes in the *CPrR*, what duty requires is "plain of itself to everyone"; what happiness requires is not (36).

of others, know with certainty that the categorical imperative ever really determines anyone to act in a given instance, or is ever accepted by an agent as binding (407f.). Given that experience can be of no help to us here, how is it then possible to establish the reality of the law? When Kant attempts to answer this question in Section III, he tells us that he must rely on something other than empirical evidence. His investigation, he says, must be "entirely a priori" (420).

5.9 The categorical imperative as an "a priori synthetic proposition" (420)

Instead of setting out at this point to prove the reality of the categorical imperative, Kant aims in these paragraphs to explain what a categorical imperative is and how it is different from hypothetical imperatives. He notes, first, that the categorical imperative is an a priori law. It derives from reason, not from experience. He also says that the categorical imperative is an "a priori *synthetic* practical proposition" (emphasis added). This is a claim he returns to later in Section II and discusses at length in Section III. The fact that the law is "synthetic" suggests that the relation between the end or object it posits and the means for attaining that end is somehow not analytic as in the case of hypothetical imperatives. As it turns out, Kant's account of the synthetic nature of the categorical imperative is connected to his view that the demonstration of the reality of the law has to be "synthetic" rather than "analytic." These two doctrines – regarding the synthetic nature of the categorical imperative and the synthetic method for demonstrating its reality – are among the most obscure of the *Groundwork*. I discuss them in detail in the final section of this chapter (beginning at Section 19.2) and then early on in Chapter 5. Here I simply draw attention to one puzzling feature of Kant's insistence upon the synthetic nature of the categorical imperative.

   Remember that hypothetical imperatives, for Kant, have merely conditional or relative validity. They are commands, but their validity is contingent upon the particular and various ends of individuals. For this reason, we do not know "beforehand" what these imperatives contain. A given hypothetical command (such as "one ought not to eat meat") will be valid only relative to some specified or "presupposed" end (to become a vegetarian). We know what specific obligation follows from a hypothetical imperative once its end is set or presupposed. As Kant says, the obligation is "already thought" (and so, analytically contained) in the end. But we cannot specify the ends of hypothetical imperatives in advance. Only once the end is set am I in a position to know what obligation is conceptually implied: "Given that I will to achieve X, I ought to do Y."

But the situation is different, Kant insists, with categorical imperatives. On his account, there is no such analytic connection, in the case of these imperatives, between the object willed and what is willed as the means of attaining it. This claim seems curious for the following reason. A distinguishing feature of a categorical imperative, as we have seen, is that its end or purpose is known in advance. When I think of a categorical imperative, Kant says, "I know at once what it contains." The end is known in advance because it is an end that is universally and necessarily shared by all rational wills. But given that the end is known in advance, why is it not also the case that we know in advance the means for attaining it? Why can we not say, in this case as in that of hypothetical imperatives, that the willing of the means is "already thought" in the willing of the end? Why, in other words, does Kant assert that there is no conceptual or analytic conception between: "I will to realize object X" (where "X" is an unconditional end) and "I therefore ought to do whatever is necessary for realizing X?"

Kant returns to the perplexing topic of the synthetic nature of the categorical imperative at (440). We will consider this topic in greater detail in sections 19.2–19.4 below.

6. FIRST FORMULA OF THE CATEGORICAL IMPERATIVE: FORMULA OF UNIVERSAL LAW ("FUL") (421)

We might find ourselves growing impatient at this point. Kant has dwelled on the distinction between hypothetical and categorical imperatives, and he has drawn our attention to the difficulty of demonstrating the reality of the latter. However, he has yet to specify the categorical imperative in an informative or contentful way. We are still in the dark, that is, about what the supreme principle of morality exactly commands.

While it is true that Kant introduced us to the categorical imperative back in Section I, he provided very little information about it there. In the course of his analysis of the concept of a good will, he informed us that a good will acts from duty. He indicated that the principle expressing duty is formal or a priori. He formulated the principle as follows:

I ought never to act except in such a way that I could also will that my maxim should become a universal law. (402)

Kant did not explicitly label this principle the "categorical imperative" in Section I, but it is virtually indistinguishable from the law he identifies at (421) as the categorical imperative:

[A]ct only in accordance with that maxim through which you can at the same time will that it become a universal law. (421)

Formulated in either of these ways, the law is highly abstract. It restricts the maxims we are morally permitted to act on by means of the idea that we must be able to will our maxims as universal law. But how are we to understand this restriction? And how can such a vague and general constraint guide us in determining what we ought to do in particular cases?

We can demystify the categorical imperative somewhat with the help of material we have covered up to this point. The principle is a priori; its origin is thus pure reason rather than experience. Kant insists that the principle deserves to be called a "law." This implies, on his account, that it has "strict" versus merely "comparative" universality and necessity. The categorical imperative, then, is necessarily valid not merely for some but for all rational natures. Furthermore, the universal and necessary validity of the principle implies, for Kant, that it commands an end or purpose that is shared by all rational natures. Kant has not yet revealed to us the precise nature of this special end. He does not do so until many paragraphs later in Section II (beginning at (429)). So far, he has indicated no more than that the supreme principle of morality commands us to act only on maxims that respect that end.

6.1 The "single" categorical imperative versus many categorical imperatives (421)

Kant insists at (421) that there is a "single" categorical imperative. This is not his first mention of this point. A few paragraphs back, he noted that there is "one imperative" that commands categorically, namely, "the imperative of *morality*" (416). At (421), he furthermore asserts that from this "single" categorical imperative "all imperatives of duty" may be derived. He suggests, then, that in addition to the one categorical imperative – the supreme principle of morality – there are specific categorical imperatives. These specific imperatives are categorical in that they, too, necessitate the will categorically or unconditionally. These imperatives (such as the duty to tell the truth, or to care for the welfare of others) are particular applications of the one supreme categorical imperative. The supreme moral law commands us to act only on maxims that are universally and necessarily valid, maxims that respect an end shared by all rational wills. A specific duty or categorical imperative commands a particular way of carrying this obligation out. The categorical imperative to tell the truth, for example, specifies one way in which we can respect that end shared by all rational wills.

6.2 *The matter and the form of the categorical imperative (416)*

Back at (416) Kant asserted that the categorical imperative "has to do not with the matter of the action and what is to result from it, but with the form and the principle from which the action itself follows." We are now in a position to understand this remark. The form commanded by the categorical imperative, we now know, is that of "universalizability." The categorical imperative commands that our maxims have this form; our maxims must be capable of being willed as universal law. We can equivalently express this point as follows: The form commanded by the categorical imperative is that of lawfulness; our maxims must have the form of law. They must, in other words, be universally and necessarily valid.

Kant's further claim that the categorical imperative has nothing to do with the "matter" of the action is less straightforward. By "matter" of the action, he seems to mean the action's purpose or end. His remarks at (416) are suggestive of this, as is a passage in his Introduction to the *Metaphysics of Morals* (222). He writes in that latter text that a categorical imperative has nothing to do with the matter of actions in that it does not represent an action as necessary "through the representation of some end that can be attained by the action."

Kant's assertion that a categorical imperative has nothing to do with purpose or end of an action is easily misinterpreted. He appears to imply that a categorical imperative, including the supreme categorical imperative, *has* no object. He seems to hold the view, then, that the command expressed by a categorical imperative is not in the service of achieving some end. We considered this interpretation of his view in our discussion back at Section 5.3. As the result of our examination there it became clear that Kant's meaning is not that categorical imperatives command no ends or purposes whatsoever. Rather, a categorical imperative has nothing to do with the matter of our actions in that it does not command the fulfillment of a *certain class* of ends or purposes, namely, ends or purposes that derive from our empirical nature and are thus contingent. This point is evident in the following remark from Section I:

> [A]n action from duty is to put aside entirely the influence of inclination and with it every object of the will; hence there is left for the will nothing that could determine it except objectively the *law* and subjectively *pure respect* for this practical law. (400f.)

Kant identifies "every object of the will" in this passage with objects of inclination. The agent who puts aside "every object of the will" and acts from nothing other than "*pure respect*" for the practical law, then, is the agent who does not act from inclination.[17] Kant does not claim here that the agent who puts aside every object of the will acts from *no* ends or purposes. On the contrary, he tells us that she acts from "*pure respect*" for the practical law. This is her end. Her end or objective is to bring her maxims into conformity with the practical law. She does this by ensuring that her maxims have the form of law, that is, by ensuring that they are universalizable.[18]

---

[17] In the final paragraphs of Section II, starting at (442), Kant no longer narrowly identifies "objects of the will" with objects of inclination. If a will is determined by some matter or object (versus by respect for the moral law), it is determined either by inclination, he says, or by (certain) objects of reason. In both cases, the will is determined by a "foreign impulse," that is, by "nature" (444). Here Kant implies that, in some cases, reason's determination of the will can be heteronomous. I return to this point in my discussion of these passages in Section 18.

[18] Kant will have a great deal more to say in Section II about the end or objective we will when we act from the moral law. Eventually, he will argue that to act from duty is to respect rational nature as an end in itself. (See my discussion beginning at Section 9 below.)

6.3 The formula of universal law as the formula
of nature ("FN") (421)

Further on at (421) Kant provides another expression of the categorical imperative. Again following convention, I refer to this as the formula of nature ("FN"):

[A]ct as if the maxim of your action were to become by your will a *universal law of nature.*

This is not a new categorical imperative; it does not express an independent moral principle. Rather, FN is a further expression of what Kant says is the "single" categorical imperative. We will soon discover that he provides *various* formulae of the categorical imperative in the *Groundwork.* Later in Section II, he tells us explicitly that these are not expressions of different imperatives, but "formulae of the very same law" (436).

Why does Kant go to the trouble of providing FN in addition to FUL? He does so, apparently, because he believes that FN can help us better understand what FUL implies. FUL commands that we act only on maxims we can will as universal law. FN refers to laws of nature, and laws of nature are instances of universal laws. Laws of nature are universal with regard to the scope of their application. All laws have this feature of universal validity, on Kant's account. In fact, Kant's use of the phrase "universal law" is redundant. As we saw earlier, he holds that a command is strictly speaking a law (versus, say, a mere "rule" or "counsel") only if it is universally valid.[19] The natural law, "for every action there is an equal and opposite reaction," thus governs not just *some* objects in the realm of nature but *every* object in the realm of nature. No object within the realm of nature escapes its determination. A further feature of laws of nature is that they compel or necessitate. Every object they command (every object in nature) is *necessarily* versus merely contingently subject to them.

Kant introduces FN in addition to FUL, then, in order to clarify the command of FUL. FUL commands that we act only on maxims we can universalize. Kant wants us to understand that to universalize a maxim is, in effect, to raise it to the status of a law of nature. When

---

[19] See in addition Kant's remarks at (416).

I ask myself whether I could will a maxim as a universal law, I am thus asking whether I could will a world in which my maxim governed as a law of nature. This would be a world in which everyone necessarily acted on that maxim.

In what follows, I refer to the above interpretation of the FN test as the "strong" interpretation. As we will soon see, Kant's language sometimes supports a weaker reading of FN as well.

7. FOUR DUTIES: VERSION I (422–423)

Kant finally turns his attention to examples of specific duties. He does so for two reasons. First, he believes the examples demonstrate how the categorical imperative serves as a practical rule determining our moral obligations in particular situations. We learn, in other words, that with the help of the categorical imperative it is possible to derive specific duties (specific categorical imperatives). Second, Kant believes that the examples clarify the meaning or content of the supreme moral law (421). By considering how to apply the categorical imperative to individual cases, we gain a better understanding of what the law actually commands.

Before getting started, Kant announces that he will present the four duties in keeping with "the usual division" (421).[20] The "usual division," then, refers to the following classification of duties: First, duties divide into duties we have to ourselves and duties we have to others. Second, duties are either "perfect" or "imperfect." We will consider the meaning of this latter and less obvious division at Section 8.1, following our discussion of the four examples.

We may welcome the fact that Kant finally turns his attention to the application of the categorical imperative to concrete cases. A warning is nonetheless in order. At first glance, the examples appear relatively straightforward, but this is surely an instance in which appearances deceive. To this day, their proper interpretation is the subject of much controversy. Although it will not be possible to avoid

---

[20] For discussions of Kant's ties to as well as departure from the natural law tradition on the division of duties, see Manfred Baum, "Recht und Ethik in Kants praktischer Philosophie," in *Kant in der Gegenwart*, ed. Juergen Stolzenberg, and Mary Gregor's Introduction to the 1991 edition of the *MM*, pp. 7–10.

mention of interpretative difficulties altogether, it is not my task here to undertake a comprehensive survey of the critical commentary. My discussion of the cases will be relatively brief, and I will try to avoid unnecessary complications. This is not, in any case, the only opportunity we will have for considering the examples. Kant revisits them a second time in Section II (beginning at (429)), and we will return to them later in our discussion as well (at Section 11).

7.1 Perfect duty to oneself: The duty to preserve one's own life (422)

A man is "sick of life" because of a "series of troubles"; he is in a state of "despair." His despair is not so debilitating, however, that he is unable to ask himself whether it would be "contrary to his duty" to take his own life. He first formulates his "maxim," that is, his "subjective principle of volition" (401n). He then considers whether his maxim "could … become a universal law of nature." He performs this thought experiment in order to determine whether his maxim has moral worth. In this example, the man employs the FN version of the categorical imperative.

Kant formulates the man's maxim as follows:

[F]rom self-love I make it my principle to shorten my life when its longer duration threatens more troubles than it promises agreeableness.

What motivates the man in this case is "self-love" or what Kant sometimes also refers to as "personal advantage."[21] Recall that in the first paragraphs of Section II, Kant explicitly *opposes* the motive of self-love to that of duty (407). In the case we are now considering, the question is whether the man's maxim of self-love could become a "universal law of nature." Kant's answer is that it could not, because universalizing the maxim would produce a contradiction.

What contradiction does Kant have in mind? He gives us the following clue:

[A] nature whose law it would be to destroy life itself by means of the same feeling whose destination is to impel towards the furtherance of life would contradict itself and would therefore not subsist as nature.

---

[21] *Groundwork* (422).

Kant's point here is that a law of nature that commanded the destruction of life would be self-contradictory. If we universalized the man's maxim (that is, raised it to the status of a law of nature), we would produce a contradiction. But *why* would a law of nature that commanded the destruction of life be self-contradictory? It is not possible to answer this question without recalling Kant's account of the role laws of nature play in governing living things.

Back in Section I, Kant suggested that nature has endowed beings "constituted purposively for life" with the means for doing so, with the means for preserving life and for satisfying needs (395). This is why nature has given us instincts, including the instinct of self-love. Since nature has given us self-love in order to preserve life, we would contradict nature's purpose were we to engage this feeling in the destruction of life. The man's maxim, if universalized, would produce such a contradiction. Were he to universalize the maxim to destroy himself from self-love, he would in effect elevate that maxim to the status of a "universal law of nature." This law of nature would be self-contradictory, since with respect to beings "constituted purposively for life," laws of nature are "destined" to preserve life. Such a self-contradictory law "would therefore not subsist as nature," as Kant says. Because the man's universalized maxim would produce a contradiction, it fails the categorical imperative test. Because it fails the test, the man is obligated *not* to take his own life. Expressed positively, he is obligated to preserve his life. This is a duty he has to himself.

Notice how the categorical imperative test works. If a maxim fails the test, we have a duty *not* to act on it. In the present case, the man's maxim fails the test; he is therefore obligated not to take his own life. As we will see, if a maxim *passes* the categorical imperative test, acting on the maxim is morally permissible (but not necessarily a duty). Suppose my maxim is: "Since my shoelace needs tying, I will tie it." Assuming that this maxim would pass the test, morality permits me to act on it. It is not, however, morally *required* that I act on it.[22]

---

[22] Kant is explicit about how the categorical imperative test works in his discussion of the formula of autonomy at (439): "An action that can co-exist with the autonomy of the will is *permitted*; one that does not accord with it is *forbidden*." See also his Introduction to the *MM* (223).

Following his presentation of the four examples, Kant observes that some maxims cannot "even be *thought* without contradiction" as universal laws of nature, while others cannot be *willed* without contradiction as universal laws of nature (424). On his account, the maxims in the first and second examples commit the former kind of contradiction. The man's maxim to destroy his own life, then, cannot even be *thought* as a law of nature without contradiction. Kant's reasoning is as follows: To apply the FN test is to ask whether a maxim could serve as a law of nature. The purpose of laws of nature, as we have seen, is to preserve life. Because the aim expressed in the man's maxim is to destroy life, the maxim cannot even be thought as a law of nature. It contradicts the very idea of a law of nature.

7.2 Perfect duty to others: The duty to not tell a false promise (422)

In this second case, a man needs to borrow money. He knows he will succeed in borrowing only if he promises to repay the money within a set time. He also knows, however, that he in fact will never repay it. The man's maxim is this:

[W]hen I believe myself to be in need of money I shall borrow money and promise to repay it, even though I know that this will never happen.

As in the first example, Kant identifies this maxim as a principle of "self-love" or "personal advantage." He once again subjects the maxim to the FN version of the categorical imperative test. Could the maxim become a universal law of nature? It is "at once" clear, Kant writes, that the maxim "could never hold as a universal law of nature and be consistent with itself." The universalized maxim, that is, would be self-contradictory.

To see why, consider Kant's reasoning in the following passage:

[T]he universality of a law that everyone, when he believes himself to be in need, could promise whatever he pleases with the intention of not keeping it would make the promise and the end one might have in it itself impossible, since no one would believe what was promised him but would laugh at all such expressions as vain pretences.

It should not escape our notice that the above passage suggests a subtle change in the FN test. Kant does not ask:

(i) What if everyone told a false promise when they believed that personal advantage required it?

Instead, he asks:

(ii) What if everyone "could" tell a promise when they believed that personal advantage required it?

The first interpretation is what I earlier labeled the "strong" interpretation of the FN test. It captures an important feature of laws of nature. Laws of nature compel their objects to obey; no object subject to their legislation has the option of non-compliance. In his discussion of the first example, Kant seemed to rely on this strong interpretation of the FN test. The contradiction he was concerned about there involved "a nature whose law would be to destroy life." In that context, he seemed to have in mind the self-contradictory character of a law that compelled the destruction of life.

If we apply the strong interpretation of the FN test to the maxim in Kant's second example, we in effect ask this question: What if everyone were compelled to tell a false promise? On this interpretation of the test, the following contradiction results: If the maxim to tell a false promise from self-love were made a universal law, then everyone would tell false promises in the service of self-love. A world in which this maxim were elevated to universal law, however, would be a world in which individual false promises would not be believed. The promise of the man in Kant's example would fail to achieve its intended effect. The man's maxim, if universalized, would thus be self-contradictory.

As just mentioned, however, Kant's language in the above-quoted passage from (422) supports a *weaker* interpretation of the FN test. He writes that in determining whether the maxim is universalizable, we are to ask whether everyone who believed himself in need "could" tell a false promise. According to this weaker interpretation, we are to ask whether acting on the maxim is something that could be universally *allowed* from a moral point of view. When Kant discusses a similar example in the *Critique of Practical Reason*, he employs this weaker language as well: What if everyone "*permitted* himself to deceive" when he believed it to be to his advantage (69; emphasis added)?[23]

---

[23] In a further passage, Kant considers a case of lying about a deposit someone has given me for which there is no proof. There he tells us that the test is whether "everyone may [*dürfe*] deny a deposit which no one can prove has been made," *CPrR* (27).

The point worth emphasizing is that a contradiction is generated, on Kant's account, even on this weaker reading of the FN test. For it is reasonable to suppose that even in a world in which telling false promises from self-love were merely universally permitted (versus required), individual false promises would not be believed. False promises would be laughed at as "vain pretences."

At this point in our discussion, it would be natural to wonder how many instances of false promising have to occur before the practice of promising is rendered ineffective. Kant does not attempt to answer this question here; in fact, he does not even raise it. He seems to assume, however, that even in a world in which false promising were merely universally permissible, there would be enough instances of false promising to threaten the practice of promising. Perhaps he has in mind something like this: Any particular instance of false promising weakens the practice of promising and thus undermines the possible effectiveness of a single promise (false or otherwise). It is for this reason that universalizing the maxim to tell a false promise is self-contradictory.

As in the first example, Kant classifies the kind of contradiction that results when the man tries to universalize his maxim to tell a false promise as a contradiction in conception. He means by this that the maxim cannot even be thought or conceived as a law of nature. Universalized, the maxim becomes the law that everyone is either permitted or required to make false promises in the service of self-love or personal advantage. The contradiction in conception becomes apparent as soon as we note that the law at once affirms and undermines the practice of making promises. The universalized maxim affirms the practice of making promises in that it affirms the practice of a particular kind of promise (a false promise). At the same time, the law destroys the possibility of making promises in that it asserts either the universal permissibility or necessity of making false promises. The law is self-contradictory because it asserts, in effect, that the practice of making promises both is and is not valuable, or both ought and ought not to exist.

Although Kant insists that this second example is like the first in that the kind of contradiction committed is a contradiction in conception, the cases are not perfectly analogous. In the first example, universalization of the man's maxim (to destroy his life) contradicts the very idea of a law of nature in this sense: it contradicts the purpose of laws of nature with respect to beings constituted for life. As we have seen, the purpose of laws of nature, on Kant's account, is to preserve life. In the promising case, universalization of the maxim results in a contradiction in conception as well, but this time the universalized maxim poses no threat to nature's subsistence. This time, universalizing the maxim threatens the existence of a social practice, the practice of promising.

7.3 *Imperfect duty to oneself: The duty to develop one's talents (423)*

This man has a talent the cultivation of which "could make him a human being useful for all sorts of purposes." But he enjoys comfortable circumstances and prefers to indulge his desire for pleasure rather than bother with "enlarging and improving" his "fortunate natural predispositions." The man chooses, in other words, to neglect his talents. His maxim is something like this: Because I wish to enjoy life, I will not put myself to the trouble of developing my talents.

Kant asks us to consider whether this maxim is "consistent with what one calls duty." His answer, once again, is that it is not. Although a "nature could indeed always subsist with such a universal law," he says, it is not possible to "will" the maxim as universal law.

As in the previous two cases, we apply the categorical imperative test by asking whether the maxim could be universalized (could serve as a universal law of nature). In the previous cases, however, the question was whether the maxims could be *conceived* as universal law. Now the question is whether the maxim could be *willed* as universal law. In his discussion of this third case, Kant claims that although the man's maxim to neglect his talents could be conceived as law without contradiction, it nonetheless fails the categorical imperative test because it could not be *willed* as law without contradiction.

To see how a contradiction arises, we first need to imagine ourselves living in a world in which people did not consider themselves obligated to develop their talents. This would be a world in which people devoted themselves to nothing but "idleness, amusement, procreation," as Kant says. Those with intellectual or artistic gifts would allow their gifts to waste; they would invest no effort in nurturing their special abilities. To demonstrate the sense in which the contradiction resulting from the universalized maxim is not a contradiction in conception, Kant contrasts this case with the first case. Universalizing the maxim to neglect one's talents would not be inconsistent with the very idea of a law of nature because nature, under such circumstances, "could indeed always subsist." Were we to elevate the man's maxim to the status of law, life would surely go on. At most, its quality would be diminished.

So no contradiction in conception results from the universalized maxim in this third case because universalization is not inconsistent with the purpose contained in the very idea of laws of nature. Nor is there, in this case, a contradiction analogous to the one that occurs in Kant's second example. A contradiction in conception occurs in the second example because in trying to universalize the maxim to tell a false promise, the man at once affirms and undermines the practice of promising. In willing the maxim to neglect his talents, however, the man in Kant's third example lands himself in no such conceptual inconsistency. He wills the maxim in order to indulge his desire for pleasure. The universalization of his maxim is not conceptually at odds with the possibility of his fulfilling that aim.

Although the man's maxim in this case produces no conceptual contradiction if universalized, Kant claims that it nonetheless cannot be *willed* as universal law without contradiction. Kant's sole explanation for this conclusion is contained in the following sentence:

> [A]s a rational being (the man) necessarily wills that all the capacities in him be developed, since they serve him and are given to him for all sorts of possible purposes.

Here Kant implies that what is contradicted if the maxim is universalized is the willing of a rational being. What does he mean by this?

We might be tempted to read Kant as suggesting here that in willing the maxim to neglect his talents as universal law, the man potentially interferes with his own chances for happiness or wellbeing. His natural capacities, after all, are given to him for "all sorts of possible purposes" – including, presumably, the achievement of happiness. If we interpret Kant in this way, however, we overlook the significance of the first few words of the quoted passage. The object of Kant's remark is the will of man "as a *rational* being" (my emphasis). Kant is not interested in what it is we want or desire as creatures motivated by empirical ends (by inclination). In this instance, in other words, he appeals specifically to our *rational* nature and what it implies about what we are and are not able to will. His suggestion is that it would be incompatible with the willing of a rational nature for the man to make a law that commands the neglect of his capacities. Willing the maxim as law in effect undermines ends he shares with all rational natures.

Kant has not yet made explicit what our specifically rational ends are; it is therefore impossible to comprehend his line of reasoning here. He will begin clarifying the nature of our rational ends at (428).

7.4 *Imperfect duty to others: The duty of benevolence (423)*

A fourth man, for whom life is good, notices that the same is not true for many others; he is aware that some must contend with great hardship. The man recognizes, as well, that he is in the fortunate position of being able to help out. Nonetheless, his attitude is one of indifference. He simply has no interest in providing assistance to those in need. His maxim is thus once again a maxim of indifference – not to the cultivation of his own talents (as in the third case), but this time to the welfare of others.

Kant asks whether this "way of thinking" could become a universal law of nature. As in the third example, he tells us that nature could "subsist" were this maxim to be made a universal law. Nonetheless, he says it is "impossible to *will* that such a principle hold everywhere as a law of nature." He makes his reasoning explicit in the following remark:

> For, a will that decided this would conflict with itself, since many cases could occur in which one would need the love and sympathy of others and in which, by such a law of nature arisen from his own will, he would rob himself of all hope of the assistance he wishes for himself.

It is difficult to ignore the fact that the considerations Kant draws to our attention here seem entirely prudential. Kant, in other words, encourages the following interpretation of his argument: Given that it might someday be the case that the man will need the help of others, universalization of his maxim would possibly undermine his own interests. Were his maxim of indifference either universally required or universally permissible, he might not get that help. Although the "human race could ... very well subsist" were such a maxim raised to universal law, the universalized maxim would contradict the man's willing. In universalizing the maxim, the man would in effect be willing his own potential unhappiness.

Contrary to appearances, Kant's reasoning here cannot be prudential. We will thus have to provide an alternative interpretation of this case below (see Section 8.4).

8. REMARKS ON THE FOUR EXAMPLES (421–425)

8.1 Perfect versus imperfect duties (421, 424)

At (424), Kant asserts that the two kinds of contradiction (in conception and in the will) correspond to the two types of duties: duties that are "strict or narrow (unremitting)" and duties that are "wide (meritorious)." Strict or narrow duties are those he refers to in the footnote at (421) as "perfect" duties. These, he tells us in the note, admit "no exception in the interest of inclination." Wide or meritorious duties are "imperfect" duties. Because Kant says so little in the *Groundwork* to clarify these terms, we need to seek illumination in his other works.

Kant's remark in the note that perfect duties admit "no exception in favor of inclination" is curious. It is curious, because he thereby seems to imply that this feature is supposed to distinguish perfect from imperfect duties. But imperfect duties no more admit of exception in favor of inclination than perfect duties do. It is not Kant's view, in other words, that we have no obligation of benevolence, for example, if we lack the inclination to be benevolent. In light of the fact that *no* duties permit of exception in the service of inclination, on Kant's account, it is odd that he makes this point with regard to perfect duties in particular.

It will aid our effort to solve this puzzle if we consider what Kant has to say about the nature of imperfect duties. How are they "wide" or "meritorious" in a way that perfect duties are not? In defining imperfect duties in the *Metaphysics of Morals*, Kant writes that since these are duties of "wide" obligation, they leave "playroom (*latitudo*) for free choice in following (complying with) the law." In the case of these duties, he says, "the law cannot specify precisely in what way one is to act and how much one is to do by the action for an end that is also a duty" (*MM II* (390)). If we apply this point to the imperfect duty of benevolence, Kant's position appears to be that although the categorical imperative determines that we have a duty not to be indifferent to the welfare of others, the law does not tell us exactly how we are to perform this duty. Are we to give money to charity? If so, which charity, and how much money? Must we volunteer time to help the needy? If so, how much time is enough? Kant notes that the answers to these questions will depend on the particular circumstances of individuals and therefore cannot be specified in advance. All that can be specified in advance, in his view, is that we are not obligated to give so much that we sacrifice our own "happiness" and "true needs" (*MM II* (393)).[24]

As just noted, Kant describes imperfect duties not just as "wide" but also as "meritorious." Once again, the *Metaphysics of Morals* helps us understand his meaning.[25] If we adopt the maxims to cultivate our talents and to attend to the needs of others, we deserve moral praise, Kant says. Our adoption of these maxims is hence "meritorious" (*MM II* (390)). If we fail to will these maxims, we are "deficient of moral worth." But although we act contrary to duty, we cannot be subject to legal sanction. There are two reasons for this, both of which I discussed in my Introduction (at Section 2.3). First, imperfect duties (or "duties of virtue," as Kant sometimes calls them) imply no correlative right. This means that if we fail to perform them, it is not within a state's right to impose a penalty. Second, there is a sense in which even were it within a state's right to coerce imperfect duties, it could not effectively do so. This is because imperfect duties legislate over our dispositions, and dispositions are not the kind of thing that can be externally coerced. So while a state can and ought to coerce the performance or omission of *actions* insofar as those actions potentially affect the expression of the freedom of others, it cannot coerce us into adopting *maxims*. It is therefore for us to decide whether and to what extent we will dedicate our time to helping

---

[24] Regarding the imperfect duty to cultivate our talents, Kant's point about "latitude" is the same: The "different situations in which human beings may find themselves make a human being's choice of the occupation for which he should cultivate his talents very much a matter for him to decide as he chooses;" *MM II* (392). For a helpful discussion of the sense in which imperfect duties admit of latitude, see Mancia Baron, *Kantian Ethics Almost Without Apology*, Chapter 3. See also Barbara Herman on how to establish the proper content of a maxim in *The Practice of Moral Judgment*, Chapter 7.

[25] For this discussion I rely on *MM II* (390–394; 381).

others. The only possible form of coercion in this kind of case is "internal."[26]

Returning our attention to Kant's conception of perfect duties, recall that he characterizes these duties as "strict" or "narrow." If imperfect duties are "wide" in that they allow for "playroom" in our choice of how to observe them, then presumably perfect or "narrow" duties permit no such latitude. This characterization is consistent with the treatment of the perfect duties Kant has so far provided in the *Groundwork*. Each of the perfect duties he has discussed is strict or narrow in that each prohibits specific actions. We have a duty not to commit suicide in the service of self-love, and we have a duty not to tell a false promise for the sake of personal advantage.

We just saw that imperfect duties or duties of virtue, for Kant, do not admit of external coercion. This would seem to imply that perfect duties *do* admit of external coercion. On Kant's account, however, this turns out to be true of some perfect duties but not of others. As he remarks in the note at (421), perfect duties are either "internal" or "external." He implies that this division of perfect duties is his own innovation; it is contrary to tradition, he says. He explains these classifications in his Introduction to the *Metaphysics of Morals*. External perfect duties, he tells us there, are duties to others for which there can be not merely internal but also "external lawgiving" (*MM* (224)). Suppose I sign a legally binding contract to buy your property. I can decide either to observe the contract or not. This is my choice, and my decision is in this respect internally coercible. But in the case of this kind of duty, my decision is *in addition* subject to "external lawgiving." If upon reflection, I decide not to observe the contract, a court of law may rightfully punish me. My action (or inaction) is thus also externally coercible. Kant refers to the class of perfect duties that are externally coercible as the class of "juridical" duties. He does not discuss this class of duties in the *Groundwork*, but they are the focus of his discussion in Part I of the *Metaphysics of Morals* (the *Doctrine of Right*).

---

[26] It is not just that the only appropriate form of coercion in this case is internal. Kant holds in addition that only internal coercion would be effective. This is because, as he points out, we cannot be forced to adopt maxims or ends. As he puts it in the Introduction to his *Doctrine of Right*, external lawgiving cannot "bring about someone's setting an end for himself," *MM I* (239). I have benefited from Mary Gregor's discussion of these points in her Introduction to her 1964 translation of the *Doctrine of Virtue*, p. xxi.

What about the "internal" perfect duties Kant mentions in the note at (421) of the *Groundwork*? The fact that these duties are "internal" rather than "external" means that they do not permit of external sanction. They share this feature with imperfect duties. Nonetheless, they fall under the heading of "perfect" duties. Why is this so?

To see why, consider once again the two perfect duties we have been discussing: the prohibitions against suicide and against telling false promises. As already noted, these duties prohibit specific actions. The duties to cultivate one's talents and to care about the welfare of others, on the other hand, prescribe maxims – and, as we have seen, they allow for "playroom" in how we choose to perform them. So even though the internal perfect duties Kant discusses in the *Groundwork* are unlike other perfect duties in that they are not susceptible to external sanction, they are like other perfect duties in that they are "narrow" as opposed to "wide."

Our explanation of the difference between perfect and imperfect duties perhaps provides a clue to Kant's curious claim, in the note at (421), that perfect duties admit "no exception in the service of inclination." Again, the remark is perplexing in light of Kant's repeated insistence that *no* duty admits of exception in the service of inclination. It is *never* the case, on his account, that morality either permits or requires us to act from inclination over duty. Why does Kant then choose to remind us of this point with regard to perfect duties alone? As we have seen, he introduces us in the note to the category of internal perfect duties. This class of perfect duties is similar to that of imperfect duties in that these perfect duties are not externally coercible. But although they are not externally coercible, internal perfect duties are nonetheless perfect duties. They are importantly different from imperfect duties in permitting no latitude in their application; they prescribe narrowly specific actions. Perhaps in writing that perfect duties admit "no exception in the service of inclination," then, Kant means merely to emphasize this respect in which all perfect duties, including internal perfect duties, differ from imperfect duties. They are "strict" or "narrow" in their application.

8.2 On the "impossibility" of willing an immoral maxim as universal law (424)

When we apply the categorical imperative test, according to Kant, we ask whether our maxim could be willed as a universal law. In each of the four examples of Section II, the maxim under consideration fails the test; in each case, what the agent wills cannot be universalized and is therefore contrary to duty. Now, in the second paragraph at (424), Kant observes that whenever we will a maxim that is contrary to duty, we do not actually will that our maxim should become a universal law. Doing so would be "impossible," he says. The man who from self-love wills the maxim to tell a false promise, then, does not really also will that everyone should act on this maxim. What the man wills, Kant now tells us, is that he should be allowed to break his promise while others continue to keep theirs. The man does not in fact will that breaking promises should become a universal law. Instead, he wills that there should be an exception to the rule of promise-keeping in his own case.

8.3   On the sense in which willing an immoral maxim produces no contradiction (424)

It is "impossible" to will an immoral maxim as universal law, Kant has just explained, because when we will an immoral maxim, we will it as an exception to a law we regard as universally valid for others. Further on at (424), he adds the point that there is also a sense in which our willing an immoral maxim does not even produce a contradiction.

Above, we reviewed Kant's reasons for claiming that, in the false promising case, the universalized maxim produces a contradiction in conception. The maxim to tell a false promise cannot even be thought as universal law, he argues, because if universalized, there would be no practice of promising at all. To will the maxim as universal law is effectively to will at once the existence and the non-existence of the practice. Kant's point may perhaps be expressed in this way: In universalizing the maxim to tell a false promise, the man misunderstands what the concept of promising implies.

But in what sense does willing the immoral maxim *not* produce a contradiction, in Kant's view? The message he now conveys is that when the man tries to universalize his maxim, it is not in fact the case that he both affirms and denies the same thing. Rather, one part of him affirms the institution of promising, and another part of him threatens to destroy it. As a rational agent (as a will "wholly conformed with reason"), the man grants the universal validity of the duty to keep one's promises. In willing to make himself an exception to the rule of promise-keeping, he implicitly acknowledges the validity of that rule. But the man is not *just* a rational agent. He also has a sensible nature, and is therefore also "affected by inclination," as Kant says. This other part of him is motivated by self-love or personal advantage. While the rational part of his nature recognizes the validity of the rule of promise-keeping, he nonetheless decides to grant his sensible nature the upper hand. So it is not that, in willing the false promise, the man strictly speaking involves himself in self-contradiction. Rather, in willing the false promise, one part of his nature asserts its opposition to another part of his nature.

8.4 On the fact that the categorical imperative test is not a prudential test

Kant's discussion of the four examples conveys the impression that we determine the morality of a maxim, in his view, with regard to the effects of its universalization for our happiness. In his final remarks on the fourth case, for instance, he tells us that the reason the man should not will his maxim of indifference to the welfare of others is that, if universalized, this could mean that the man might himself some day not receive help. The universalization of the maxim could, in the end, interfere with his own happiness or wellbeing. In expressing the point in this way, Kant seems to imply that his test for morality is ultimately prudential.

We considered this matter back in Section I when we discussed Kant's first treatment of the false promising case at (402). As in his description of this case in Section II, the situation described at (402) is one in which a man considers whether to tell a false promise in order to extricate himself from some difficulty. When the man asks himself whether his maxim is universalizable, he realizes that universalization has the potential to inconvenience him even more. He recognizes that if people ceased to have confidence in each others' promises, his own promise would probably not be believed. His maxim, if raised to universal law, would thus bring upon him "greater inconvenience," as Kant says.

On the face of it, this reasoning indeed seems prudential. It seems that Kant is claiming nothing more than that the man ought not to tell the false promise because doing so would only increase his personal difficulties. But in his discussion of the promising case in Section I, Kant explicitly alerts us to the fact that his reasoning should *not* be interpreted in this way. To be truthful "from duty," he says, is something "entirely different" than being truthful "from anxiety about detrimental results" (402). The categorical imperative test is supposed to determine whether or not a maxim is compatible, not with happiness, but with duty.[27]

Despite his explicit warning in Section I against interpreting the categorical test prudentially, the prudential interpretation seems forced upon us in light of Kant's own portrayal of the four examples in Section II. His language tempts us to read the false promising case, for example, in the following way: The maxim to tell a false promise cannot be universalized because universalization would undermine the man's happiness. The man seeks relief from his financial troubles by engaging in an act of deception. But were deception universally permissible, his particular act of deception would be ineffective or even counterproductive.

While it is true in this second discussion of the promise case, as in the first, that Kant draws our attention to the fact that universalization would inconvenience the man, it is also true in this second discussion that Kant's reasoning, contrary to appearances, is not prudential. His reasoning, in other words, is not: The man ought not to tell a false promise because universalization would interfere with his happiness. We know from our discussion of the case that the universalized maxim would command that anyone should be either required or permitted to tell a false promise in the service of self-love. Universalization of the maxim would entail a contradiction in conception, on Kant's account, because it would result in a universal law that both affirmed the practice of making promises and undermined that practice. No doubt, the destruction of the practice of promises would inconvenience us, and Kant is aware of this. But if we conclude that this prudential analysis of the case captures the essence of Kant's reasoning, we miss the mark by a wide margin.

---

[27] See also the final pages of Section II where Kant reminds us that happiness is not the ground of morality. Making someone happy, he writes, "is quite different from making him good, or making him prudent and sharp-sighted for his own advantage is quite different from making him virtuous" (442).

Consider two possible answers to the following question: Why is it that we care about the fact that universalizing the maxim to tell a false promise has the potential to destroy the practice of promising? One answer to this question is prudential: We care, because the practice of promising serves the interests of our happiness. This answer, I have been urging, is not Kant's. Kant's answer, instead, is this: We care about the practice of promising because the practice serves the interests not just of happiness, an empirical end, but also of a rational end, an end that is universally and necessarily valid for all rational natures. If this answer seems inadequate at this stage of our discussion, it is because Kant still has not filled us in on the nature of this rational end. He finally does so beginning at (427).

8.5 Worries about rigorism

Readers typically respond to Kant's discussion especially of the first two examples in Section II with the charge that his treatment suffers from rigorism. The complaint is that he seems to argue that these two duties hold absolutely or without exception. On this interpretation, the lesson Kant wishes us to take away from the suicide example is that morality prohibits self-destruction no matter what. Likewise, the lesson we are supposed to derive from the false promise example is that morality in every instance forbids breaking a promise or telling a lie.

Although there is undeniably a sense in which Kant's treatment of duties is rigoristic or absolutist, specifying the precise respect in which this is so is no simple matter. It is especially difficult if we restrict our attention to his remarks about the examples in the *Groundwork*. This is because, in that text, Kant has little interest in justifying or even discussing particular duties. As I noted in my Introduction, he does not intend the *Groundwork* as a work in applied ethics. So if our objective is to achieve an informed assessment of the nature of his rigorism, we need to consult his other works in practical philosophy (in particular, his *Metaphysics of Morals* and *Lectures on Ethics*).[28]

Since our concern in this commentary is with the *Groundwork* and not with these other texts, this is not the place for an extensive

---

[28] I rely here on the Collins transcription of Kant's university lectures from 1784–5.

evaluation of the rigorism charge. I want to provide enough of a response to the charge, however, to at least cast it into doubt. My aim is to suggest that Kant's treatment of particular duties is more nuanced – and more defensible – than his sketchy remarks in the *Groundwork* might lead us to conclude.

A careful look at the suicide example in the *Groundwork* reveals that Kant does not in fact argue that all forms of self-destruction are morally impermissible. In the case under consideration, the maxim that cannot be universalized without contradiction is the maxim to take one's life from self-love. Kant does not imply, then, that *no* cases of self-destruction are morally permissible. When he reconsiders this case at (429) he in fact warns us against this interpretation of his view. He suggests that some forms of self-destruction may even be morally obligatory – for example, cases in which it is necessary to amputate a diseased limb in order to save one's own life. He notes explicitly in his *Doctrine of Virtue* that only those instances of willful self-destruction that debase the humanity in one's own person count as "crimes." I commit a crime against my own person, he says, when I dispose of myself "as a mere means to some arbitrary end" (*MM II* (423)). I do not commit a crime against my own person when I amputate a diseased limb for the sake of preserving my life. Very possibly, Kant suggests here, I also commit no crime against myself if I hurl myself to certain death in order to save my country. There may be cases of "deliberate martyrdom," in other words, that are morally permissible or even obligatory.

As for the example of false promising in the *Groundwork*, Kant does not argue that all cases of false promising are impermissible. To suggest otherwise is to overlook the conditions under which the man in the example formulates his maxim. The man is in need of money; his maxim expresses his intention to tell a false promise in order to ease his financial burden. The man's principle or motive, Kant explicitly says, is "self-love or personal advantage." The most we are entitled to conclude from Kant's description of this example, then, is that morality does not permit telling a false promise in the service of self-love or personal advantage. This leaves open the possibility that the duty to keep one's promises – or, more generally, to tell the truth – may admit of exception in other kinds of cases.

If we look to other texts for further clarification of Kant's views on the duty of veracity, we encounter enormous complexity. Sometimes the position Kant defends appears unyielding indeed. In his 1797 essay "On the Supposed Right to Lie from Philanthropy," for instance, he writes that the duty of veracity is a "sacred command of reason prescribing unconditionally, one not to be restricted by any conveniences."[29] We are obligated to tell the truth even when a murderer appears at our door asking for the whereabouts of the innocent friend we are hiding. Since the murderer intends to injure, he forfeits his right to the truth, on Kant's account. This, however, implies no exception to our duty to tell the truth. The duty of veracity is unconditional, Kant writes, because in lying we "violate the principle of right with respect to all unavoidable necessary statements *in general*."[30]

Kant takes a similarly hard line in his *Lectures on Ethics*. If my enemy "takes me by the throat" and demands the whereabouts of my money, I do him no "wrong" if I tell him a lie. I nevertheless "violate the right of humanity; for I have acted contrary to the condition and the means, under which a society of men can come about."[31] This is clearly Kant's default position. "Every lie is objectionable and deserving of contempt," he insists; the duty of veracity thus admits of no exception.[32] In this very same context, however, Kant goes on to weaken his view. He warns of the dangers of being "faithful to every detail of truth." I am justified in telling a "necessary lie," he now tells us, if "force is used against me, to make an admission, and a wrongful use is made of my statement, and I am unable to save myself silence."[33] My untruth in this instance is not a lie, strictly speaking, because my extortioner has no reason to expect truthfulness from me. I am justified in telling the untruth, Kant reasons here, in order to fulfill my duty to preserve my own life. What is odd is that there is no trace of this kind of reasoning in Kant's later treatment of this topic in the "Supposed Right to Lie" essay. Given that he argues in the *Lectures on Ethics* that necessary lies are permissible when one's own life is threatened, we might also expect him to argue that necessary

---

[29] *Practical Philosophy*, "Supposed Right to Lie" (427).
[30] *Ibid.* (429).
[31] *Lectures on Ethics*, Collins transcription (447).   [32] *Ibid.* (448).   [33] *Ibid.* (448).

lies are permissible when this is the only way to save the life of an innocent friend.[34] On the basis of the above discussion, what general conclusions can we reach about the nature of Kant's rigorism? Kant is a rigorist or absolutist in this sense: When a maxim is determined to be contrary to duty, then it is absolutely contrary to duty and morality absolutely or necessarily requires that we not act on it. But we can only determine whether a maxim is or is not contrary to duty by specifying it very carefully. It is one thing to destroy oneself from self-love, and quite another to destroy oneself in order to protect one's country. Likewise, it is one thing to tell a lie in order to avoid financial difficulty, and quite another to tell a lie of necessity if this is the only way to fulfill the duty of self-preservation.

9. INTERLUDE: FROM THE FIRST TO THE SECOND FORMULA OF THE MORAL LAW (424–429)

In these paragraphs, Kant at last reveals the nature of the end that is universally and necessarily valid for all rational natures, the end that motivates a will that is good. He moves on to this important topic, however, only after he has taken stock of his accomplishments in Section II so far.

He notes, first, that in his discussion of the four examples, he has laid out "completely" the four types of duties that derive from the categorical imperative (424). In demonstrating the derivation of these duties, he has shown, moreover, that the categorical imperative is fit to determine duty for "every use" (425). Finally, he has articulated "distinctly" the meaning or "content" of the categorical imperative (425). It is noteworthy that even though Kant asserts each of these accomplishments with confidence, he finds it necessary in the coming pages to go through the examples a second time.

In his remarks here Kant also recalls his distinction between categorical and hypothetical imperatives. If duty is a concept that really

---

[34] It is possible that the harder line Kant takes in the "Supposed Right to Lie" essay may be explained with reference to his principal objective in that work, which is to respond to the argument of Benjamin Constant for the occasional accommodation of principles of justice to political expediency. I defend this line of interpretation in my essay, "On Lying and the Role of Content in Kant's Ethics," *Kant-Studien* 82 (1991), 42–62.

governs our actions, he says, it "can be expressed only in categorical imperatives and by no means in hypothetical ones." Here he simply summarizes the results of his discussion earlier in Section II. As he argued back at (413), duty or "practical good" determines the will by means of "grounds that are valid for every rational being as such" (413). If duty exists at all, its commands must therefore be valid for all rational natures; its commands must, as he says, be objectively valid. Hypothetical imperatives have no such objective or unconditional validity. The imperatives of morality thus have to be categorical.

Kant alerts us once again to the fact that he has not yet tried to demonstrate the *reality* of the supreme moral law. He has not yet endeavored to show, in other words, that there really *is* such a practical law that commands our will "absolutely of itself and without any incentives." This would be equivalent to demonstrating that rational beings recognize the validity of the law and use it to "appraise their actions" (426). It would be to prove that the will can indeed be determined by something other than empirical ends (or what Kant refers to here as "incentives"). The fact that Kant has not yet tried to establish the reality of the moral law explains his frequent use of hypothetical formulations in these pages. Notice his remark, for example, that, "*if* duty is a concept that is to contain significance and real lawgiving for our actions it can be expressed only in categorical imperatives" (425; emphasis added). (His use of hypothetical language is evident also at (426) and (428).)

Although Kant has not yet undertaken to establish the reality of the moral law, he highlights the point again (as he did back at (419–421)) that the required proof cannot rest on an appeal to empirical facts about human nature. If we attempt to ground the law on "the *special property of human nature*," he says, we will lack the means to account for its validity for the will of *every* rational being. For this reason, the proof of the categorical imperative cannot be empirical. These are old points, but for Kant they are of fundamental importance. As he remarks here, one "cannot give too many or too frequent warnings" against the temptation to rest morality on an empirical basis (426).[35]

---

[35] Kant makes these points not merely earlier in this section (at (419–421)), but even in his Preface where he writes that, "it is of the greatest practical importance not to make (the principles of practical reason) dependent upon the special nature of human reason" (412). See also (389).

9.1 Clarifying the concept of the will of a rational being (425–429)

Back at (420) Kant had indicated that since the possibility of the categorical imperative cannot be investigated empirically, it must be investigated "a priori." At (426) he offers us some clues as to how such an examination must proceed. A crucial passage is this:

> If there is such a law (a categorical imperative), then it must already be connected (completely a priori) with the concept of the will of a rational being as such.

The phrase "connected with" is not terribly illuminating; but as Kant's subsequent comments suggest, he means to indicate that the demonstration of the reality of the categorical imperative, in Section III, requires as a necessary component an examination of the concept the will of a rational being. The above-quoted comment signals his intention, at this point in Section II, to subject the concept of a rational will to analysis.[36]

Kant observes that in examining this concept he will take a step into "metaphysics." This is for reasons we considered both earlier in this chapter (at Section 4) and in our discussion of his Preface. As we saw, objects of metaphysics, for Kant, are "transcendent" objects or objects of speculation. Such objects are not given in space and time, and therefore cannot be known empirically. In his Preface, Kant informed us that his investigation would involve taking a step into metaphysics because he would be examining "the idea and the principles of a possible *pure* will." A will that is pure, on his account, is importantly distinct from a will that is empirical. Only the former is "completely determined from a priori principles without any empirical motives" (390). As will become evident in a moment, Kant means by this that only the pure will has the unique "capacity" to act from a priori principles. Only the pure will, in other words, can be motivated non-empirically. In addition, the pure will recognizes the validity of a particular a priori principle, namely, the categorical imperative.[37]

---

[36] As Kant makes clear both at (440) and in the final paragraph of Section II, the procedure of analyzing or explicating the concepts of morality is necessary but not sufficient for the demonstration of the reality of the categorical imperative.

[37] The "pure will" refers, for Kant, to the capacity to act from a priori laws or principles (427). (See also (412).) The pure will in addition recognizes the validity of the a priori law of practical reason or categorical imperative. The pure will is not, however, identical to the good will Kant discusses

But what does Kant have in mind when he writes that a pure will is "completely determined from a priori principles"? If a principle is a priori, its source is reason, not experience. This implies that a will determined by a priori principles is a will determined by principles of reason. Such a will derives its laws from its own rational nature; it is thus a will that governs itself. Kant conveys this idea in the following passage:

The will is thought as a capacity to determine itself to acting in conformity with the *representation of certain laws*. (427)

An empirical will merely responds, in all that it does, to laws imposed by nature. A pure will, in contrast, is capable of acting in conformity with the *representation* of laws. A pure will can be motivated to act, that is, by the very *idea* of law. Kant insists that only rational beings have the capacity to be motivated in this way. Sticks and stones cannot be moved by the idea of law, nor can plants and most animals. This point may be expressed differently by saying that, for Kant, reason can have a genuinely practical employment only in creatures that are rational. Only rational natures (or more precisely, practically rational natures) can determine themselves to act.

Kant moves on to explore the meaning or content of the representation that provides the motivating force behind a pure will. He has already told us that the law that determines or motivates the pure will is given by its rational nature and is thus a law of reason. We also know that all laws, on his account, are universally and necessarily valid. To say that the pure will is capable of being motivated by a law of reason is to say that it can act from an end that is universally and necessarily valid (an "objective" end). Insofar as the will is capable of being motivated in this way, it can thus act from categorical versus merely hypothetical imperatives. It can act from commands that are valid for all rational nature. Otherwise put, the pure will is a will that can act from maxims that could be willed by all rational nature.

The foregoing elucidates the "connection" Kant says he needs to establish between the law (the categorical imperative) and the "concept of the will of a rational being" (426). If there is a categorical

in Section I. As we saw in Chapter 3, a will is good if it acts from duty, not from inclination. To act from duty is not merely to have the *capacity* to act from a priori principles, but to actually do so. A good will, in other words, is motivated by the categorical imperative.

imperative then it constitutes the "objective principle" or determining ground of the pure will. Or, if there is a categorical imperative, then it is the law by means of which the will of a rational being can determine itself to act.

9.2 Our rational or objective end (426–428)

Up to this point it is clear that, for Kant, the pure will is a will capable of acting from maxims that are objectively valid and thus universalizable. The pure will, in other words, is able to act from maxims that have the categorical imperative as their determining ground. But Kant now takes this analysis a step further. He seeks an answer to the question: What, exactly, *qualifies* as an objectively valid end, an end that is shared by all rational natures? To ask this question in a different way, what kinds of ends are universalizable for a rational will? We earlier considered the nature of relative or conditional ends. These differ depending on our particular empirical natures and circumstances, and our diverse conceptions of happiness. These are the "incentives" or empirical ends that lie at the basis of all hypothetical imperatives.[38] Now, however, we are seeking to identify something that is of unconditional worth to all rational natures. We are seeking what Kant refers to as the "ground" or basis of the categorical imperative.

In the name of supplying that ground, Kant invites us to engage in following thought experiment:

[S]uppose there were something the *existence of which in itself* has an absolute worth, something which as *an end in itself* could be a ground of determinate laws; then in it, and in it alone, would lie the ground of a possible categorical imperative, that is, of a practical law.

We need to be certain we understand Kant's reasoning in this passage. Were there something of absolute worth, he is saying, it would be valued by all rational natures. It would therefore be a ground of laws,

---

[38] Kant is not consistent in his use of the term "incentive" [*Triebfeder*]. At (427) he tells us that an incentive is the "subjective ground of desire." Incentives, he tells us in this passage, are not valid for every rational being. At (440), however, his broadens the scope of "incentive" so that even "respect for the law" falls within it.

not merely of principles or counsels. It could ground laws because it would have universal and necessary validity. Again, we are considering practical laws here, laws prescribing how people ought to behave. So were there something of absolute worth, that something would provide a ground or basis for a law commanding all rational natures to respect or honor that thing. It would serve as the ground of a command that is categorical versus merely hypothetical.

What is that thing of absolute worth? Kant finally gives us his answer at the end of (428):

[R]ational nature exists as an end in itself.

This is Kant's answer, but it is so far quite vague. We need to know precisely what feature of rational nature qualifies it as having an absolute rather than merely conditional worth. We also need to know why Kant believes he is entitled to claim that rational nature is valuable unconditionally or as an end in itself.

We can extract an answer to our first question from the way in which Kant has already characterized rational nature. Kant has been considering rational nature in a practical context. As we have seen, he distinguishes the will as practical reason, the pure will, from the empirical will. Only the pure will, on his account, has the "capacity to determine itself to acting in conformity with the *representation of certain laws*." If it really is the case that we possess a pure will, then we must be more than mere objects of nature – more than mere "things," Kant now says. We must, then, possess the capacity of self-determination or freedom, the capacity Kant begins at (433) to identify as "autonomy." As I noted in my introductory chapter (at Section 6.2), Kant understands by this capacity something other than mere freedom from external constraint. He has in mind nothing less than the capacity to rise above the mechanical forces of nature. This is the feature of rational nature that qualifies it as an end in itself.

As for our second question, Kant says very little here to justify his claim that rational nature is an end in itself. He simply asserts the claim at (428) when he writes:

Now I say that the human being and in general every rational being *exists* as an end in itself, *not merely as a means* to be used by this or that will at its discretion.

Kant contends that every human being "necessarily represents his own existence in this way" (429). He cannot be appealing in this remark to popular opinion because, in his view, popular opinion is unreliable. Instead, he thinks of himself as clarifying an assumption of common human reason or "natural sound understanding" (397).[39] This is all Kant gives us here by way of justification. We are warranted in affirming that rational nature is an end in itself, he implies, because this assumption is in agreement with common human reason.

10. SECOND FORMULA OF THE CATEGORICAL IMPERATIVE: FORMULA OF HUMANITY ("FH") (429)

We now turn to what Kant identifies at (436) as the second official formula of the categorical imperative. The first official formula, expressed either as FUL or as FN, requires that we act only on maxims that are universalizable or that could be willed as laws of nature.[40] It should be clear at this point that universalizable maxims are maxims that respect an objective end, an end that has unconditional or absolute worth. Kant identified that end at (428f.): "*rational nature exists as an end in itself.*" As we have just seen, rational nature is an end in itself by virtue of its capacity to "determine itself to acting in conformity with the *representation of certain laws*" (427). To be motivated by the categorical imperative, then, is to be motivated by respect for this capacity. This is precisely the idea Kant aims to capture in his second formula of the law, FH:

So act that you use humanity, whether in your own person or in the person of any other, always at the same time as an end, never merely as a means.

Notice the inclusion here of the word "merely." The formula does not state that it is impermissible to use oneself or others as a means. Instead, it commands us never to use ourselves or others *merely* as a means. There is an important difference. When my tooth aches, I seek a dentist's help in alleviating the pain. I use my dentist as a means to pain reduction. What the second formula commands is that I not treat

---

[39] This is evident also in Kant's concluding remarks at (445). He tells us there that he has been "explicating the generally received concept of morality."

[40] At (436), Kant groups FUL and FN together as the first of the "three ways of representing the principle of morality."

my dentist *merely* as a means. Although I need to rely on her special skills to treat my symptom, I am commanded to treat her "at the same time as an end." I am commanded to bear in mind that she is a creature endowed with the special capacity of self-determination, and that she is for that reason entitled to respect. I am not to treat her merely as an object to be used in the service of my desires. The same goes for how I am to treat myself. I am not to forget that as a creature endowed with the capacity of self-determination, I must treat myself with respect as well.

Immediately following his introduction of the FH formula, Kant briefly reconsiders his examples of the four kinds of duties. This time he employs FH in his evaluation of the various maxims. Given his claim further on (at (436)) that the various formulae of the moral law are equivalent, we are warranted in expecting that the reasoning he employs in his second consideration of the cases will essentially be the same as in the first. Now that we have FH at our disposal, however, we can better understand what qualifies, for Kant, as a universalizable maxim. We now know that when we apply the test for universalizability, we are in effect asking whether our maxims respect rational nature. This is essentially what the second formula specifies as the test.

11. FOUR DUTIES: VERSION 2 (429–430)

11.1 Perfect duty to oneself: The duty to preserve one's own life (429)

Instead of reproducing his earlier version of this case verbatim here, Kant describes it a bit differently. A man considers taking his own life in order to extract himself from "a trying condition." Applying the second formula of the categorical imperative, he asks himself whether "his action can be consistent with the idea of humanity *as an end in itself.*" The maxim fails, Kant insists, because to take one's own life for this kind of reason (the reason he identified in the first version as the incentive of "self-love") is to treat oneself as "a thing" and hence as a mere means. This is what FH expressly forbids. Not only does FH forbid suicide, it forbids even partial forms of self-destruction. We are to refrain from "maiming" or "damaging" ourselves from self-love as well. As Kant writes:

A human being ... is not a thing and hence not something that can be used merely as a means, but must in all his actions always be regarded as an end in itself.

Kant claims at (438) that FH is "at bottom the same" as the first formula of the categorical imperative. It is far from obvious how this could be so. If we compare FH to FN, for example, we note that only FH makes reference to the importance of treating humanity as an end. The FN test asks us to imagine whether an inconceivability is involved in the idea of a natural law commanding the destruction of life for personal advantage. As we saw in our discussion back at Section 7.1, that argument turned on Kant's understanding of the purpose of natural laws. For beings "constituted purposively for life," the purpose of natural laws, on his account, is to preserve life. In his second consideration of the case, however, Kant argues that the man's maxim fails the test because it is inconsistent with the idea of humanity as an end in itself. On Kant's account, however, humanity is an end in itself not because of its membership in the class of living things, but because it possesses the faculty of pure will. It is therefore puzzling that Kant insists that the first two formulae of the moral law are equivalent. We will take up this issue again at Section 12 below.

11.2 Perfect duty to others: The duty not to tell a false promise (429f.)

This time Kant does not even go to the trouble to set up the example; he expects us to remember details from his first discussion. He says here that in considering whether to make a false promise, the man realizes this would be to use another human being "merely as a means." The man realizes, in addition, that the intended recipient of the false promise could not "possibly agree" to this deception.

Why does telling a false promise amount to using another person merely as a means? Even if we grant that others would not agree to this kind of treatment, this does not by itself explain very much. Others might not agree to such treatment for a number of reasons. Suppose you are deceived by a friend or loved one. Your feelings would most likely be hurt, and this would cause you pain. If you are deceived by a stranger, you might feel less personally aggrieved, but you would still react with displeasure. The deception might even cause you significant inconvenience. In each of these cases, your happiness would be compromised.

It should be clear by now, however, that when Kant tells us that others could not "possibly agree" to be deceived, he does not have their happiness in mind. Rather, others would not agree, on his analysis, because others would not agree to be treated as mere means. To be treated as a mere means is to be treated as a mere thing; it is to be used to satisfy someone else's contingent ends, ends of desire or happiness. When we are treated as mere means, our absolute or unconditional value is either ignored or undermined in some way. As practically rational natures, we cannot agree to that.

If we assume that Kant's message here is that none of us could possibly agree to be deceived because acts of deception interfere with our happiness, we once again make the mistake of interpreting his categorical imperative test prudentially. In effect, we understand the categorical imperative as a version of the Golden Rule: Do unto others only what you would want them to do unto you. What the categorical imperative commands, however, is not that we will only those maxims that are consistent with what we, as empirical natures, could desire or want, but rather that we will only those maxims consistent with what we, as rational agents, could think or will.[41] When Kant warns us in the footnote at (430) not to conflate the categorical imperative with the Golden Rule, he means to caution us against this prudential reading of the moral law.

11.3 *Imperfect duty to oneself: The duty to develop one's talents (430)*

Kant refers to this duty as "contingent," but he does not thereby intend to imply that the duty is optional. As is clear from his parenthetical inclusion of the word "meritorious," he means the word "contingent" to pick out the fact that the duty to develop (or not neglect) one's talents is an imperfect duty. As we have seen, this kind of duty allows for latitude in how we are to carry it out. The duty requires us to adopt a maxim – in this case, the maxim to develop or not neglect our talents. If

---

[41] This distinction in Kant between what we can will and what we desire or want is emphasized in Onora O'Neill's "Consistency in Action," Chapter 5 of her *Constructions of Reason*.

we fail to act on it, a contradiction results. Since the duty is imperfect, the contradiction is not a contradiction in conception. Universalizing the maxim of indifference, that is, does not contradict the very idea of laws of nature, on Kant's analysis. As he says, failing to develop our talents "might admittedly be consistent" with the "preservation" of humanity. What *does* result from the universalized maxim, however, is a contradiction in the will. Applying the FH, Kant argues that universalizing the maxim conflicts with the "humanity in our person." Why is this so?

All Kant tells us here is that it is an "end of nature with respect to humanity in our subject" that we are given "predispositions to greater perfection." The FH commands that we respect humanity as an end in itself, as having absolute value owing to its capacity to give itself law. Kant seems to be suggesting, now, that indifference to the development of our talents interferes with the fulfillment of that command. He assumes here, as he did in his first discussion of this duty, that developing our talents is somehow essential to the exercise of our practical rationality. His reasons for this assumption, however, are so far unclear.

The *Doctrine of Virtue* gives us some guidance. Under the heading of "natural capacities," Kant includes our capacities to understand and to will. Morality requires us to cultivate the former, he says, in order to enable us to grasp the concepts connected with duty. Morality requires us to cultivate the latter, because doing so allows us to "raise ourselves" from our "animality." Raising ourselves from our animality is a matter of perfecting that capacity we have as practically rational natures to set ends. To set ends, in the sense Kant has in mind here, is to govern one's own conduct by laws of practical reason. Only by governing ourselves in this way is it possible for us to acquire a "virtuous disposition" (*MM II* (387)). For these reasons, cultivating our talents or natural capacities is a duty.

11.4 Imperfect duty to others: The duty of benevolence (430)

This time the maxim under consideration is the maxim of indifference to the welfare or happiness of others. Kant begins this brief discussion by granting that we all have as a natural end the desire to achieve happiness. He then asks us to imagine living in a world in which none of us contributed to the happiness of others. Kant notes here that, in such a world, humanity "might indeed subsist." He thus once again draws our attention to the fact that willing this kind of maxim as universal law does not result in a contradiction in conception. Nonetheless, we have the duty of benevolence, the duty to "further the ends of others."

Although Kant does not explain why this duty is implied by the FH, we can fill in his reasoning for him. FH commands us to treat ourselves and others always as ends and never merely as means. Humanity is an end in itself because of its capacity of practical rationality. Clearly, Kant is committed to the view that a world in which the maxim of indifference were universalized would be a world inhospitable to the exercise of our practical rationality. His reasoning depends on the following two assumptions: First, universalization of the maxim of indifference would diminish human happiness and sense of well being. Second, if we are unhappy, we are much less likely to do what duty requires. Kant argued for this latter assumption back in Section I. We each have an indirect duty to secure our own happiness, he argued there, because dissatisfaction with our condition can "easily be a great *temptation to transgression of duty*" (399). Kant's general point thus seems to be this: It is unrealistic to expect finite rational beings to act from duty unless certain material conditions – conditions essential to their happiness or well being – are satisfied first.

12. THE EQUIVALENCE OF THE FIRST AND SECOND FORMULAE OF THE CATEGORICAL IMPERATIVE (431, 436)

Before moving on to consider Kant's third formula of the moral law, it will be illuminating to explore a bit further the way in which he characterizes the relation between the first two formulae. As noted back at Section 11.1, Kant's claim at (436) that the different formulae are various ways of representing "the very same law" seems implausible on its face. FH depends essentially on the idea that humanity is an end in itself. No such idea, however, is referred to in the first formula, expressed either as FUL or as FN. Kant furthermore asserts that the first formulation of the moral law is all we need to determine duty. (He makes this point explicitly at (437).) But if this is his view, why does he go to the trouble to introduce the further formulae? What role do FH and the further formulae play in his account?

At this point in our discussion, we can attempt an answer to these questions merely with regard to the relation between the first formulation of the moral law (expressed either as FUL or as FN) and FH. FUL and FN command us to act only on maxims that can be universalized or that be raised to the status of laws of nature. Neither version of this first formula specifies, however, *which* maxims meet this qualification. Kant provides some help when he tells us that universalizable maxims are maxims that can be willed by all rational nature. But then we need to know, of course, precisely what can be willed by all rational nature, in his view. Our question then becomes: What do all rational natures care about? Or more precisely: What is of unconditional value to all rational natures? Kant finally supplies his answer to this question at (428): Of unconditional value, he says, is rational nature as such. As unconditionally valuable, every rational being is an end in itself. This is the idea expressed in the second formula, FH.

We can thus clarify the relation of FH to the first formula of the moral law in this way: FH makes explicit an idea Kant relies on in his first formula of the moral law. The first two formulae are equivalent in the sense that they place the same constraints on what can count as a morally permissible maxim. Without the second formula (FH), however, we cannot adequately understand the first (FUL or FN).[42]

13. THE THIRD FORMULA OF THE LAW: FORMULA OF AUTONOMY ("FA") (431–434)

The third formula of the law takes this analysis one step further and thereby brings the meaning of the first and the second formulae "closer to intuition" (437). The second formula, FH, captures the idea that the object that has unconditional value is rational nature. The third formula, FA, specifies the *basis* of the unconditional worth of rational nature. Kant indicates this basis in his mention of the "idea of the will of every rational being as a *will giving universal law*" (431). Giving law is something that only rational nature can do. The third formula commands that we respect this particular feature of rational nature, since it is this feature that earns rational nature unconditional worth. Kant expresses the third formula, FA, as follows:

[A]ct only so that the will could regard itself as at the same time giving universal law through its maxim. (434)

---

[42] Kant is explicit about the equivalence of the first and second formulas at (431).

Not only does the idea expressed in the third formula identify the basis of our unconditional worth as rational natures, it also helps us understand how it is that each of us accepts the moral law as valid. Recall Kant's claim back at (428) that if there really is a categorical imperative valid for all rational wills, then all rational wills really must accept that imperative as binding on them. He acknowledged that finite rational wills such as ours act from a variety of motives. Obviously, we often seek to satisfy our desire for happiness. But Kant insists that, as practically rational natures or as beings possessing a pure will, we nevertheless also accept that the categorical imperative obligates us. We implicitly grant its validity, in his view, even when we transgress the law. (We discussed this latter point back at Section 8.2.)

In these paragraphs at (431–434), Kant aims to explain and defend his assertion that every human will necessarily accepts the categorical imperative as valid. A few pages earlier, at (426), he gave us a clue. He indicated there that, if there is a categorical imperative, then it "must already be connected (completely a priori) with the concept of the will of a rational being as such." What we learned from his analysis of the concept of a rational will was, first, that that concept refers to a will that is pure rather than empirical. We learned, second, that the pure will, for Kant, is the capacity of a rational being to give itself law, the capacity he identifies as "autonomy" (433). Finally, we learned that since the law that all rational natures give themselves is valid for *all* rational natures, its command for finite rational natures is categorical rather than hypothetical. The law that the will of a finite rational being gives itself, then, is the categorical imperative.

What this analysis did not make explicit, however, is *why* all human rational wills necessarily accept the categorical imperative as valid. The point that Kant merely asserted back at (428), he now attempts to explain. His reasoning relies on the following assumptions: The categorical imperative, he has argued, has its *source* in pure practical reason (in the pure will). It is therefore correct to say that practically rational nature is the *author* of the moral law. This fact, namely, that we as practically rational natures are the authors of the law, is of tremendous significance. In Kant's view, it explains why each of us values the law unconditionally. It explains, moreover, why each of us gives ourselves the law and accepts it as binding on our will.

Kant notes at (432) that, in making explicit the fact that we are the authors as well as legislators of the moral law, he is able to solve a problem that previous approaches to practical obligation could not solve. For if we consider ourselves merely as subject to or standing under a practical law – without adding the qualification that the law has its source in our own will – then there is no reason to suppose that we would necessarily recognize an obligation to obey that law. Why would we be willing to accept as valid the law's constraint on our actions? "Previous efforts" have failed to discover the principle of morality, Kant claims, because the only answer philosophers have so far been able to supply to this question is that we act from duty because we have some "interest" in doing so. By "interest" in this context, Kant has in mind what he earlier referred to as "inclinations" or "incentives."[43] When we act from "interest," the motivational source of our action is our empirical nature. We act from grounds Kant identifies as "heterono-mous." He is concerned in these paragraphs to argue once again that it is not possible to account for practical obligation in this way. It is not possible, because commands that are merely heteronomous lack the universality and necessity of law.

The significance for Kant of the idea that the categorical imperative is a law we both author and legislate is that this explains how it is possible for us to act from something other than heteronomous grounds. Kant's insight (inspired by Rousseau) is this: If the law governing our actions proceeds from our own will, we will necessarily recognize its validity.[44] The question "Why should I obey?" will not arise. Since the law's validity is independent of our interests or inclinations – all of which

---

[43] Kant's use of the term "interest" here may seem to conflict with his earlier use of it in the footnote at (413). There he introduced the notion of "practical interest." A fallible or dependent will, on his account, does not always act in conformity with reason. Its dependence on principles of reason, he says, is called "interest." It can know that it ought to perform a certain action (it can have a "practical interest" in that action) and yet not be motivated to perform it. At (433), Kant writes of acting "from a certain interest." But in this context he has in mind (what he refers to in the note at (413) as) "pathological" interest. When I act from pathological interest, the ground of my action is heteronomous, not autonomous.

[44] I have in mind here Rousseau's idea that we recognize as legitimate only laws that we give ourselves and that reflect the interests not of private wills but of the "general will." See *On Social Contract*, Book II, Chapter IV.

derive from our merely contingent needs and circumstances – we will moreover grant that its validity is unconditional. Of course, our recognition of the validity of the law is no guarantee that in every instance we will employ it as a limiting condition on our actions. But our recognition of the law does imply that even when we allow ourselves to transgress, we grant (in our heart of hearts) that what we have done is something we ought not to have done (432).

According to FA, "all maxims are repudiated that are inconsistent with the will's own giving of universal law." FA thus implies that our maxims must be consistent with the will's own giving of universal law if they are to pass the categorical imperative test. If what motivates us is interest or self-love, our actions are at best governed by hypothetical imperatives. When we act from duty, what motivates us is *not* interest or inclination but something else. What motivates us, Kant now reveals, is respect for the capacity of the will of a practically rational nature to give itself law. This is the capacity he identifies as autonomy.

14. REGARDING ONESELF AS LAWGIVING IN A KINGDOM OF ENDS (433–438)

Borrowing the language of FH, the supreme moral law commands us to treat ourselves and others never merely as means but always at the same time as ends. As rational agents, we both stand under and give ourselves this law. Kant now asks us to imagine a world (a "kingdom" or "realm"[45]) governed by this law, a world in which all rational beings are united under it. This world or "kingdom of ends" would be like the kingdom of nature in a certain respect: as in the kingdom of nature, all objects in the kingdom of ends would be law-governed.

But Kant notes an important difference, as well, between the two realms or kingdoms. In the kingdom of nature, he writes, objects are governed by "externally necessitated efficient causes." Objects are determined by mechanical forces over which they have no control (438). In the kingdom of ends, in contrast, the governing law is a law rational beings give to themselves as the expression of their capacity of self-determination or autonomy. Furthermore, while the kingdom of nature actually exists, the kingdom of ends is a mere ideal. It could

---

[45] The German is "*Reich*," which is acceptably translated either as "kingdom" or as "realm."

only exist, Kant tells us, were its law "universally followed" by all rational beings (438). An actual kingdom of ends, then, would be a kingdom in which rational beings were never motivated to act solely in the service of their contingent empirical ends. It would be a world in which rational beings always limited their empirical ends by the moral law. An actual kingdom of ends, in other words, would be a world in which all rational beings acted only on universally valid maxims. Alternatively put, it would be a world in which all rational beings always treated themselves and others as ends.

Kant distinguishes between rational beings that belong as "members" of the kingdom of ends and the "sovereign" of the kingdom of ends. The sovereign not only gives herself law, but always acts from the law. In contrast to the members of the kingdom of ends, her will does not have to be commanded. Kant recalls here the idea of the "holy" or "perfectly good will" he introduced back at (414). As he writes at (439), the maxims of this will "necessarily harmonize with the laws of autonomy."

Members of the kingdom of ends, however, both give law and are at the same time "subject to" the law. Unlike the sovereign, members must be commanded in morality. Kant has in mind here finite rational wills, including human rational wills. Because we are rational beings, we have the capacity of autonomy and can thus give ourselves law. But because we are finite wills and must be commanded in morality, we are at the same time subject to moral laws. Those laws, in other words, obligate us.

15. AUTONOMY AS THE GROUND OF DIGNITY (434–436)

As we now know, autonomy on Kant's account refers to the capacity of rational nature to give itself law. We could not give ourselves law, in the way in which he intends, did we not possess the faculty of pure will or practical reason. Kant now moves on to argue that it is in virtue of the fact that we are autonomous wills that we have dignity. To say of something that it has dignity, in his view, is to praise it; and he tells us that this term of praise is appropriately applied only to rational beings. Dignity, Kant claims, designates the special kind of value rational nature has.

Returning to the theme of the first paragraph of Section I, Kant remarks that some human traits have a merely relative or conditional value while others have absolute worth. He tells us at (435) that traits such as skill and diligence have at most a "market price."[46] Their value varies depending on the extent to which they satisfy some actual "need." The value of traits, such as wit and imagination, which have a "fancy price," are equally contingent, but these traits satisfy what we might think of as more elevated purposes – the purpose, for instance, of aesthetic enjoyment. What skill, diligence, wit, and imagination share in common is their status as merely relative or conditional goods.

Kant reminds us here of the conditional character of some goods in order to emphasize the unconditional value of dignity. Obviously, his claim is that the goodness of dignity is not contingent upon circumstance or upon the diverse and varying desires of individuals. The "dignity of humanity," he says, "consists ... in this capacity to give universal law" (440). Since Kant refers to the capacity to give law as autonomy, we have dignity insofar as we are capable of autonomy.[47] As he elsewhere puts the point:

Autonomy is ... the ground of the dignity of human nature and of every rational nature. (436)

16. ON THE EQUIVALENCE OF THE THREE FORMULAE OF THE CATEGORICAL IMPERATIVE (436–437)

Above (at Section 12) we explored the relation between the first two formulae of the moral law. We saw that FH brings FUL and FN "closer to intution" in that FH makes explicit an idea contained in Kant's understanding of FUL and FN. With Kant's help at (436), we

---

[46] Samuel Fleischacker argues that this is a "possible reference" to Adam Smith. See his "Values Behind the Market: Kant's Response to the 'Wealth of Nations'." *History of Political Thought* XVII (1996), p. 394.

[47] Back in the opening paragraphs of Section I, Kant identified the good will as the only unconditional good. He told us there that the goodness of the good will is attributable to "its volition," to what it wills (394). As we saw, he defined a good will as a will that acts from duty. Now, however, he tells us that what has "unconditional, incomparable worth" is dignity (436). Dignity, we now know, refers to the *capacity* of a will to give itself law. Because a will that has the capacity to give itself law is not necessarily also a good will, Kant thus seems to award unconditional value to two different things. Perhaps we make a mistake, however, in interpreting his remarks in Section I to imply that the unconditional value of a good will derives from anything other than its capacity to act from duty, its autonomy.

can now specify the relation between the first and second formulae in more technical terms. The first formula (expressed either as FUL or as FN) requires that our maxims have a certain "form." Our maxims must have the form of universalizability. Alternatively put, our maxims must be capable of being raised to the status of laws of nature. The second formula, FH, clarifies which maxims qualify as having that form. FH requires that our maxims have a certain "matter" or "end." Our maxims will qualify as universalizable, then, only if they have that matter or end. The matter or end our maxims must have, according to FH, is rational nature as such. The first two formulae of the moral law are equivalent because they place the same limits on our maxims. This equivalence will only be evident to us, however, if we properly understand the formulae. We can only properly understand the first formula with the help of the second.

Kant notes that in addition to the fact that our maxims may be tested with regard both to their form and their matter, they may also be tested with regard to what he calls their "complete determination." As he puts it, they can be tested by the formula that, "all maxims from one's own lawgiving are to harmonize with a possible kingdom of ends as with a kingdom of nature." While we might have expected Kant to restate the third or FA formula of the moral law here, he instead provides a new formula. This new formula brings together the concepts of autonomy (of "one's own lawgiving") and of a kingdom of ends. We will refer to this new formula as the formula of the kingdom of ends, FKE.

Remember that FA makes explicit the feature by virtue of which rational nature qualifies as an end in itself. Kant isolated this feature at (431) when he drew our attention to the "idea *of the will of every rational being as a will giving universal law.*" FA commands the will to act, then, only so that it can regard itself "*as at the same time giving universal law through its maxim*" (434). If we imagine all rational wills united together as members in a realm or kingdom governed by "common objective laws" (laws the rational wills give themselves), we are led to the idea of a possible kingdom of ends. This idea is captured in FKE, which Kant provides a version of at (428):

[E]very rational being must act as if he were by his maxims at all times a lawgiving member of the universal kingdom of ends.

As we have seen, Kant claims that this additional formula, FKE, tests our maxims with regard to their "complete determination." He gives us a clue as to how this is so when he links the idea of a maxim's "complete determination" to the category "totality." In the *Critique of Pure Reason*, Kant defines the category of totality as, "nothing other than plurality considered as a unity" (B 111). FKE captures the idea of a maxim's complete determination, then, in that this formula refers to something that is a "plurality considered as a unity." A kingdom of ends is a plurality because it collects together particular rational beings, beings subject to a law they give themselves. A kingdom of ends is a unity, presumably, because rational beings in such a kingdom are united under one law, the categorical imperative. This law may be expressed in various ways; but as we know, Kant holds that the various formulae are formulae of the same law.[48]

17. THE "PARADOX" REGARDING WHAT SERVES AS AN "INFLEXIBLE PRECEPT OF THE WILL" (439)

In his remarks at (439), Kant identifies as a "paradox" the suggestion that a "mere idea" could serve as an "inflexible precept of the will." The "idea" he refers to figures prominently in the paragraphs immediately preceding; it is the idea of the "dignity of humanity." We know that to act from duty is to be motivated by respect for this idea. The "paradox" Kant refers to at (439) arises not because the idea of human dignity is self-contradictory or incoherent. Rather, it arises in light of the remarkable fact that we indeed accept the idea of human dignity as a limiting condition on our maxims, and we accept this condition without regard to "any other end or advantage."

Kant has made these points before. What he identifies in this passage as "paradoxical," he elsewhere refers to as "strange." In Section I, he called "strange" the idea of a will whose worth derives not from "what it

---

[48] Kant writes in these pages that from the "form" to the "matter" to the "complete determination" of a maxim, a "progression" takes place. The progression, he says, is "through" the categories of "unity," "plurality," and "totality." (He draws here on his discussion of the categories of quantity in the *CPR* A 80/B 106.) The idea may be that the three different formulae of the moral law correspond in some way to the three categories of quantity. Kant also tells us that one formula, namely FKE, "unites the other two in it." (Here Gregor's translation is mistaken.) For further analysis, see Paton, *The Categorical Imperative*, p. 185, and Wood, *Kant's Ethical Thought*, p. 185f.

effects or accomplishes" (in the service of inclination), but only because it acts from duty (394). The idea of a will motivated in this way is so strange, he notes, that many deny its very possibility. Kant took up this theme in the opening paragraphs of Section II as well. He drew attention there to the fact that many doubt that there ever could be a "disposition to act from pure duty" – without, that is, regard for self-love (406). He conceded the great difficulty involved in trying to demonstrate with certainty that persons have the capacity to act in this way (407). At (439), he comments on this difficulty again, in anticipation of the work that awaits him. For in Section III he will set out to prove that we are warranted in thinking of ourselves as capable of being motivated by the moral law. He will set out to prove that we are warranted in regarding ourselves as bound or subject to the law.

18. AUTONOMOUS VERSUS HETERONOMOUS DETERMINATION OF THE WILL (440–444)

18.1 Autonomy of the will as the sole and supreme principle of morality (440)

In this paragraph, Kant again describes autonomy as the capacity of the will to give itself law. What he here refers to as the "principle of autonomy" looks very much like a variation on FUL:

[C]hoose only in such a way that the maxims of your choice are also included as universal law in the same volition.

Kant goes on to tell us that mere "analysis" cannot prove that every rational will is "bound to" this rule. By this he means that analysis cannot prove that every rational will accepts this rule as a valid constraint on its actions. The fact that analysis cannot prove this, he suggests, is somehow tied to the rule's "synthetic" nature. All that analysis can prove, he says, is that the "principle of autonomy is the sole principle of morals" (440).

As I just noted, Kant will eventually undertake to justify his claim that every rational nature is warranted in thinking of itself as bound to the moral law. This will be his central task in Section III, and he will execute it with the help of a method he describes as "synthetic." I am going to postpone until Section 19 a comparison of the

"analytic" method of Sections I and II with the "synthetic" method of
Section III. My task at present is to review the basic shape of the
argument Kant believes he has already provided to establish an
"analytic" connection between the "principle of autonomy" and the
"sole" and "supreme" principle of morality.

18.2 On the analytic procedure of Sections I and II

At the end of our discussion of the Preface, we considered a preliminary explanation of Kant's notion of the analytic method of
Sections I and II. Recall that in performing the analytic procedure,
we begin from a concept we wish to clarify or understand, and by
means of an analysis or explication of that concept, regress to conditions or assumptions upon which it rests. By the end of Section II,
Kant has arrived at the principle of autonomy. He tells us that he has
arrived at this principle by a "mere analysis of the concepts of
morality." With the help of his analytic method, he believes he has
demonstrated that the supreme principle of morality "commands
neither more nor less" than (what is expressed in) the principle of
autonomy (440).

  We can illustrate Kant's employment of the analytic method by
highlighting some of the main steps in the argument leading from the
beginning of Section I to the end of Section II. As we saw, Section I
begins with the common cognition of a good will and ends with the
first appearance of the categorical imperative. It is by means of analysis
of the former that we arrive at the latter. Kant's analysis of the concept
of a good will reveals that a good will is good without qualification. It
is good not because of it effects but because of its willing. What a good
will wills is duty. From Kant's analysis of the concept of duty, we learn
that duty is the "*necessity of action from respect for law*" (400). Since a
rule or principle has the status of law only if it is valid universally and
necessarily, it follows that the will that acts from respect for law, acts
on maxims that have universal and necessary validity. This line of
reasoning prepares the way for the first appearance of the categorical
imperative, expressed at (403) as FUL.

  Section II carries out this analytic procedure further, deepening our
understanding of the moral law. We learn, first, that since the law
commands us to respect ends that are unconditionally valid for all

rational natures, its command is categorical versus hypothetical. The categorical imperative commands that we act only on maxims that could be willed by all rational natures. Such maxims respect ends that are of absolute versus merely conditional value. Kant then argues that only one thing qualifies as unconditionally valuable or valuable as an "end in itself," namely, rational nature itself. This idea is captured in FH, which commands us to treat rational nature always as an end and never merely as a means. With the help of further analysis, Kant next determines that the feature of rational nature responsible for its unconditional value is its autonomy, its capacity to give itself law (428, 432f.). He expresses this idea in FA, which commands the will to act only so that it can regard itself *"as at the same time giving universal law through its maxim"* (434).

By means of these steps, Kant completes the transition from the "common cognition" with which his analysis began back in Section I, to the "metaphysics of morals" arrived at midway in Section II. On the basis of this analysis, he believes he is justified in concluding in the final paragraphs of Section II that the "sole" and "supreme" principle of morals "commands neither more or less" than autonomy (440). His explication of the concept of a good will is thus complete.[49] A good will acts from duty, and we now know what duty is. In acting from duty, a good will is motivated by respect for the capacity of autonomy.

18.3 Heteronomy of the will as the source of all spurious principles of morality (441)

Thanks to its capacity of autonomy, a rational will can give itself law. When a rational will allows that law (the categorical imperative) to govern its will, the law then functions as a limiting condition or constraint on its maxims. Kant tells us that, in such cases, the law "immediately" determines the will. It determines the will, that is, without intervening incentives or "independently of any property of the objects of volition" (440). In these cases, the will is good; it acts from duty.

---

[49] See Kant's own summary at (437): "[W]e now end up where we set out from at the beginning, namely with the concept of a will unconditionally good." That is, he has now completed, or nearly completed, his explication of the concept of a good will.

But Kant acknowledges that fallible rational natures sometimes transgress or are indifferent to duty. A fallible rational nature, then, does not always allow its law to govern its will. When its will is determined not by itself "immediately" but rather "by means of an incentive," some object in effect "gives the law to it" (441, 444).[50] When this occurs, the ground of its determination is "heteronomous." If I resist telling a lie in order to protect my reputation, the object determining my will is personal gain. I act from inclination and the principle determining my will is hence heteronomous; I answer a command or imperative that is merely hypothetical or conditional. But if I refrain from telling a lie because my maxim fails the categorical imperative test, I allow myself to be immediately governed by a law that I, as a rational nature, give myself. The principle governing my will is the categorical imperative. Otherwise stated, the principle governing my will is the principle of autonomy.[51]

One thing that should not escape our notice here is Kant's remark that heteronomous principles can derive not just from "inclination" but also from "representations of reason" (441). We have not encountered this point before. So far, Kant's examples of actions determined by something other than duty have in every instance been examples of maxims determined by inclination. Now he is suggesting that we can also act from grounds that are both rational and heteronomous. This claim is curious if only because, from his Preface onward, Kant has insisted that the supreme ground of obligation must be discovered "a priori simply in concepts of pure reason" (389). What he asserts here, however, is that some rational grounds are unfit to perform this role. In order to establish that he is not guilty of inconsistency, we need to consider more closely what he has in mind by a ground that is both rational and heteronomous.

---

[50] This language appears in the *CPrR* as well, for example, at (33).

[51] We should note a distinction, here, between acting autonomously and allowing the principle of autonomy to govern our will. If we allow the principle of autonomy to govern our will, we act from duty. Our maxim has moral content or moral worth. But does not follow, for Kant, that we only express our autonomy when we act from duty. If we consider ourselves as beings in possession of a pure will, *all* our actions are expressions of our autonomy – even actions resulting from our decision to ignore or transgress duty. From this point of view, we are free and therefore culpable not just when our will is good but also when it is evil. Kant is most explicit about this point in the early paragraphs of his *Religion Within the Limits of Mere Reason Alone*.

18.4 Division of all possible principles of morality taken from heteronomy assumed as the basic concept (441–445)

In these paragraphs, Kant explains the difference between what he here calls "empirical" and "rational" heteronomous grounds. In all cases of heteronomous determination, it is not the will that gives itself law; rather, some object gives law to the will. At (444), Kant describes this object as a "foreign" impulse. The foreign impulses he has in mind derive, he says, from a subject's "nature" or "natural constitution." Belonging to our natural constitution, on his account, are our faculty of sensibility ("inclination and taste") and our rational faculties ("understanding and reason"). Empirical heteronomous grounds derive from our faculty of sensibility; rational heteronomous grounds derive from our rational faculty.

Kant expands upon these points in the *Critique of Practical Reason*. Cases in which the will does not determine itself "immediately" or autonomously, he says, are cases in which the will is determined "by means of an intervening faculty of pleasure or displeasure" (25). When this occurs, the determining ground of the will is some object (or matter) of desire. Kant indicates that both our sensible as well as our rational faculty can be the source of objects of desire. Sometimes we act merely to satisfy our desire for food or sex. These are clear examples of acting in response to the command of our sensible natures. But sometimes we seek the gratification of our "higher" appetites. We exercise our cognitive powers, for instance, in the service of some idea of perfection (24). Insofar as what determines us in the latter as well as in the former case is desire, however, we act from heteronomous grounds. In the latter case, as in all cases of heteronomous willing, our will is governed not by a "practical law," but by an "empirical" principle (21).[52]

There is a sense, then, in which the vocabulary Kant relies on to "divide" heteronomous principles at (442) of the *Groundwork* is misleading. It is misleading because the "rational" heteronomous grounds he refers to in that discussion are in one respect no less empirical than what he there calls "empirical" grounds. As we have just seen, Kant's view is that *both* "rational" as well as "empirical" heteronomous grounds, qua heteronomous, stem from our "natural

---

[52] Kant makes this point also at *CPrR* (41).

constitution."[53] By "natural constitution," here, he means our nature empirically considered (our nature as "appearances"). When we act either from rational or from empirical heteronomous grounds, it is "nature that gives the law" (444). Because both grounds are heteronomous and hence derive from our empirical nature, both grounds are ultimately empirical.

18.5 Empirical heteronomous grounds (442)

Empirical heteronomous principles, according to Kant, are "taken from the principle of happiness" and "built upon physical or moral feeling." We know from our preceding discussion that when we are motivated by these grounds, the object that gives law to our will derives from our sensible nature. When we satisfy our desire for warmth or food, we most obviously answer to empirical heteronomous principles. In such cases, our conception of happiness is "built upon" physical feeling. But we are highly complex sensible creatures and thus have in addition more complicated sensible desires. We crave the love and recognition of others, or we strive to achieve such goods as "power, riches, (and) honor" (393). Our actions are sometimes motivated, then, by the wish to satisfy our psychological needs. These are the needs Kant classifies here under the heading of "moral feeling." When we are motivated either by our physical or by our psychological needs, the ground of our action is heteronomous and hence empirical.

One might hold the view not just that all rational beings desire happiness, but that all rational beings mean by happiness precisely the same thing. One might furthermore contend that this conception of happiness is fixed over time. Were these assumptions true, we would be warranted in claiming that from this invariable conception of happiness it is possible to derive rules that have universal and necessary validity. We might, then, propose as our moral principle: "Promote the happiness of all rational beings."

---

[53] Perhaps it is in order to avoid this confusion that, when he returns to this topic in the *CPrR*, Kant introduces new vocabulary for describing the division of heteronomous grounds. He there explicitly describes as "empirical" *all* "material" (that is, heteronomous) grounds, including those "based on reason" (41).

As we know, Kant grants that all human rational natures desire happiness. He believes this is a fact about human nature that can be "presupposed surely and a priori" (415f.). But he also believes that the concept of happiness, and hence also the principle commanding us to promote it, is empirical and as such indeterminate. As empirical, the principle of happiness is not "fit to be the ground of moral laws" (442). We cannot, from a merely empirical account of the "special constitution of human nature" and of what human natures desire, ground laws valid for all rational beings.[54] Nor can we rely on an empirical account of human nature to ground laws valid merely for *human* rational beings. Because of its empirical grounding, then, a principle such as "Promote the happiness of all rational beings" is unfit to earn the status of law and is thus heteronomous, in Kant's view.

Of all possible efforts to ground morality on empirical heteronomous principles, Kant insists that the "most objectionable" is the effort to ground morality, not on a principle that commands the promotion of *everyone's* happiness, but on a principle that commands the promotion of *"one's own happiness."* Think back to the case of the prudent merchant of Section I. The merchant is honest to his customers, but only because he believes he stands to profit from his honesty down the line. Kant's remarks at (442) suggest that he doubts that any of us would be fooled into identifying this kind of self-serving behavior as virtuous. But what is "most objectionable" about the attempt to ground morality on a principle of one's own happiness, Kant tells us, is that it "bases morality on incentives that undermine it and destroy all its sublimity." Although he does not say so explicitly, Kant is presumably reacting here to the effort to make a virtue out of selfishness. This approach, in his words, puts "motives to virtue and those to vice in one class and only teaches us to calculate better." The motives of the virtuous and of the vicious are "in one class," on this conception, because both the virtuous and the vicious person are after the same thing, namely, the gratification of their own desires. The

---

[54] Kant repeats this point a number of times in the *Groundwork*. His first mention of it is in the Preface (389). For further passages, see also (408, 410, 425). I discussed these matters earlier in this chapter, at Section 5.4.

virtuous person is merely the person who is more successful in calculating the means to achieving this aim.[55]

Kant reserves a few sentences of this discussion for an attack on one particular empirical approach to morality: the "moral sense" theory of the Scottish philosopher Frances Hutcheson (1694–1746). Because Kant reveals almost nothing here about the features of Hutcheson's theory he finds objectionable, we once again have to look to other texts for illumination. In the *Critique of Practical Reason* he tells us that moral sense theory posits a special feeling or sense for morality (38). It suggests that, just as we can feel hot and cold, and see shapes and colors, so we can feel the difference between virtuous and vicious conduct. Moral sense theory in addition proposes that our judgments about virtuous and vicious conduct reflect nothing other than the feelings awakened in us by certain behaviors. I judge a person to be bad or evil, then, only insofar as that person's behavior produces displeasure in me. I judge a person to be good when her conduct produces in me an agreeable feeling.

Although Kant endorsed this approach to morality back in 1762, he now rejects it.[56] The reason he provides in the *Groundwork* is the familiar one that we cannot expect to get from a moral theory based on feeling a "uniform standard" of good and evil (442). After all, the fact that a particular conduct produces displeasure in me is no guarantee that it will have the same effect on you.[57]

18.6 Rational heteronomous grounds (443)

Kant says of rational heteronomous grounds that they are "based on reason." As we saw in our discussion at Section 18.4, he means by this that they gratify "higher" objects of desire, objects of desire posited

[55] For further discussion, see *CPrR* (35) where Kant writes that happiness is the "direct opposite" of the principle of morality. It "obliterates" the difference between virtue and vice. It "bases morality on incentives that undermine it and destroy all its sublimity."

[56] His endorsement of moral sense theory is evident in his 1762 essay (the so-called "prize essay"): "Inquiry concerning the Distinctness of the Principles of Rational Theology and Morals."

[57] Kant provides further reasons for rejecting moral sense theory in other texts. In the *CPrR*, he calls moral sense theory a "deception." He doubts that those who claim to adhere to it actually do so consistently. Rather than derive moral judgments from feeling, they in fact rely on a prior cognition of obligation, he says at (38). See also his remarks in *MM II* (400).

not by our sensible nature but by our rational faculty. Remember that by our rational faculty, in the present context, Kant has in mind the rational part of our natural constitution. He is not referring here, then, to that special (or "metaphysical") faculty which is the source of non-empirical motivation (390, 412). In other words, Kant is not referring to our faculty of pure will or of pure practical reason. In the present context, he means by reason a faculty we have as empirical beings, as "appearances."

Objects of desire produced by our faculty of reason derive, Kant says, from the concept of perfection – a concept "based on reason" because it refers to objects we cannot encounter in experience. Perfection is an ideal; in the practical sense, it refers to the "fitness or adequacy of a thing for all sorts of end" (*CPrR* (41)). What we encounter in experience are not instances of perfection, but instances of efforts to achieve it.

Kant divides rational grounds into two kinds, corresponding to two concepts of perfection: "ontological" and "theological." He says almost nothing in the *Groundwork* about the ontological version. We can infer from his discussion in the *Critique of Practical Reason*, however, that the ontological version relies for its standard of morality on the idea of human perfection. According to this view, we act from duty insofar as we meet, or strive to meet, that standard. Kant singles out Stoicism as an example of this approach to moral theory. The Stoics model virtue after the idea of the "heroism of the sage" who successfully governs his merely animal desires by reason (*CPrR* (127*)). The Stoic approach is heteronomous, because even though the idea of human perfection is "rational" in that it corresponds to nothing we can ever discover in experience, what ultimately motivates us to strive for perfection is the desire for happiness or the "advantages of life" (*CPrR* (41)). Although "rational," the idea of human perfection is in this respect like all other heteronomous grounds.

Kant's discussion of the theological concept of perfection in the *Groundwork* is somewhat more expansive. The theological approach derives its standard of moral conduct not from the rational idea of human perfection but from a different concept of reason, namely, that of a "divine, all-perfect will." We act from duty, according to this approach, when we bring our conduct into conformity with this idea. On this account, duties are essentially divine commands. They are heteronomous, in Kant's view, for the same reason that all principles are heteronomous: the object determining the will is set by our empirical nature (by desire) and thus ultimately serves the interests of happiness.[58] We act from duty in order to please God. We wish to please God either because we fear God's power and vengefulness or because we hope for future reward.[59]

19. KANT'S FINAL REMARKS (444–445)

In this final paragraph of Section II, Kant draws our attention both to what he believes he has already accomplished and to the task ahead of him. He tells us that by "explicating" the "generally received concept of morality" he has been able to show that "an autonomy of the will" is "unavoidably attached" to that concept, or more precisely, "lies at its basis."[60] What he has not yet shown, he says, is how the categorical imperative (a "synthetic practical proposition") is "possible" and "why it is necessary." He has not yet affirmed the law's "truth," or demonstrated that it is anything more than a "chimerical idea." Kant furthermore reminds us here that Section II, like Section I, is "analytic." We need to shed light on these obscure remarks in order to ease our transition to Section III.

19.1 On what Kant believes he has accomplished in Section II

Consider, first, Kant's assertion at (445) that he has succeeded in showing that "an autonomy of the will" lies at the basis of the "generally received concept of morality." Since he introduced the notion of autonomy rather late in Section II (beginning at (432)), this comment reflects the relatively recent achievement of the final pages of the section. The remark highlights what could reasonably be regarded as the *culminating* achievement, not merely of Section II, but of the first two sections of the *Groundwork*. The "generally received

---

[58] We should bear in mind that the interests of happiness are varied and complex, according to Kant. For an informed defense of the view that Kant's conception of happiness is not crudely hedonistic, see Andrews Reath's essay, "Hedonism, Heteronomy, and Kant's Principle of Happiness," Chapter 2 of his collection of essays, *Agency and Autonomy in Kant's Moral Philosophy*, pp. 33–66.

[59] In my Introduction (at Section 4), I say a bit more about why Kant was convinced that morality cannot have religion as its ground.

[60] I comment on Gregor's translation of this passage in a note to Section 6 of Chapter 2.

concept of morality" Kant refers to at (445) is simply another name for the "common rational moral" cognition explicitly mentioned in the title of Section I. What he claims to have demonstrated by "explicating" the "generally received concept of morality," then, is that at the basis of the common cognition with which he began Section I (the concept of a good will) is the assumption of autonomy. Thanks to his explication or analysis of the concept, we learned, first, that a will that is good acts from duty. We learned, second, that the maxims of a good will are universalizable, that is, they pass the categorical imperative test. We learned, third, that the categorical imperative is a law the pure will gives itself. We learned, fourth, that the pure will just is the capacity of autonomy. As a result of Kant's explication of the generally received concept of morality, then, we discovered that a good will has autonomy "at its basis."

19.2 What remains to be done: the project of Section III (444f.)

From his sketchy remarks at (444f.), it is difficult to determine precisely what Kant believes he still needs to do. He specifies the task ahead of him in two different ways. He says he needs to demonstrate:

(i) how a "*synthetic practical proposition*" (the categorical imperative) is "possible" and "why it is necessary,"

and

(ii) that morality is not a "phantom" or "chimerical idea."

Perhaps Kant intends these remarks as different descriptions of the same task. We can only assess this proposal with the aid of further discussion.

Kant's observation at (444), that he has not yet established the truth of the assumption that a synthetic practical proposition is possible, appears elsewhere in Section II. At (420), for example, he comments on the difficulty of demonstrating "entirely a priori the possibility of a *categorical imperative*" (420). He emphasizes the term "categorical" in this latter passage because he has just finished telling us that *no* difficulty is encountered in explaining the possibility of hypothetical imperatives. Why should a difficulty exist, however, in explaining the possibility of categorical but not of hypothetical imperatives?

As I noted back at Section 5.7, Kant links the ease with which we can explain the possibility of hypothetical imperatives to the fact that these imperatives are "analytic." Recall his discussion of imperatives of skill. A doctor wishes to help his ailing patient. In the service of that end, he ought to provide the means for doing so. His imperative is: "In order to cure my patient, I ought to provide the proper treatment." Kant believes we can easily explain the possibility of this kind of imperative in the following way: In the volition expressing the doctor's end (to cure his patient), the volition expressing the means to achieving that end is "already thought" (417). Once the end is given or presupposed, the volition expressing the means may thus be analytically deduced.[61]

The categorical imperative, Kant has told us, is a "synthetic" proposition. As such, there is presumably no such analytic connection, in the case of this kind of imperative, between the end or object willed and the means willed for attaining it. Somehow, the difficulty of proving the possibility of this imperative must be connected with this feature. But as I suggested in my earlier comments on this issue at Section 5.9, the difficulty Kant alludes to is by no means obvious. In at least one respect, establishing an analytic connection between the willing of the end and the willing of the means might seem to be *easier* in the case of the categorical imperative than in the case of hypothetical imperatives.

To see this, consider again the fact that hypothetical imperatives, on Kant's account, are relative or conditional. The ends or purposes to which they refer vary from person to person and from situation to situation. For this reason, I cannot know what you desire in advance; I cannot even really know in advance what I will desire tomorrow. We can deduce the volition expressing the means from the volition expressing an end, but we can do this only once some end is presupposed or posited, as Kant says. In the case of the categorical imperative, however, the situation is different. When I think of a categorical imperative, he writes, "I know at once what it contains" (420f.). We know in advance the end referred to in a categorical imperative because its end does *not* vary from person to person and from situation to situation. Instead, its end is universally and necessarily shared by all rational wills. But given that the end of a categorical

---

[61] Did the man claim to will the end but not the means, we would have to doubt either his sincerity or his rationality.

imperative may be known in advance, why does Kant seem to imply that we cannot also know in advance the means for attaining it? Why is it not possible to say, in this case as in the case of hypothetical imperatives, that the willing of the means is already thought in the willing of the end? Why, in other words, does Kant deny a conceptual or analytic connection between: "I will to realize object X" (where "X" is an unconditional end) and "I therefore ought to do whatever is necessary for realizing X?" The conclusion forced upon us at this point is that we have not yet successfully identified the difficulty Kant associates with proving the possibility of the categorical imperative.

Perhaps our efforts will be better rewarded if we follow a clue Kant provides in his note at (420). He reminds us there that the human will is imperfect. He suggests that *were* our will perfect, there *would* be an analytic connection between our ends or purposes and the volitions expressing the means for achieving them.[62] A perfect or infallible will, remember, necessarily wills the good; it necessarily has the good as its end or purpose. Since it necessarily wills the good as its end, it also necessarily wills the means for achieving that end. An imperfect will such as ours, however, does not necessarily will the good. We cannot simply presuppose in our own case, then, that we ever in fact will the good. Since we cannot assume that we ever will the good as our end, we also cannot assume that we will actions as means to achieving that end.

The difficulty of proving the possibility of the categorical imperative thus seems to be tied to the fact that we lack a perfect will. This fact about us poses a challenge unlike any challenge associated with proving the possibility of hypothetical imperatives. While it is true that I cannot know in advance what you desire, or even what I will desire tomorrow, I *can* know in advance (or "a priori," as Kant says) that all rational human natures desire happiness. This is a necessary fact about what Kant refers to as the "special constitution of human nature" (384, 442). The end of happiness is given by our "natural constitution" (444). Moreover, this fact about the role of happiness in our lives is confirmed by experience, since experience provides abundant examples of actions performed in the service of heteronomous

---

[62] Kant repeats this point in Section III where he claims that, if we were members of the intelligible world, all our actions "*would* always be in conformity with the autonomy of the will" (454).

ends. But as Kant has told us repeatedly in the *Groundwork*, experience is of no use to us in our effort to demonstrate that actions are ever really done from duty. (See his discussion, for example, at (407).) In the case of the categorical imperative, we thus lack the advantage that its "reality" is given in experience (419f.). The question then arises: by what *right* do we assume that the categorical imperative is valid for our will?

The challenge of this question is all the more apparent when we reflect upon all that we are presupposing when we assert that the categorical imperative is real for us – when we assert that the law really does obligate or bind our will. Most obviously, we presuppose that it is possible for us to act not just from inclination but also from duty. To act from duty, as we know, is to be motivated by a special kind a law, a law that does not derive from "the *special constitution of human nature* or the contingent circumstances in which it is placed" (442). (See also (389).) The moral law is not given by our nature as creatures susceptible to empirical or scientific study. Rather, it is a law we give ourselves as beings possessing a special capacity, the capacity Kant calls autonomy. With reference to this capacity we can demonstrate that we are not merely determined in all that we do by laws of nature over which we have no control, but that we can in addition act from laws we give ourselves as beings possessing a pure will.

The difficulty of proving the possibility of the categorical imperative is therefore linked to the difficulty of justifying this particular self-conception. To prove the possibility of the categorical imperative is in effect to prove that we are more than mere cogs in nature's machine. This is equivalent to establishing that there is indeed a point to our holding ourselves responsible for what we do, a point to attributing to ourselves genuine agency. Recalling the puzzle with which our discussion began, we can now see that the problem of proving the possibility of the categorical imperative is indeed identical, on Kant's account, to the problem of demonstrating that morality is more than a mere chimera or phantom for us.

19.3 Elaboration

We need an additional refinement of our understanding of Kant's message when he tells us at (444) that he has not yet shown how the categorical imperative is "*possible* a priori" and "why it is necessary." Consider two possible accounts of what he could have in mind by this claim:

Interpretation 1: He means that he has not yet shown that we do indeed *think* of ourselves as beings capable of respecting universal and necessary ends, beings capable of acting from duty. He has not yet shown in other words, that we do in fact take the categorical imperative as binding on our will. Otherwise put, he has not yet shown that we in fact consider ourselves as beings possessing a pure will.

Interpretation 2: He means that he has not yet shown that we are *warranted* in thinking of ourselves in the above way. He has not yet shown that we have justification in supposing that there really is a categorical imperative that commands our will. Otherwise put, he has not yet shown that we are justified in considering ourselves as beings possessing a pure will.

The evidence against Interpretation 1 is overwhelming. Throughout the *Groundwork*, Kant repeats the claim that we do consider ourselves capable of acting from duty.[63] As we have seen, he is convinced that we think of ourselves in this way even when we transgress the moral law. (See, again, his discussion at (424).) He writes in Section III that even the "most hardened scoundrel" believes himself able to act from motives that are non-heteronomous (454f.).

Interpretation 2, however, is well supported by the text. Kant observes at (425) that he has "not yet advanced so far as to prove a priori that there really is such an imperative, that there is a practical law, which commands absolutely of itself and without any incentives." By this he means that he has not yet shown that we are *entitled* to think of ourselves as capable of being motivated by the moral law. He has not yet shown, in other words, that we are justified in regarding ourselves as "necessarily bound to [the law] as a condition" (440). To put this point differently, he has not yet established our right to think of ourselves as endowed with a pure will. Since he has

---

[63] See, for example, in Section III (456): "All human beings think of themselves as having free will." For a parallel passage in the *CPrR*, see (79f.).

not yet established this, the possibility remains that morality is merely "chimerical," and that what we call "duty" is an "empty concept" (421).[64]

19.4 On why Kant's method in Section III must be "synthetic"

In his Preface, Kant indicated that the "synthetic" method of Section III is supposed to move us "forward" from an "examination" of the "supreme principle and its sources," and then "back to the common cognition in which we find it used" (392). The reference "back" to common cognition is puzzling if only because this movement is not reflected in the title of Section III: "Transition from metaphysics of morals to the critique of pure practical reason." Perhaps what Kant is telling us here is that, by the time the book is complete, he will have provided his grounding of the common cognition. He will have justified the common cognition that we are bound to the moral law and thereby demonstrated that morality is not a chimera. He will then be in a position to direct his attention back to the common cognition with which he began and declare that he has succeeded in securing its justification or ground.

But in what respect does Section III move us "forward?" What are we moving forward to? The forward movement refers to the project of finally grounding the metaphysics of morals. As Kant's title for Section III suggests, this justificatory work needs to be "prefaced" by a critique of the faculty of practical reason. That is, it calls for an argument demonstrating our right to think of ourselves as having a pure will. For the reasons we just reviewed, the demonstration cannot be empirical. As Kant states explicitly at (444), the aim is to prove that the categorical imperative is possible (and why it is necessary) "a priori." Nor can the proof be "analytic." It cannot proceed in the manner of Sections I and II by beginning from some conditioned concept and regressing to conditions of that concept's possibility. Why is it that the procedure cannot be analytic?

Kant is most explicit at (440) about what we cannot expect to determine by means of analysis. He first specifies the principle of autonomy ("choose only in such a way that the maxims of your choice

---

[64] Further evidence in favor of Interpretation 2 is provided in Section III, for example, at (449f.).

are also included as universal law in the same volition"). He then asserts that it is not possible to determine by analysis that "the will of every rational being is necessarily bound" to this rule "as a condition." What Kant means, apparently, is that this connection cannot be established by an analysis of the concepts contained in the categorical imperative. In another passage in which he discusses the synthetic character of the law, he implies that we cannot arrive at the conclusion that the law is binding on all rational wills merely by analyzing the "concept of the will of a rational being" (420).

This returns us to a point we discussed above at Section 19.2. Although Kant tells us we are warranted in concluding from analysis of the concept of a *perfect* rational being that it is "necessarily bound" to the moral law "as a condition," he claims we are not warranted in making the same claim about *every* rational will. Unlike perfect rational beings, imperfect or finite rational wills can be determined by heteronomous grounds. Mere analysis of the concept of a rational will cannot justify the conclusion, then, that imperfect rational wills are necessarily bound to the moral law. Since analysis cannot provide the proof we need, some other method of proof is required. This is why Kant insists that his method in Section III will be "synthetic."

CHAPTER 5

Section III: Transition from metaphysics of morals to the critique of pure practical reason

1. THE STRUCTURE AND DIFFICULTY OF SECTION III

We know from our discussion of Kant's concluding remarks in Section II that he understands the task of Section III of the *Groundwork* as that of proving a priori the possibility of the categorical imperative. As we have seen, he takes this task to be equivalent to that of demonstrating that morality for us is "no phantom" (445). We know, moreover, that the proof he will provide will be "synthetic" in contrast to the "analytic" demonstrations of Sections I and II.

The reader should not look for evidence of Kant's synthetic proof in the opening paragraphs of Section III, however. In these first paragraphs, Kant instead highlights key implications of the conceptual analysis he has performed in the earlier sections of the text. He tries once again to draw a clear line between the results of his discussion in the *Groundwork* so far and the work he has yet to complete.

The synthetic proof gets underway, finally, at (450). It is there that Kant sets out to *justify* our right to think of ourselves as beings possessing free will and necessarily bound to the moral law. He summarizes his argument in the section, "How is a Categorical Imperative Possible?" In the final paragraphs of Section III, he further elucidates the nature of the proof he has provided. In addition, he cautions us against making unwarranted knowledge claims about the reality of our freedom.

Of the three sections of the *Groundwork*, this final section is unquestionably the most difficult. Part of the difficulty stems from the fact that Kant is never terribly successful in his efforts to explain the nature of his synthetic proof and why such a proof is necessary. Moreover, the argument of Section III derives key premises from work he has completed elsewhere. The reader who hopes to unravel the mysteries of Section III without prior acquaintance with the *Critique of Pure Reason* is thus faced with a daunting task. Kant divides Section III with the help of a number of subheadings. I have borrowed his subheadings to organize my discussion. In order to provide my reader further guideposts with which to navigate this chapter, however, I have inserted a few subheadings of my own. Those unfamiliar with Kant's first *Critique* may benefit from consulting the background theoretical material I reviewed in my Introduction, beginning at Section 6. I recommend that that material be consulted prior to reading either Section III of the *Groundwork* or my remarks in what follows.

2. THE CONCEPT OF FREEDOM IS THE KEY TO THE EXPLANATION OF THE AUTONOMY OF THE WILL (446–447)

2.1 The connection between freedom and autonomy

Kant introduced us to the concept of autonomy in the second half of Section II. When he now defines autonomy at (447) as "the will's property of being a law to itself," he adds nothing new to his earlier characterization.[1] What *is* new in these opening paragraphs of Section III, however, is the idea that autonomy is nothing other than "freedom of the will" (447). As Kant's title for this subsection indicates, he is convinced that the concept of freedom can be of use in explaining or clarifying the concept of autonomy. The explanation depends crucially on the distinction he introduces in these first two paragraphs between the "negative" and "positive" concepts of freedom. Kant claims that the positive concept of freedom "flows from" the negative concept of freedom. His idea seems to be that the positive conception of freedom emerges from a fully developed account of the implications of the negative concept. Kant's main point in these opening paragraphs of Section III is that we cannot properly grasp the idea of autonomy unless we appreciate the concept of freedom in its fully developed (that is, positive) sense.

Understood negatively, Kant tells us, freedom is a causality independent of "alien causes *determining* it." By "alien causes," he has in

---

[1] Compare this definition at (447) with Kant's characterization of autonomy at (432).

mind laws of nature. Freedom in the negative sense, then, is a form of causality different from and independent of the causality of nature, of what he refers to here as "natural necessity." As I noted in my Introduction, Kant adheres to the view that objects of our form of experience are without exception governed by the causality of nature. On his account, nothing happens in the realm of experience that is not sufficiently determined by some antecedent cause. To be free in the "negative" sense, then, is to be independent of the laws that determine every event or happening in the realm of nature.[2] Kant implies in these paragraphs that such freedom is possible only for rational beings.

But this negative sense of freedom fails to convey what Kant identifies at (446) as the "essence" of freedom. The negative conception does not make explicit two further features of freedom, on his account. These two additional features constitute the "positive" concept of freedom. One feature is the law-governed nature of freedom. While a free act is independent of laws of nature, it is not altogether independent of law. The other feature has to do with the origin of laws of freedom. According to Kant, laws of freedom originate in the pure will. Recall that at the close of Section II he told us that when a will is heteronomously determined, it is "nature that gives law" (444). When the will is determined by laws of freedom, however, it is the pure will that gives law. When we act from laws of freedom, we bring our maxims into conformity with a law that we, as rational agents, give ourselves. Since the pure will is capable of providing a rule or law that can determine our conduct, the pure will may be said to have a kind of causality.

Adding together the above two features, we discover that freedom of the will in the positive sense is, as Kant insists here, nothing other than autonomy. It is nothing other than the capacity of the will of a rational being to give itself law. Freedom of the will in this positive sense is identical to autonomy because, on Kant's definition, autonomy just is "the will's property of being a law to itself" (447).[3]

---

[2] In his Introduction to the *Metaphysics of Morals*, Kant characterizes freedom in the negative sense as "independence from being *determined* by sensible impulses" (213). See also his Introduction to the *MM* (226).

[3] In his Introduction to the *MM*, Kant writes that freedom in the positive sense is "the ability of pure reason to itself be practical" (214).

The fully developed idea of freedom of the will thus helps us better grasp the concept of autonomy.

2.2 A free will is a will under moral laws (447)

Now that Kant has drawn our attention to features of the positive concept of freedom, he is in a position to move on to assert a connection between freedom and morality. If "freedom of the will is presupposed," he says, "morality together with its principle follows from it by mere analysis of its concept." Kant has just argued that a free will, in the sense he intends, is an autonomous will: it is a will that not only is independent of natural necessity but can also give itself law. His claim now is that the law the free will gives itself is nothing other than the supreme moral law. He believes it is possible to establish this connection simply by analyzing the concept of a free will.

Kant's reasoning relies on the following assumptions, all of which he argued for in Section II.[4] A will that is autonomous is a will that has the capacity to give itself law. The law the autonomous or free will gives itself has its source in the faculty Kant calls the pure will, the faculty that is "nothing other than" practical reason (412). Because the law of the free will has its source in practical reason, it is valid for all beings that possess practical reason. The law that qualifies as having this kind of validity therefore commands more than merely contingent ends, ends valid for some rational natures but not others. As valid for all rational natures, the law commands ends that could be willed by all rational natures. As Kant puts it here, the law commands that we "act on no other maxim than that which can also have as object itself as universal law." The law the free will gives itself, in other words, is the categorical imperative.[5]

By means of the above line of reasoning, Kant believes he is warranted in asserting at (447) that a will that is free (in the fully analyzed or positive sense) and a will "under moral laws" are "one and the same." His phrase "under moral laws" should not mislead us. In referring to "moral laws," in this context, he is not suddenly invoking

---

[4] See esp. (426f.). I discussed these points in Chapter 4 (at Section 9.1).
[5] Strictly speaking, on Kant's account, the moral law needs to be specified as a command only for *finite* rational wills.

a set of standards *other* than the standard supplied by the categorical imperative. Rather, he has in mind the particular duties (the particular categorical imperatives) that have their basis or justification in the supreme moral law. Furthermore, in asserting the equivalence of a free will and a will under moral laws, Kant does not mean to imply that a free will always acts from duty. Although he does not address this point here, it is clear from his remarks in other contexts that a free will, on his conception, can choose to transgress the moral law.[6] Kant does not hold, then, that we only express our freedom when we act morally. In his view, a free or pure will is a will that "stands under" law in the sense that it is always *subject to* the standard of the categorical imperative. More precisely, such a will considers itself bound by the moral law; it recognizes the law as valid for it. As free, however, it can choose whether or not to act from duty. A free or pure will, that is to say, need not always be a good will.

2.3 *The principle of morality is a synthetic proposition (447)*

The connections Kant has drawn so far – between freedom and autonomy, and then between a free will and a will under moral laws – have resulted from his analysis of these concepts. But Kant believes he has now reached the limit of what analysis is able to reveal. He therefore turns his attention to the complicated issue of the synthetic status of the supreme moral law. He begins with the following observation:

> [T]he principle of morality – that an absolutely good will is that whose maxim can always contain itself regarded as a universal law – is nonetheless always a synthetic proposition; for, by analysis of the concept of an absolutely good will that property of its maxim cannot be discovered.

We first need to be certain we understand what Kant identifies here as a synthetic proposition. He indicates that it is the "principle of morality" that is synthetic. Since he already identified the moral law as an a priori synthetic proposition in earlier passages of the *Groundwork*, this remark should come as no surprise.[7] His formulation of the principle of morality in this passage is awkward, but we can simplify

---

[6] Kant is most explicit about this in the early pages of Book One of the *Religion*, where he argues that the disposition to evil is the product of free choice.

[7] See, for example, (420, 444).

it as follows: The principle commands that the maxims of an absolutely good will always be fit as universal law. To phrase the principle differently, it states that an absolutely good will ought always to act on maxims that are fit as universal law.[8]

Our difficulties multiply considerably, however, when we try to grasp the reasoning behind Kant's insistence upon the "synthetic" nature of this principle. A proposition is synthetic, he writes here, if it contains two cognitions that are "bound together by their connection with a third." So the principle of morality is synthetic rather than analytic, presumably, because it is not possible, merely by analyzing the concept of an absolutely good will, to derive the "cognition" that the maxim of such a will ought always to be universalizable. That is to say, we cannot, merely by analyzing the concept of an absolutely good will, demonstrate that such a will is obligated always to act from duty. Because the two cognitions are not analytically or conceptually connected, we need some other means of establishing their necessary connection. Kant indicates here that the argument he will provide relies on the "positive concept of freedom." Somehow, the positive concept of freedom will furnish the "third cognition" that connects the other two.

Kant is quite cognizant of the obscurity of these points; he acknowledges that he cannot set out to establish the synthetic nature of the principle of morality without "further preparation." Because his own formulation in this passage of the problem he seeks to solve is not terribly helpful, we are forced to seek elucidation elsewhere in the *Groundwork*. Fortunately, other passages in the text can aid us in understanding the sense in which the argument he seeks has to be synthetic rather than analytic.

At (440), Kant writes that we cannot show by analysis that "every rational being is necessarily bound to [the categorical imperative] as a condition." At (426), he suggests that analysis is unable to show that it is a necessary law "*for all rational beings*" always to appraise their actions by the standard of universalizability. It is not possible, he

---

[8] Note that Kant does not formulate the principle of morality in this quoted passage as a command. Again, his view is that the moral law must be formulated as a command only for imperfect wills such as ours. What Kant is articulating here, apparently, is that the moral law is valid for all rational wills, including perfect wills that do not have to be commanded.

says, to establish this merely from an analysis of the "concept of a rational being as such." Comparing these two passages with the above-quoted remark from (447), we notice the following key difference: The subject of Kant's remark at (447) is the "absolutely good will." In the passages at (440) and (426), however, his subject is "every rational being." It thus seems that there is a change in what he says analysis cannot show: His message at (447) is that analysis cannot show that an absolutely good will ought always to act on universalizable maxims. In the earlier passages, his point is that analysis cannot prove that rational beings are bound to the moral law. Is this difference significant?

Consider, first, Kant's substitution of "absolutely good will," at (447), for "rational being." We are likely to regard this change as significant if we make the mistake of interpreting Kant's use of the phrase "absolutely good will," in the above-quoted remark, to refer to a will that is infallible or perfect. It might then seem that Kant's attention shifts from a concern, in the earlier passages, to determine what analysis is able to discover in the concept of *all* rational wills (including imperfect rational wills such as ours), to a concern with what can be discovered by analyzing the narrower concept of an infallible or perfect will. But this interpretation cannot be correct for the following reason: If by "absolutely good will," at (447), Kant means nothing other than the perfect will, then we have no way to account for the problem he alerts us to there. Recall his remark back at (420*) that, from a mere analysis of the concept of a perfect or infallible rational will, we *can* demonstrate a necessary connection to the cognition that its maxim can always "contain itself regarded as universal law." We can demonstrate such a connection, because a perfect will, on his definition, is "necessitated" to act in conformity with the moral law (414). Kant's concern at (447), however, is that we *cannot* establish this necessary connection by analyzing the concept at hand, the concept of an absolutely good will. His concern at (447) is evidence, then, that he does not intend the phrase "absolutely good will," in this context, as simply another name for the perfect or infallible will.

If the absolutely good will Kant refers to at (447) is not equivalent to the perfect or infallible will, in what sense is it "absolutely" good? The most defensible answer to this question is this: This will is "absolutely good," according to Kant, in virtue of its *capacity* to act from duty. In other words, Kant simply means by the "absolutely good will," in this context, the pure will. His use of the phrase "absolutely good will" is not consistent in the *Groundwork*, but he sometimes uses it in this way.[9] In Section I, for example, he introduces us to the idea of a will that is "absolutely" good in the sense of "good without limitation" (393, 402). The will he describes in that early discussion is clearly not a perfect will; unlike a perfect will, it can act from inclination. It can act from inclination, but it is also capable of acting from duty. When it acts from duty (as in the case of the grieving philanthropist), its capacity for goodness is on display. In such instances, we are warranted in judging that this will is good.[10]

In a passage in Section II, Kant writes of the "absolutely good will" that it has a worth "raised above all price" because its principle of action is "free from all influences of contingent grounds" (426). Although this description does not by itself allow us to determine whether he means to refer to the perfect or to the imperfect will, it is noteworthy that in the passage in which it appears, Kant is leading up to his introduction of the concept of a pure will. As we know, he defines the pure will not as a will that necessarily acts from the moral law, but as a will that has the "capacity" to do so. The pure will *can* be good; it *can* free itself from "all influences of contingent grounds."

There is thus reason for supposing that the "absolutely good will" Kant writes of at (447) is not the perfect or infallible will which necessarily acts from duty, but rather the pure will, the will which is merely capable of acting from duty.[11] One implication of this proposal is that it suggests that the subject of his remarks at (447), namely, the "absolutely good will," is no different from the "rational will" he refers to in the passages at (440 and 426).

---

[9] One passage in which Kant does *not* use it in this way is at (429), where he explicitly identifies the absolutely good will with the holy will.

[10] In Section I, for example, it is not always clear whether Kant means by "absolutely good will" the capacity to act from duty (the pure will) or the will that acts from duty (the good will). Some commentators suggest that by the pure will and the good will, Kant means the same thing. See, for example, Allen Wood's essay, "The Good without Limitation," in Horn and Schönecker, eds., *Groundwork for the Metaphysics of Morals*, p. 32.

[11] For further evidence in support of the thesis that by "absolutely good will," at (447), Kant does not mean a perfect or infallible will, note that in the final pages of Section II he tells us that the "absolutely good will" has to be commanded in morality; its principle, he says, "must be a categorical imperative" (444). A perfect or infallible will, remember, does not need to be commanded, on Kant's account. For such a will, then, the moral law is not formulated as an imperative.

Comparing the passages again, recall that at (447), Kant tells us that analysis cannot establish that an absolutely good will is morally required always to act on universalizable maxims. As I have suggested, this point follows from the fact that the absolutely good will, for Kant, is not a perfect will. A will that is absolutely good but not perfect is capable of acting from duty, but it does not necessarily act from duty. It can respond to other motivating forces. The human rational will is imperfect in that it is sensibly affected. Nature, that is to say, works on us; it demands the satisfaction of our various inclinations. In light of this fact about our imperfect rational natures, the question arises: What reason is there for supposing that moral requirements are valid for us? Or, what reason is there for supposing that the moral law necessarily binds our will?

The problem Kant identifies at (447) is thus merely a reformulation of the problem he raised in the earlier passages at (440 and 426). In the earlier passages, he claimed that analysis cannot demonstrate that all rational beings – including imperfect or fallible rational beings – are bound to the moral law. But the claim that analysis cannot prove that all rational beings are bound to the law is equivalent, for Kant, to the claim that analysis cannot prove that the law is valid for all rational natures. If analysis cannot prove that the moral law is valid for all rational natures, it also cannot prove that the absolutely good will (the pure will) is morally required always to act on universalizable maxims.

To summarize the results of our discussion: Kant's complaint at (447) is that we so far lack an argument demonstrating that all rational beings, including imperfect rational beings, are necessarily bound to the moral law. In the case of perfect wills, the argument is supplied by conceptual analysis. This is because, on Kant's account, we can derive from our analysis of the concept of a perfect will the idea that such a will necessarily acts from duty. In the case of imperfect or fallible wills such as ours, however, a different kind of demonstration is required. Kant's chief objective in Section III is to furnish that demonstration.

3. FREEDOM MUST BE PRESUPPOSED AS A PROPERTY OF THE WILL OF ALL RATIONAL BEINGS (447–448)

We first need to be clear about the reasoning behind the assertion expressed in Kant's title for this subsection. Why does he tell us that freedom must be presupposed as a property of the will of all rational beings? We can discover the answer to this question only by considering one by one the claims he makes in this section.

3.1 Morality must hold for all rational beings (447)

This is not a new assertion; we have encountered it a number of times in the *Groundwork*, beginning in Kant's Preface (at (389)). Note the word "all" here. The moral law is valid for *all* practically rational beings, for *all* beings endowed with a pure will, not just for human rational beings. The explanation Kant provides for this claim at (447) is that the moral law serves as a law for us only "*as* rational beings" (my emphasis). It is only in virtue of the fact that we are practically rational, in other words, that we (and all other rational beings) stand under moral laws. This is not the case for "non-rational" beings, since such beings are governed only by "natural necessity" (446). Although Kant asserts here that morality holds for all rational beings, he has just reminded us in his previous paragraph that he has yet to provide an *argument* in support of this claim.

3.2 Morality must be derived solely from the property of freedom (447)

By this remark, Kant intends to draw our attention to the fact that moral judgment and moral imputation are out of place unless freedom is presupposed. We can have no warrant for asserting that morality must hold for all rational beings, in other words, unless we presuppose that rational beings have freedom. For beings governed solely by natural necessity, the moral "ought" is without meaning. I pointed out in my Introduction that the freedom Kant has in mind as a condition of the possibility of morality is something other than mere independence of external constraint. As Kant emphasizes us in these first paragraphs of Section III, the freedom he is referring to is independence from natural necessity altogether. (It has, in addition, the "positive" features we reviewed above.)

3.3 Freedom must be presupposed as a property of the will of all rational beings (447)

We are now in a position to explain Kant's chosen subtitle. Why must freedom be presupposed? It must be presupposed in order to ground or warrant the two assumptions we just considered. As we just saw, the very possibility of moral imputation depends on the presupposition of freedom. In addition, the presupposition of freedom is necessary if we are to justify the claim that morality holds or is valid for all rational nature.

3.4 From presupposition to proof (447f.)

Kant quickly moves from the assertion that freedom must be "presupposed" as a property of the will of all rational beings, to the assertion that we need to *prove* that freedom is a property of all rational beings. Why is a proof required?

First, remember that Kant's ultimate goal, in Section III, is to demonstrate a necessary connection between the idea of the will of a rational being and the idea that such a will is bound to the moral law. Establishing this connection, as we saw, is no challenge in the case of a will that is perfect. It *is* a challenge, however, in the case of an imperfect will such as ours. While no one doubts that our will is frequently motivated by the desire to satisfy the appetites of inclination, it is by no means self-evident that our will can also be motivated by duty. What grounds might there be, then, for supposing that human wills ever respond to anything other than their naturally given desires? To borrow from the way Kant phrases this question in his Preface: Why should we think of our will as even capable of acting "completely determined from a priori principles without any empirical motives" (390)? What justifies us in assuming, in other words, that we have a pure will?

As for the kind of proof that will suffice, Kant reminds us here of a point he has insisted upon repeatedly in the text, namely, that we cannot demonstrate the reality of our freedom by relying on "certain supposed experiences of human nature." As he noted back at (407), observations of human behavior can furnish no certain insight into the "inner principles" that motivate us. Actions that appear motivated by duty may actually be intended to serve the interests of self-love. Appeals to experience are therefore of no help in demonstrating the reality of freedom. As we know, Kant in addition rejects a second strategy of proof. We cannot demonstrate merely by analysis of the concept of a rational being that such a being either is necessarily bound to duty or ever really acts from duty. Analysis is thus of no use to us in our effort to demonstrate that rational beings are capable of acting from duty and therefore free. Since neither experience nor conceptual analysis can demonstrate that freedom is "something real in ourselves and in human nature," some other method of proof is required (449).

3.5 *Every being that cannot act except under the idea of freedom is really free in a practical respect (448)*

Here we have a first indication of the structure of the argument Kant will deploy in his effort to establish the reality of our freedom. He gives us a clue in the following passage:

I say now: every being that cannot act otherwise than *under the idea of freedom* is just because of that really free in a practical respect, that is, all laws that are inseparably bound up with freedom hold for him just as if his will had been validly pronounced free also in itself and in theoretical philosophy.

In this passage, Kant asserts that if there really is a being that cannot act otherwise than "under the idea of freedom," then that being is "really free in a practical respect." He does not suggest that we yet have any warrant for supposing that there *are* beings that "cannot act otherwise than under the idea of freedom." His point is merely that *if* there are, then it follows that such beings are "really free in a practical respect."

What does it mean to be free in a "practical respect?" In a rational nature that has a will, Kant writes, "we think of a reason that is practical, that is, has causality with respect to its objects." A rational being with a will, then, does not merely think; it also acts. Such a being is equipped with a pure will, with the faculty Kant calls practical reason. Kant wants to convince us that practical reason is a faculty of freedom. Its laws are not given by nature; they do not come into being as effects of "alien impulses." Practical reason is a faculty of freedom in that it is the source or author of its own laws or principles. It has "causality with respect to its objects," as he says, because it can determine our will.[12] In determining our will, practical reason in effect governs our actions; it brings new conduct into being.

What does Kant have in mind by a being that "cannot act otherwise than under the idea of freedom?" To act "under the idea of freedom" is to think of oneself in a certain way. It is to regard oneself not just as a product of the determination of laws of nature, but also as capable of freedom or as possessing the faculty of practical reason.

In the above-quoted passage, Kant explicitly asserts that we can infer a conclusion about the reality of our freedom from the idea of ourselves as free. A being who "cannot act otherwise than *under the idea of freedom*," he says, is "because of that really free in a practical respect." On the face of it, this argument is not terribly compelling. I can surely regard myself as Cleopatra without, in fact, being Cleopatra. So why does Kant suppose that he can prove the reality of our freedom merely from the fact that we think of ourselves as free? Obviously, we have more work to do before we can answer this question.

4. OF THE INTEREST ATTACHING TO THE IDEAS OF MORALITY (448–453)

Kant covers a great deal of ground in this next difficult subsection. It is here that he finally offers us his demonstration of the reality of freedom. Because of the length and complexity of this subsection, I add headings of my own to those he provides in the text.

4.1 On how it is possible that we subject ourselves to the moral law (449)

We have just seen that the argument Kant intends to offer to establish that freedom is "something real in ourselves and in

---

[12] See Kant's description of the faculty of practical reason in the *CPrR*, for example, at (42) and (46). In the latter passage, he says that practical reason can determine the will "immediately" – without, that is, help from any empirical incentives.

human nature" relies on the premise that we regard ourselves in a certain way, namely, as acting under the idea of freedom. One of Kant's objectives in the first paragraphs of this subsection is to ask how this way of regarding ourselves is possible. What could support or warrant this self-conception?

Kant begins with the question: Why ought I subject myself to the moral law simply as "a rational being?" His phrasing of this question is misleading because it seems to suggest that he believes that I, as well as other rational beings, need to be *persuaded* to subject myself to the moral law. As just noted, however, his view is instead that, as a practically rational being, I necessarily take the law to be a valid constraint on my will. The question he is really asking here, then, is how it is *possible* that I, along with all other rational beings, consider myself subject to the law. The answer cannot be, he says, that I am "impelled" by some "interest." The claim that I am impelled to respect the law is equivalent to the claim that I am determined to act by my natural constitution. This kind of determination is heteronomous. Although heteronomous determination explains why I act from hypothetical imperatives, it cannot explain how it is possible for me to act from the categorical imperative.

I "must," nonetheless, "necessarily take an interest" in the law, Kant says. I "must" take an interest in the law, presumably, because if I did not, there would be no way of accounting for the fact that I am indeed sometimes motivated to act from it. But, again, what explanation can be provided for how I can be motivated to act from it, or for why I sometimes limit my maxims by the law? If I am not "impelled" by an interest in the law, how is my taking an interest in it possible?

It is essential that we understand why Kant considers this question particularly pressing. He is asking, in effect, how it is that a rational human will can be determined to act by something other than its natural constitution, by something other than the incentives nature has given it to secure its own wellbeing or happiness. It is undeniable that we do in fact act to satisfy our desire for happiness, and that as beings "affected by sensibility" we are determined by natural impulses (449). But how is it that we can also be motivated to act by "incentives of a different kind?" How, in other words, is it possible for rational human wills to be moved by what Kant refers to as reason in its practical use?

4.2 *Kant draws attention to a limitation of his discussion so far (449)*

Instead of directly responding to the question he has just asked, Kant brings to the foreground various presuppositions underlying it:

It seems ... that in the idea of freedom we have actually only presupposed the moral law, namely the principle of the autonomy of the will itself, and could not prove by itself its reality and objective necessity.

It is odd that Kant says here that he has presupposed the moral law in the idea of freedom. In light of his remarks in the previous paragraphs, it would seem more accurate to identify what he has presupposed by reversing this formulation – by saying that he has presupposed freedom in the idea of the moral law. Recall that in the first sentence of this subsection, he announced that he had traced the concept of morality back to the idea of freedom (448f.). He had argued that freedom must be presupposed as a condition of thinking of ourselves as subject to morality. So why does he now tell us that "in the idea of freedom" he has "presupposed the moral law?" We know the sense in which he has presupposed the idea of freedom, but how has he also presupposed the moral law?

The answer to this question is that Kant *has* been assuming all along that we think of ourselves as bound to the moral law. Starting with the Preface of the *Groundwork*, he has been assuming that we do in fact accept the categorical imperative as a valid limiting condition on our maxims. Kant has no intention of retracting this assumption. Not only has he no intention of retracting it, he reasserts it at the beginning of the very next paragraph (at (450)): "We do indeed find that we can take an interest in a personal characteristic that brings with it no interest at all in a condition." His point here is that it is indeed the case that we can be motivated by something other than the desire to achieve a merely conditioned end, an end of inclination or happiness. We derive our sense of personal worth, even, from the fact that we take an interest in acting from duty, from the fact that we accept the categorical imperative as a valid test of our maxims.

Kant is therefore correct to observe that he has all along been presupposing that we grant the validity of the moral law. He has no doubt that rational nature, including human rational nature, thinks of itself as subject to moral laws and as thus also capable of freedom. But from the fact that we think of ourselves as bound and motivated by moral laws, it of course does not follow that we are *entitled* to think of ourselves in this way. The truth of the matter might be that we suffer from a bad case of self-deception, and that the incentives that motivate us are never anything other than heteronomous. The truth might be, in other words, that we never answer to anything but hypothetical imperatives. Kant has good reason to worry, then, about the *grounds* we have for thinking of ourselves as bound by the moral law. He knows he has not yet provided any justification for this self-conception. He has not yet demonstrated that freedom is "something real in ourselves and in human nature" (449).

4.3 A worry about circular reasoning (450–453)

A central theme of the next eight paragraphs, beginning at (450), is Kant's concern that he has perhaps taken for granted assumptions to which he is not entitled. That is, he considers the possibility that his reasoning has been circular – that he has presupposed what he set out to prove.[13] He makes this concern explicit at (450):

We take ourselves as free in the order of efficient causes in order to think ourselves under moral laws in the order of ends; and we afterwards think ourselves as subject to these laws because we have ascribed to ourselves freedom of will.

For the sake of making the suspected circularity perspicuous, we can rewrite the first phrase of this complicated passage as follows:
i. We presuppose that we are free in order to justify thinking of ourselves as subject to moral laws.

The point here is that, were we not free, we would have to concede that we are merely complicated machines, determined in all that we think and do by laws of nature. The assumption of freedom, in other words, is a condition of the possibility of morality. This is an assumption to which Kant has frequently drawn our attention.

But then the question naturally arises: What *justification* do we have for thinking of ourselves as subject to moral laws? Or, what justification do we have for supposing that the categorical imperative

---

[13] Kant worries, in other words, that he has committed the fallacy of "begging the question." He wonders whether he has assumed the validity of the moral law as a "*petitio principii*" (453).

really binds our will? The point Kant wishes to convey in the above-quoted passage is that it will *not* do to answer this question in the following way:

ii. We are justified in thinking of ourselves as subject to moral laws because we have presupposed that we are free.

Kant's point here is that we cannot *justify* the assumption that we are subject to morality by pointing out that the thought of ourselves as subject to morality relies on the presupposition of freedom. He is not calling into question the claim that freedom must be presupposed as a condition of the possibility of morality. His point instead is that he still has work to do. He has not yet provided *evidence* to support our *right* to think of ourselves as free. He has not yet given us grounds for assuming, in other words, that freedom is real for us.

Kant provides a second formulation of the circle at (453):

[W]e perhaps took as a ground the idea of freedom only for the sake of the moral law, so that we could afterwards infer the latter in turn from freedom.

The worry expressed in this remark is no different from the one expressed in the passage at (450). Once again, Kant's concern is that he has so far simply presupposed that we are free in order to provide a ground for our thinking of ourselves as bound to the moral law. To merely presuppose we are free, however, is not to provide a ground for anything. Kant therefore suggests that he has so far only begged the question of the reality of freedom in order to argue that we are justified in thinking of ourselves as subject to moral laws. He alerts us again to the fact that he has not yet supplied an argument demonstrating the reality of our freedom. Since he has so far failed to do this, morality and its supreme principle remain without a ground. Kant thus has not yet accomplished what he said in his Preface was a chief task of the *Groundwork*: to establish or justify the supreme principle of morality (392).

4.4 Freedom and the will's own lawgiving as reciprocal concepts (450)

Although Kant concedes that he has not yet provided a ground either for the moral law or for the assumption of human freedom, he notes that he has nonetheless accomplished "something considerable" by drawing our attention to the way in which freedom and morality are connected. He has shown that we cannot think of ourselves as subject to moral laws except by presupposing that we are free, and that when we think of ourselves as free we imply that we are subject to moral laws. He tells us at (450) that the concepts of freedom and that of the "will's own lawgiving" are "reciprocal." In his words, the two concepts are "apparently different representations of the same object." Because these concepts are reciprocal, moreover, neither can "be used to explain the other" or "furnish a ground for the other." Since Kant does not explain in the *Groundwork* what it means for concepts to be "reciprocal," we once again have to look elsewhere for guidance.

In his *Jäsche Logic*, Kant defines as "reciprocal" concepts that have the same "sphere" or extension.[14] This definition makes sense of the example he gives us in the *Groundwork* at (450). He asks us to consider "different fractions of equal value" – for instance, 783/783 and 5/5. If we reduce each of these fractions to its "lowest expression," we discover that each is equivalent to 1/1. By reducing the fractions, we learn that the fractions are reciprocal in that they have the same sphere. Each, that is to say, is a different representation of the same object. The concepts of freedom and of the will's own lawgiving are likewise reciprocal, Kant claims, because they are at bottom "both autonomy." This was the point he took pains to emphasize in the opening paragraphs of Section III. If we attend to the "positive" features of the concept of freedom, he argued there, we learn that freedom of the will is nothing other than autonomy (447).

5. THE SOLUTION TO THE CIRCULARITY PROBLEM: REGARDING HUMAN NATURE FROM TWO STANDPOINTS (450–453)

5.1 Recapitulation: Kant's task in Section III

Before moving on to consider the solution Kant poses to the circularity problem, it will be useful to review once again the way in which he understands his overall project in Section III. Simply put,

---

[14] *Jäsche Logic* §12.

he is worried about a problem generated by the fact that the human will is not infallible or perfect. Were our will perfect, it would be possible prove by analysis a necessary connection between our will (our nature as practical beings) and morality. By means of analysis, we could in other words prove that the maxims of our will can always be regarded as universal law. Since our will is *not* perfect, however, we have no warrant for claiming that the moral law is valid for us. We thus need some way to demonstrate that this is so. By the end of his discussion at (450), Kant believes that if he can establish the reality of our freedom, he will have completed his proof. He relies on the following reasoning:

i. If we can establish the reality of freedom for human rational beings, we will have demonstrated that even human rational beings are necessarily bound to the moral law.

ii. We will have demonstrated that even human rational beings are necessarily bound to the law because a "free will and a will under moral laws are one and the same" (447).

iii. A free will and a will under moral laws are one and the same because:

a. to be free in the positive sense is just to be capable of giving laws to oneself (to be autonomous) (447).

b. the law that the autonomous will gives itself is the supreme moral law or categorical imperative (447).

By the end of (450), then, the task ahead of Kant is clear: he must demonstrate the reality of freedom for human nature. (He explicitly indicates that this is his task at the beginning of (449).)

5.2 *The two standpoint strategy (450ff.)*

Recall that at (448) Kant gave us a first clue as to how his argument for the reality of our freedom would proceed:

I say now: every being that cannot act otherwise than *under the idea of freedom* is just because of that really free in a practical respect.

Kant includes human rational wills among those that "cannot act otherwise than under the idea of freedom." He asserts in a passage at (455), for example, that "[a]ll human beings think of themselves as having free will." As we have seen, he takes this to be an indisputable fact about us – a fact true even of the "most hardened scoundrel." Even the scoundrel recognizes that her actions are other than they both could and ought to be. She thus acknowledges the validity of the moral law as well as her freedom to act from it or not (454).[15]

To repeat a question we asked back at Section 3.5: Even if we grant Kant's assumption that we necessarily regard ourselves as free, why should we take it to follow from this fact that we are "really free in a practical respect?" As it turns out, Kant does not expect to convince us of the soundness of this argument merely as it is stated in the remark quoted above from (448). He is aware that the argument as it is stated there is incomplete. Its persuasiveness depends on further premises he has not yet brought into the foreground.

As we observed in our earlier consideration of the argument, the claim that we are beings that cannot act otherwise than under the idea of freedom is obviously a claim about how we think about ourselves. It is crucial that we notice, however, that the claim is more than that. It is, for Kant, a claim about how we *must* think of ourselves. Kant, in other words, believes that this self-conception is somehow unavoidable or necessary. He reasons that if he can persuade us of its necessity, his work will be done. He will have established, by means of his synthetic method, the reality of our freedom.

What more is there to say, then, about the premise of the argument, namely, the assumption that we *necessarily* regard ourselves as acting under the idea of freedom? This premise is equivalent to the assumption that we necessarily regard ourselves as more than complex machines determined in all that we think and do by laws of nature. But in what sense *must* we think of ourselves in this way? If our answer to this question is that unless we think of ourselves as free, we cannot provide for the possibility of morality, we run into the circularity problem Kant alerted us to earlier. The answer Kant gives to the question therefore takes a very different form. What he says is something like this: We must think of ourselves as acting under the idea of freedom. The reason we must think of ourselves in this way is because the alternative

---

[15] For parallel passages in the *CPrR*, see (79).

(namely, the idea that we are merely biological machines) is unsustainable. His answer rests on convincing us, then, of the inadequacy of the alternative self-conception. The conception of ourselves as nothing other than machines is inadequate, in his view, if it is taken to be a *sufficient* account of our nature. In the paragraphs beginning at the end of (450), Kant thus claims that we instead have to regard ourselves *both* as creatures determined in all that we do by natural laws *and* as capable of freedom. There are good reasons, on his account, for thinking of ourselves in each of these ways. Both self-conceptions or standpoints are legitimate or well grounded, and neither by itself is sufficient as an account of our nature.

Kant introduces the idea of two standpoints at (450f.). From the first standpoint, he says, we think of ourselves as "causes efficient a priori"; from the second, we think of ourselves as "effects that we see before our eyes." For the sake of simplicity, I refer in what follows to the first standpoint as the "standpoint of freedom." From this standpoint we regard ourselves as autonomous, as endowed with the causality of practical reason by means of which we give ourselves law. I refer to the second standpoint as the "standpoint of nature." From this second point of view, we regard ourselves as objects of nature, observable by the senses, and wholly determined by natural laws.

I move on, now, to offer a more expansive description of each of these standpoints. Following that, I consider Kant's reasons for finding the standpoint of nature inadequate. Since this is material I covered in my Introduction, I will be repeating some of the main points of that discussion.

5.3 The standpoint of nature

The first thing to bear in mind about the system described by this standpoint is that it is thoroughly deterministic. From within the standpoint of nature, the standpoint Kant often refers to as the "world of sense," there is no freedom. Everything that happens is the product of antecedent causal forces. By causal forces, Kant has in mind the most general laws of nature (laws of Newtonian mechanics), laws to which the special sciences such as biology, psychology, and chemistry must conform. Objects determined by these laws are objects of possible experience, or as Kant calls them, "appearances."

As we know, an appearance, on Kant's definition, is an object given in space and time. Outer appearances are both spatially and temporally extended; inner experiences (such as the joy I now feel in anticipation of a hot fudge sundae) are merely in time. Kant identifies space and time as "a priori forms of intuition." They are a priori in that they are in us prior to any sense experience. We bring them to, rather than abstract them from, experience. Furthermore, space and time are forms of intuition as opposed to forms of thought. Whereas a priori concepts ("categories") place constraints on how objects may be thought, a priori forms of intuition condition how objects must be given to us in sensation. We can only theoretically cognize (versus merely think about) objects if they are both thought through the categories and given through the forms of space and time. Another way of putting this point is to say that the only possible objects of theoretical knowledge are appearances.

When we consider human subjects as "effects that we see before our eyes," we consider them as possible objects of experience, as appearances. To consider human subjects in this way is to think of all their properties, including their actions and intentions, as caused by nature. As an appearance, or as belonging to the "world of sense," a human subject is programmed by nature to seek its own happiness or well-being; it is heteronomously determined in all that it does. It has no free will.

5.4 The standpoint of freedom

If we consider objects in abstraction from our forms of intuition, what remains, Kant tells us, are things in themselves. Although thinkable, things in themselves are outside space and time and therefore not possible objects of experience. An example Kant frequently cites of an object that is not a possible object of experience is God. If we assume, as Kant does, that God is a being that transcends space and time, then God is not a proper object of scientific investigation. Instead, God is an object of practical knowledge or faith.

Kant's analysis of the concept of free will is the same. Free will, on his account, is nowhere to be found in the realm of nature. It is not a natural or empirical property of human subjects. It belongs only to subjects conceived as members of what he now refers to as the "intellectual world" or "world of understanding."[16] As members of the intellectual world, subjects are neither in space nor in time. As free, they possess a special, non-empirical form of causality. In these paragraphs of Section III, Kant describes this special form of causality as a "pure activity" or "spontaneity" (452). A free will is a spontaneous form of causality in that it has the power to initiate a causal series from a standpoint outside time.[17]

5.5 On the limits of the standpoint of nature (451–463)

As I pointed out in my Introduction, Kant never challenges the idea that freedom is nowhere to be discovered in the realm of nature. He is utterly committed to the view that nature or the world of sense is a deterministic system. He does, however, insist that the standpoint of nature is incomplete or limited in some significant way. This latter claim is the cornerstone of his argument that we are both entitled to think of ourselves under the idea of freedom and "must" think of ourselves in this way.

In my Introduction, I reviewed two of Kant's arguments for establishing the reality of human freedom. The first concludes on theoretical grounds that we are warranted in thinking of ourselves as free. The second demonstrates, again on theoretical grounds, that we have no option but to think of ourselves as free. We can summarize the first argument as follows: Kant is convinced that in the *Critique of Pure*

---

[16] At (452), Kant draws our attention to the distinction in his system between the faculty of reason and the faculty of understanding. The faculty of understanding, on his account, is the faculty of concepts, including the a priori concepts he identifies as "categories." The categories have the function of unifying the content given to us in sensibility into a thinkable content. Their valid application, from the standpoint of theoretical cognition, is thus to appearances. The faculty of reason, however, is the faculty of "ideas." Ideas refer to objects *not* given in sensation, for example, objects such as God, freedom, and immortality. As Kant points out at (452), reason in a certain respect enjoys a greater independence from realm of sense than the understanding. Since its objects are not given in sensation, reason "goes far beyond anything that sensibility can ever afford it."

[17] As Kant explains at A 551/B 579 of the *CPR*, "The causality of reason in the intelligible character *does not arise* or start working at a certain time in producing an effect. For then it would itself be subject to the natural law of appearances, to the extent that this law determines causal series in time, and its causality would then be nature and not freedom."

Reason he has laid out the necessary and a priori conditions of human experience. He has demonstrated that objects of sense must be given to us via the a priori forms of intuition, space, and time, and that they must be thought through a priori concepts or categories. At (451) of the *Groundwork*, he calls our attention to an important implication of this account. It follows from this account of the conditions of human experience, he writes, that we are able to "cognize objects only as they affect us and we remain ignorant of what they may be in themselves." Although we can know objects as they appear to us, that is, as they are given to us in space and time, we can have no warrant for claiming to know objects considered apart from our forms of sensibility. We thus cannot know objects as they are "in themselves."

Kant is confident that he has established a necessary fact about us, namely, that we intuit or sense objects through the a priori forms of space and time. At the same time, he acknowledges that he has no means of establishing that our forms of sensibility are the only forms there are. He has no grounds, in other words, for dogmatically ruling out the possibility that other beings sense objects or experience nature differently than we do. This recognition of the limits of what we can theoretically know is precisely what permits speculation about other forms of experience. It opens up the possibility that the causality of nature as we experience it may not be the only form of causality there is. Kant reminds us of this point in Section III of the *Groundwork* when he writes that the "world of sense" may be "very different according to the difference of sensibility in various observers of the world" (451). Since the causality of nature may not be the only form of causality there is, we are permitted to speculate about a causality of freedom. We can never establish theoretically that we have freedom, but we are nonetheless allowed on theoretical grounds to think of ourselves as free.

Kant's second argument relies on the premise that theoretical or scientific inquiry is not self-sufficient. At the basis of theoretical inquiry are assumptions it lacks the resources to justify. It must, for example, presuppose a causality of freedom even though freedom is not a possible object of its knowledge. In my Introduction, I explained the reasoning behind this second argument with reference to a law Kant identifies as an a priori principle of the possibility of experience, namely, the law expressing the causality of nature. This law states that, "nothing happens without a cause sufficiently determined a priori" (*CPR* A 446/B 474). The law relies on the idea of a cause that is sufficient – a cause that itself has no cause. As Kant points out, however, the idea of a sufficient or unconditioned cause refers to an object that is not itself a possible object of experience. The law expressing the causality of nature thus posits the idea of a non-empirical form of causality. Given that everything that happens in nature happens in conformity with the causality of nature, everything that happens in nature ultimately depends on the presupposition of this non-empirical cause. If we are to account for all that happens within the realm of nature, then, we have no option but to presuppose a non-empirical, non-temporal, and sufficient cause. This is a cause that is spontaneous or free.

5.6 Is Kant inconsistent regarding the unknowability of things in themselves? (453)

In light of Kant's repeated insistence that it is not possible for us to have theoretical cognition of things in themselves, we might find it problematic that he seems to assert that we can know that things in themselves lie "at the basis of" or "ground" appearances. In one representative passage he writes that:

the world of understanding contains the ground of the world of sense and so too of its laws.[18] (453)

Kant thus seems to imply that it is possible for us to know that appearances are grounded or caused by things in themselves. But how can he consistently suggest both that we have this knowledge of the relation of appearances to things in themselves and that we are necessarily ignorant of things in themselves?

On a charitable reading, Kant is not guilty of inconsistency. When he writes that the "world of the understanding contains the ground of the world of sense," he is not ignoring his argument demonstrating the unknowability of the world of understanding. The claim is instead

---

[18] Kant makes similar remarks at (451) and (459).

a claim about the limits of our knowledge of the world of sense. Kant's objective here is once again to remind us that scientific or theoretical inquiry relies on assumptions about objects we can never know – objects or "things in themselves" that properly belong to the world of understanding. The world of the understanding "contains the ground" of the world of sense in that our knowledge of the world of sense requires for its completion assumptions about the world of the understanding. Kant commits no inconsistency because assumptions or presuppositions about the world of understanding are not equivalent to claims of theoretical knowledge.

6. HOW IS A CATEGORICAL IMPERATIVE POSSIBLE? (453–455)

Having reminded us of the results of his efforts in the *Critique of Pure Reason*, Kant believes he has now adequately prepared us for his solution to the problem he set out to solve in Section III. Consider once again the strategy of his solution:

I say now: every being that cannot act otherwise than *under the idea of freedom* is just because of that really free in a practical respect. (448)

Kant reasons that if he can establish the truth of the premise, that there are beings that "cannot act otherwise than under the idea of freedom," his work will be done. He will have justified his conclusion that such beings are "really free in a practical respect." Remember what it means to establish that we are really free in a practical respect. One thing it means is that we are *entitled* to think of ourselves as beings standing outside the world of sense, as capable of giving ourselves law due to our freedom in the positive sense of autonomy. Since the law we give ourselves as pure or autonomous wills is the categorical imperative, it furthermore means that we have a right to think of ourselves as bound to the moral law. We have this right, because Kant's investigation into the limits of theoretical knowledge has revealed that our form of experience may not be the only form there is.

To establish that we are "really free in a practical respect," however, also means something further. It means demonstrating that we "must" think of ourselves in this way (452, 457). We must, because our scientific or theoretical knowledge – our knowledge of nature – depends for its very possibility on the presupposition of an uncaused or spontaneous cause, a cause that cannot be discovered in the realm of nature. Kant believes, in other words, that his investigation into the limits of our theoretical knowledge has established that theoretical or scientific inquiry requires the practical point of view as a condition of its very possibility. Theoretical knowledge is not self-sufficient; it relies on assumptions it has no way to justify.[19]

As we know, Kant insists that it is not analysis of the concept of a pure or rational will that establishes our right to think of ourselves as free as well as the necessity of our doing so. Analysis cannot prove that the "will of every rational being is necessarily bound" to the moral law "as a condition" (440). Analysis could only be of use to us, he suggests, were our will perfect. We could then establish merely by inspection of the concept of a pure will that such a will by necessity acts from the moral law. But since our will is imperfect – since we are beings affected by nature – it is not clear that we ever act from the moral law, let alone regard the law as a valid constraint on our maxims.

6.1 A question about Kant's rejection of the analytic method of proof

This is the place to raise a question about Kant's reasons for disqualifying analysis as his method for proving the reality of our freedom. At (447), he characterizes his task as that of demonstrating a necessary connection between the cognition of an "absolutely good will" and that of a will that ought always to act on universalizable maxims. I argued back at Section 2.2 that by "absolutely good will," he has in mind not the perfect will, but the pure or autonomous will, the will that is *capable* of giving itself the moral law. I suggested that, on Kant's account, analysis is unable to establish that our rational will ever acts on or even recognizes as valid the requirement of duty. I supported my interpretation by drawing evidence from Kant's earlier expressions of the task before him, for example, when he tells us at (440) that analysis

---

[19] One place where Kant is explicit about this point is, *CPR* A 543/B 571. Without the assumption of a causality of freedom in addition to a causality of nature, he implies here, we would lose not merely the possibility of moral imputation but also our science of nature. He reminds us of this point in the final paragraph of the *Groundwork*.

cannot prove that the "will of every rational being is necessarily bound" to the moral law "as a condition."

What is curious is this: Given Kant's own definition of a pure or rational will – namely, as a will that is autonomous and thus capable of giving itself the moral law – why does it *not* follow from analysis that such a will is "necessarily bound" to the law? Kant indeed emphasizes precisely this conceptual connection in the opening paragraphs of Section III. If we have properly understood the concept of autonomy, he insists there, we know that, "a free will and a will under moral laws is one and the same" (447).

The solution to this puzzle is evident two paragraphs later in Kant's discussion at (447). The crucial passage is his remark that it is "not enough that we ascribe freedom to our will on whatever ground." Rather, he continues, "freedom must . . . be proved as a property of all rational beings." We could, of course, simply stipulate that all rational wills, including human rational wills, possess a pure or autonomous will. We could then indeed rely on the method of analysis to make the meaning or content of our concept of a pure will explicit. But this would not take us very far. For, as Kant implies here, we want to know more than simply what is contained in our concept of a free or autonomous will. We want, in addition, some way of proving that freedom is "something real in ourselves and in human nature." When he argues that we not only can, but must, "transfer ourselves into a world of understanding," his intention is to answer precisely this demand (453).

6.2 The "third cognition"

Back at (447), Kant asked the question, "How is a categorical imperative possible?" As we saw, the difficulty of proving the possibility of the categorical imperative is tied to its status as a synthetic a priori proposition. The imperative is synthetic rather than analytic because we cannot, merely by analyzing the cognition of an absolutely good will, derive the "cognition" that the maxim of such a will ought "always" to be fit as universal law. If there is a necessary connection between the two cognitions, Kant asserts, it must be made possible by means of some "third cognition." This third cognition, he indicates, is the "positive concept of freedom," the idea of freedom as autonomy.

We are now in a position to explain the sense in which the idea of freedom furnishes the required third cognition, on Kant's account. He believes he has established the third cognition in that he has secured our *right* to regard ourselves as free as well as the *necessity* of our regarding ourselves as free. That is, he believes he has demonstrated that we are beings that "cannot act otherwise than *under the idea of freedom*" (448). Having justified his premise that we "cannot act otherwise than *under the idea of freedom*," he can now conclude with confidence that we are "really free in a practical respect."

7. ON THE EXTREME BOUNDARY OF ALL PRACTICAL PHILOSOPHY (455–463)

Kant's principal aim in this final subsection of the *Groundwork* is to warn us against misunderstanding the nature of his achievement in the work. Here, as in his other major philosophical writings, he is concerned to carefully circumscribe the limits to what we can know. He believes that, in the *Groundwork*, he has established our right to think of ourselves as free as well as the necessity of our thinking of ourselves as free. But he reminds us here that he has *not* established that freedom of the will is a possible object of theoretical or scientific knowledge. This is why he begins this subsection with the assertion that "freedom is no concept of experience." Freedom is not a concept of experience because, on his account, it refers to a form of causality that is not to be discovered in the realm of nature. Freedom is thus unknowable from a scientific point of view.

In these final paragraphs of the *Groundwork*, this claim about the status of freedom takes the form of the following repeated refrain: The idea of freedom, Kant tells us again and again, can neither be explained nor comprehended. "[R]eason would overstep its bounds," he writes, "if it took it upon itself to explain . . . *how freedom is possible*" (458f.). Kant is not suggesting here that the concept of freedom is incoherent or unintelligible. Nor is he taking back what he believes he has secured in the foregoing paragraphs of Section III, namely, our right to think of ourselves as free. When he asserts that we can neither explain nor comprehend the idea of freedom, his point instead is that no explanation of freedom is forthcoming from within the standpoint of nature. As he says, we cannot explain or comprehend the idea of freedom, because explanation is possible only for objects that "can be given in some possible experience" (459). By "explanation," in this context, he clearly means scientific explanation. Objects of scientific explanation must be empirical; they must be capable of appearing to us in space and time. Freedom of the will, as Kant defines it, does not fall into this category.

Since the idea of freedom admits neither of comprehension nor of explanation from within the standpoint of nature, we also cannot expect to be able to provide, from within that standpoint, an account of how we can actually be motivated by laws of freedom. We cannot, then, explain how it is possible for us to take an interest in morality (460). All we can explain from within the standpoint of nature is how empirical objects or appearances respond to deterministic forces of nature. We can trace the origin of our thoughts and actions back to some antecedent condition, back to the sensible impulses or desires that cause them. But it is not possible for us to explain the origin of what Kant refers to in these paragraphs as "moral feeling" or "practical interest." Moral feeling has no temporally antecedent or sensible cause. It comes to be in response to a cause that is outside space and time, in response to an idea of reason (460, 460*).

If we assume that the standpoint of nature is sufficient to explain all we seek to explain, we are forced to conclude that the thesis of the objective reality of freedom is, as Kant says, "doubtful"; for freedom is not the kind of object whose reality is susceptible of scientific proof. If we assume that the standpoint of nature is sufficient, we furthermore leave ourselves no way to escape the contradiction that results when we assert, on the one hand, that our will is determined by natural necessity, and, on the other, that it is also free. We leave ourselves no way to avoid what Kant refers to here as the "dialectic of reason" (455).

Of course, Kant believes he has shown us how to steer clear of this contradiction or dialectic. The key lies in rejecting the thesis that the standpoint of nature is sufficient to satisfy the interests of reason. Once we admit the legitimacy of granting in addition the practical standpoint (the standpoint of freedom), we grant ourselves permission to consider the same subject from two points of view. From the standpoint of nature, a subject has no freedom. But since we are now allowed to consider ourselves also from the standpoint of freedom, we may think of ourselves as also belonging to a "different order of things." Considered from the standpoint of freedom, we have a pure will and are thus capable of giving ourselves law. From a practical point of view, we are warranted in thinking of ourselves as self-caused or free.

As we know, Kant believes he has secured the legitimacy of this two standpoint solution on theoretical grounds. For if we take the standpoint of nature to be sufficient in satisfying the interests of reason, we assume without warrant that our experience of nature is the only form of experience there is. We forget, moreover, that the principles upon which scientific inquiry ultimately rests are not principles science is itself able to justify. Kant underscores this second theoretical justification for the practical standpoint when, in the final paragraph of the *Groundwork*, he asserts that the complete satisfaction of the interests of reason – including the interests of scientific inquiry – requires us to postulate an unconditioned condition, a condition that exceeds the boundaries of human knowledge.

Bibliography

BIOGRAPHIES

E. Cassirer. *Kant's Life and Thought*. Trans. James Haden. New Haven, CT: Yale University Press, 1981.

M. Kuehn. *Kant: A Biography*. Cambridge University Press, 2001.

U. Schultz. *Immanuel Kant*. Reinbek bei Hamburg: Rowohlt Taschenbuch Verlag, 2003.

WORKS BY KANT CITED IN THE TEXT

Unless otherwise indicated, all quotations and references are to translations available in the Cambridge Edition of the Works of Immanuel Kant. Volumes of the Cambridge Edition from which works are cited are:

Critique of Pure Reason. Trans. and ed. by Paul Guyer and Allen W. Wood. Cambridge University Press, 1998. As is customary, citations are to the A (1781) and B (1787) pagination of the Academy edition.

Lectures on Ethics. Trans. and ed. by P. Heath and J. B. Schneewind. Cambridge University Press, 1997.

Lectures on Logic. Trans. and ed. J. M. Young. Cambridge University Press, 1992. Contains the following work cited:

    The Jäsche Logic, pp. 519–640.

Practical Philosophy. Trans. and ed. M. J. Gregor. Cambridge University Press, 1996. Contains the following works cited:

    Groundwork of the Metaphysics of Morals, pp. 37–108.

    Critique of Practical Reason, pp. 133–271.

    Metaphysics of Morals, pp. 355–603.

    "On a Supposed Right to Lie from Philanthropy," pp. 605–615.

Religion and Rational Theology. Trans. George di Giovani, ed. Allen W. Wood. Cambridge University Press, 1996.

Theoretical Philosophy 1755–1770. Trans. and ed. R. Meerbote and D. Walford. Cambridge University Press, 1992. Contains the following work cited:

"Inquiry concerning the Distinctness of the Principles of Natural Theology and Morality," pp. 243–286.

Theoretical Philosophy after 1781. Trans. and ed. H. Allison and P. Heath, trans. G. Hatfield and M. Friedman. Cambridge University Press, 2002. Contains the following work cited:

Prolegomena to Any Future Metaphysics that Will be Able to Come Forward as Science, pp. 49–169.

Other editions of Kant's works:

The Doctrine of Virtue: Part II of the Metaphysics of Morals. Trans. M. J. Gregor. Philadelphia, PA: University of Pennsylvania Press, 1964.

The Metaphysics of Morals. Trans. Mary J. Gregor. Cambridge University Press, 1991.

Religion Within the Limits of Reason Alone. Trans. Theodore M. Greene and Hoyt H. Hudson. New York, NY: Harper & Row, 1960.

On History: Immanuel Kant. Trans. and ed. L. W. Beck, Indianapolis, IN: The Bobbs–Merrill Company, Inc., 1963. Contains the following works cited:

"Idea for a Universal History from a Cosmopolitan Point of View," pp. 11–26.
"Conjectural Beginning of Human History," pp. 53–68.

The Standard German edition of Kant's works is *Kants gesammelte Schriften.* Ed. Royal Prussian (later German) Academy of Sciences. Berlin: Georg Reimer, later Walter de Gruyter & Co., 1900–. The marginal numbers in works in the Cambridge edition are to volumes and pages of this edition.

OTHER WORKS CITED

H. E. Allison. *Kant's Theory of Freedom.* Cambridge University Press, 1990.

K. Ameriks. *Kant and the Fate of Autonomy: Problems in the Appropriation of the Critical Philosophy.* Cambridge University Press, 2000.

M. W. Baron. *Kantian Ethics Almost without Apology.* Ithaca, NY: Cornell University Press, 1995.

M. Baum. "Recht und Ethik in Kants praktischer Philosophie." In *Kant in der Gegenwart*, ed. Juergen Stolzenberg. Berlin/New York: Verlag Walter de Gruyter, forthcoming.

L. W. Beck. *A Commentary on Kant's Critique of Practical Reason.* Chicago/London: University of Chicago Press, 1960.

P. Carus, trans. and ed. *Goethe and Schiller's Xenions.* Chicago, IL: The Open Court Publishing Company, 1896.

S. Engstrom. "Kant's conception of practical wisdom." *Kant-Studien* 88 (1997), 16–43.

S. Fleischacker. "Values Behind the Market: Kant's Response to the 'Wealth of Nations'." *History of Political Thought* XVII (1996), 379–407.

V. Gerhardt, R.-P. Horstmann, and R. Schumacher, eds. *Kant und die Berliner Aufklärung: Akten des IX. Internationalen Kant-Kongresses.* Berlin/New York, NY: Verlag Walter de Gruyter, 2001.

T. M. Greene. "The Historical Context and Religious Significance of Kant's 'Religion'." In T. M. Greene and H. H. Hudson, trans., *Religion within the Limits of Reason Alone.* New York: Harper & Row, 1960, pp. ix–lxxviii.

M. J. Gregor. Translator's Introduction to the Metaphysics of Morals. In *The Metaphysics of Morals,* trans and ed. M. Gregor. Cambridge University Press, 1991, pp. 1–31.

Laws of Freedom. New York, NY: Barnes & Noble, Inc., 1963.

Translator's Introduction to the Doctrine of Virtue: Part II of the Metaphysics of Morals. Trans. Mary J. Gregor. Philadelphia, PA: University of Pennsylvania Press, 1964, pp. xvii–xxxvi.

P. Guyer. "The Form and Matter of the Categorical Imperative." In *Kant und die Berliner Aufklärung: Akten des IX. Internationalen Kant-Kongresses,* eds. Volker Gerhardt, Rolf-Peter Horstmann, and Ralph Schumacher, pp. 131–150.

ed. *Kant on Freedom, Law, and Happiness.* Cambridge University Press, 2000.

B. Herman. *The Practice of Moral Judgment.* Cambridge, MA/London: Harvard University Press, 1993.

C. Horn. "Kant on Ends in Nature and in Human Agency." In *Groundwork for the Metaphysics of Morals,* eds. C. Horn and D. Schönecker, Berlin/New York, NY: Verlag Walter de Gruyter, 2006, pp. 45–71.

C. Horn and D. Schönecker, eds. *Groundwork for the Metaphysics of Morals.* Berlin/New York, NY: Verlag Walter de Gruyter, 2006.

C. M. Korsgaard, ed. *Creating the Kingdom of Ends.* Cambridge/New York, NY: Cambridge University Press, 1996.

R. Louden. *Kant's Impure Ethics: From Rational Beings to Human Beings.* Oxford and New York, NY: Oxford University Press, 2000.

O. O'Neill. *Constructions of Reason: Explorations of Kant's Practical Philosophy.* Cambridge University Press, 1989.

H. J. Paton. *The Categorical Imperative: A Study in Kant's Moral Philosophy.* Philadelphia, PA: University of Pennsylvania Press, 1971.

A. Reath. *Agency and Autonomy in Kant's Moral Philosophy.* Oxford: Clarendon Press, 2006.

"Kant's Theory of Moral Sensibility: Respect for the Moral Law and the Influence of Inclination." *Kant-Studien* 80 (1989), 284–302.

C. M. Schmidt. "The anthropological dimension of Kant's Metaphysics of Morals." *Kant-Studien* 96 (2005), 66–82.

S. Sedgwick. "On Lying and the Role of Content in Kant's Ethics." *Kant-Studien* 82 (1991), 42–62.

M. Willaschek. "Practical Reason." In *Groundwork for the Metaphysics of Morals*, eds. Christoph Horn and Dieter Schönecker, pp. 130–132.
B. Williams. "Persons, Character and Morality." In *Moral Luck: Philosophical Papers 1973–1980*. Cambridge University Press, 1981, pp. 1–19.
A. Wood. *Kant's Ethical Thought*. New York, NY: Cambridge University Press, 1999.
  "The Good without Limitation." In *Groundwork for the Metaphysics of Morals*, eds. C. Horn and D. Schönecker, pp. 25–44.

GENERAL WORKS NOT CITED

H. E. Allison. *Idealism and Freedom: Essays on Kant's Theoretical and Practical Philosophy*. Cambridge University Press, 1996.
L. W. Beck. "Apodictic Imperatives." *Kant-Studien* 49 (1957/58), 7–24.
L. Denis. "Kant's Ethics and Duties to Oneself." *Pacific Philosophical Quarterly* 78 (1997), 321–348.
J. Ebbinghaus. "Interpretation and Misinterpretation of the Categorical Imperative." *Philosophical Quarterly* IV (1954), 97–108.
S. Engstrom. "The Concept of the Highest Good in Kant's Moral Theory." *Philosophy and Phenomenological Research* 52 (1992), 747–780.
  "Conditioned Autonomy." *Philosophy and Phenomenological Research* 48 (1988), 435–453.
T. E. Hill Jr. *Autonomy and Self-Respect*. Cambridge University Press, 1991. *Human Welfare and Moral Worth: Kantian Perspectives*. Oxford and New York, NY: Oxford University Press, 2002.
O. Nell (O'Neill). *Acting on Principle: An Essay on Kantian Ethics*. New York, NY and London: Columbia University Press, 1975.
J. B. Schneewind. *The Invention of Autonomy*. Cambridge University Press, 1998.
R. Sullivan. *An Introduction to Kant's Ethics*. Cambridge, New York, NY: Cambridge University Press, 1994.
J. Timmermann. *Kant's 'Groundwork of the Metaphysics of Morals': A Commentary*. Cambridge University Press, 2007.

ANTHOLOGIES NOT CITED

S. Engstrom and J. Whiting, eds. *Aristotle, Kant, and the Stoics*. New York, NY: Cambridge University Press, 1996.
P. Guyer ed. *Kant's Groundwork of the Metaphysics of Morals: Critical Essays*. Totowa, NJ: Rowman & Littlefield, 1998.
M. Timmons, ed. *Kant's Metaphysics of Morals: Interpretative Essays*. Oxford: Oxford University Press, 2002.

Index